Richard Béliveau Ph. D. ▪ **Denis Gingras** Ph. D.

Eating Well, Living Well

An Everyday Guide for Optimum Health

McCLELLAND & STEWART

Original title: La Santé par le plaisir de bien manger
Copyright © 2009 Éditions du Trécarré

English-language translation copyright © 2009 Éditions du Trécarré
English-language edition copyright © 2009 McClelland & Stewart Ltd.

All rights reserved. The use of any part of this publication reproduced, transmitted in any form or by any means, electronic, mechanical, photocopying, recording, or otherwise, or stored in a retrieval system, without the prior written consent of the publisher – or, in case of photocopying or other reprographic copying, a licence from the Canadian Copyright Licensing Agency – is an infringement of the copyright law.

Library and Archives Canada Cataloguing in Publication

Béliveau, Richard, 1953-
    Eating well, living well : an everyday guide for optimum health / Richard Béliveau and Denis Gingras.

Originally published in French under title: La santé par le plaisir de bien manger.

ISBN 978-0-7710-1138-2

1. Diet in disease. 2. Non-insulin-dependent diabetes – Nutritional aspects. 3. Cancer – Nutritional aspects. 4. Cardiovascular system – Diseases – Nutritional aspects. 5. Nervous system – Degeneration – Nutritional aspects. I. Gingras, Denis, 1965- II. Title.

RM217.B4413 2009   615.8'54   C2008-907575-7

We acknowledge the financial support of the Government of Canada through the Book Publishing Industry Development Program and that of the Government of Ontario through the Ontario Media Development Corporation's Ontario Book Initiative. We further acknowledge the support of the Canada Council for the Arts and the Ontario Arts Council for our publishing program.

Original French-language edition
Editorial: Martin Bélanger
Copyediting: Carole Mills
Proofreading: Emmanuel Dalmenesche
Design: Marike Paradis
Typesetting: Hamid Aittouares
Photo of the authors: Jacques Migneault
Nutrionist: Frances Boyte
Illustrations: Amélie Roberge
Collaborators: Maude St-Jean, Julie Gauthier, Patrick Thibault, Sam Murray, Michelle Hénault, Randal Lyons, Louise Durocher, Jessica Laroche

Printed and bound in Canada

McClelland & Stewart Ltd.   Les Éditions du Trécarré
75 Sherbourne Street   Groupe Librex, Inc.
Toronto, Ontario   1055, boul. René Lévesque Est
M5A 2P9   Montréal, Québec
www.mcclelland.com   H2L 4S5

1 2 3 4 5   13 12 11 10 09

This book is dedicated to Dr. Claude Bertrand, neurosurgeon,
founder of the Neurosurgery Department, CHUM,
for his enlightened and innovative vision of medicine,
and for inspiring a generation of surgeons and researchers.

ACKNOWLEDGEMENTS

For their unflinching support of the Chair of the Prevention and Treatment of Cancer, UQAM, thank you to:

- Nautilus Plus and its president, Richard Blais

- Manulife Financial

- National Bank of Canada

- Metro Inc.

Their vision of a better society has made it possible for us to continue our research.

Thank you to the neurosurgeons of the Neurosurgery Department, CHUM, for their enthusiasm in combining therapeutic intervention and medical research.

Thank you to the oncologists at the Montreal Jewish General and the Cancer Prevention Centre for their determination to instil preventive measures in the population.

Thank you to all the patients who, through their testimony and motivation, encourage us to continue this fight against chronic diseases.

A special thanks to Kathleen Asselin for her wonderful courage and determination in her individual fight against cancer.

Thank you to all the researchers in the Molecular Medicine Laboratory for their unremitting work, making it possible to advance research in the treatment and prevention of cancer and other chronic diseases.

Old age is not
a matter of death;
it's a matter of health,
since death is certain.

François Mitterrand (1916–1996)

Chapter 1

When Diet Leads to Illness

A child born today in an industrialized country can hope to live on average for nearly 80 years, a remarkable statistic considering that for the greater part of our history, life expectancy has been no more than 20 to 30 years (Figure 1). Only in the second half of the nineteenth century did life expectancy significantly improve, continuing upward thanks to the amazing breakthroughs achieved by medical science during the twentieth century (Figure 2). In particular, the development of numerous antibiotics, vaccines, drugs, surgical procedures, and other medical achievements over the past 50 years has considerably reduced the toll taken by serious diseases, particularly those of the infectious kind. Barely a century has passed since tuberculosis, pneumonia, and diarrhea alone were responsible for one third of all deaths in the United States. These

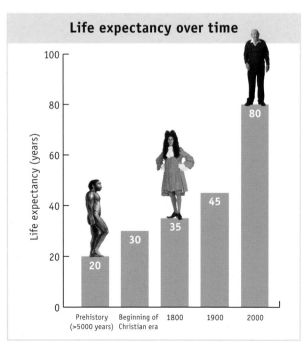

Figure 1

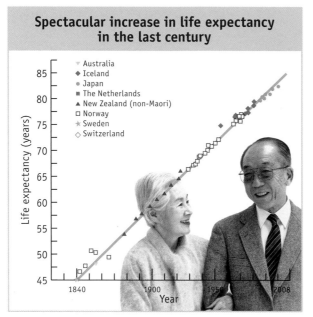

Spectacular increase in life expectancy in the last century

- ▽ Australia
- ◆ Iceland
- ● Japan
- ■ The Netherlands
- ▲ New Zealand (non-Maori)
- ▢ Norway
- ★ Sweden
- ◇ Switzerland

(Y-axis: Life expectancy (years); X-axis: Year, 1840–2008)

Figure 2   Source: adapted from *Science* 2002; 296: 1029-1031

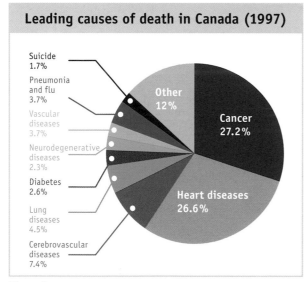

Leading causes of death in Canada (1997)

- Suicide 1.7%
- Pneumonia and flu 3.7%
- Vascular diseases 3.7%
- Neurodegenerative diseases 2.3%
- Diabetes 2.6%
- Lung diseases 4.5%
- Cerebrovascular diseases 7.4%
- Other 12%
- Cancer 27.2%
- Heart diseases 26.6%

Figure 3   Source: Statistics Canada

diseases today represent only a small percentage of deaths, well behind mortalities from "new diseases" such as cancer, cardiovascular disease, and other chronic conditions like Type-2 diabetes and neurodegenerative diseases (Figure 3). These illnesses therefore constitute the principal challenge faced by medicine today, well ahead of certain risk factors that often make headlines but whose real impact on public health is much less significant (Figure 4).

Even though longer life expectancy has clearly played a role in the soaring mortality rates from chronic diseases, it is nonetheless worrisome that these diseases also strike people in their prime, considerably diminishing the duration and quality of life. For example, the World Health Organization (WHO) states that a person who lives for 95 years will lose an average of almost ten years of good health as a result of one or more of these chronic diseases. It goes without saying that the loss of independence and suffering resulting from the treatment of these diseases (surgery, chemotherapy, dialysis, etc.) represent a substantial loss of the benefits that should derive from a longer life span. Although the continued increase in life expectancy we have seen over the last 150 years suggests that average life spans could reach 90 or even 95 years in a few decades from now, this high incidence of serious chronic diseases threatens not only to halt the trend, but also to undermine the main reason for living longer: staying in good health for as many years as possible.

Longer life with good health

We often assume that the onset of these chronic diseases is an inevitable aspect of ageing, a fate we cannot avoid unless we are "lucky" and possess genes that predispose us to ageing in good health. This is a misconception, however, because we now know that these "Methuselah genes" are responsible for only about one-third of cases of exceptional longevity; two-thirds of those who live to an advanced age in good health do so primarily because of a healthy lifestyle.

Comparison of the incidence of various chronic diseases in different world populations dramatically illustrates how lifestyle can influence the risk of being afflicted by these diseases. For example, while mortality due to cardiovascular disease is very high in most Western countries and represents the main cause of death, the incidence can be as much as ten times lower in certain

regions of the Mediterranean Basin and in Japan (Figure 5). These differences are not due to genetic factors that are protecting the inhabitants of these countries: When they immigrate to areas with a high incidence of cardiovascular disease (like North America), they quickly acquire the same mortality rates as the local inhabitants. Comparing the rate of cardiovascular disease among Japanese people living in Hiroshima with that of their compatriots living in Hawaii or California provides a striking example of this phenomenon (Figure 6). While heart attacks are rare occurrences in Japan, the incidence doubles among Japanese people who immigrate to the more Western-oriented Hawaii and quadruples when they settle on the United States mainland.

Such differences are also observed in cancer rates. American women – and women in Western countries generally – are hit hard by breast cancer after menopause, and death rates from this disease keep climbing as a result. Conversely, breast cancer deaths among Japanese women hardly increase with age, so that even at advanced ages (75 and over), these women are five times less affected by the disease than Western women (Figure 7A). A similar situation has been observed with prostate cancer. While in the West the death rate associated with this cancer increases dramatically after age 65, the increase is much less pronounced in Japan, leading to three times fewer deaths than in America (Figure 7B). Once again, these differences must be due to factors linked to lifestyle since breast and prostate cancer rates

Deaths per year in the United States (2004)	
Cardiovascular diseases	**652,486**
Cancer	**553,888**
Accidents	112,012
Cold and flu	59,664
AIDS	14,627
Falling down stairs	1,307
Falling out of a bed	450
Falling on ice	92
Shark attacks	2
Avian flu	0
Mad cow disease	0

Figure 4   Source: Centers for Disease Control and Prevention

among the Japanese who settle in the United States tend to align with those of the residents of their adopted country. Overall, these examples show the degree to which a Western lifestyle, especially a North American one, can influence the onset of chronic diseases associated with ageing. The startling increase in these diseases observed in the last few years is therefore not an inevitable consequence of people living longer but rather the result of poor lifestyles that promote the onset of and accelerate the development of such diseases. Among all the lifestyle factors that can influence the risk of contracting a chronic disease, diet is one of the most important.

À la carte diseases

The first signs that diet was involved in the development of major chronic diseases came from observations made by explorers, doctors, and missionaries who were working with isolated populations in Africa, Australia, and Canada's Far North at the beginning of the twentieth century. They noticed that the inhabitants of these regions were rarely affected by cancer, cardiovascular disease, or even Type-2 diabetes, but that the incidence of these diseases quickly increased following adoption of a Western lifestyle. This change was generally characterized by a more sedentary way of life and an increased consumption of sugary and fatty foods at the expense of

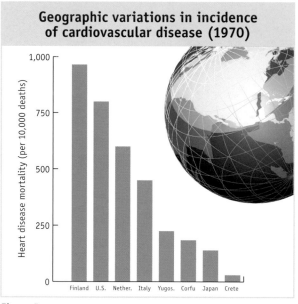

Geographic variations in incidence of cardiovascular disease (1970)

Heart disease mortality (per 10,000 deaths)

1,000 — 750 — 500 — 250 — 0

Finland   U.S.   Nether.   Italy   Yugos.   Corfu   Japan   Crete

Figure 5

Source: adapted from Keys (1980)

Variations in incidence of cardiovascular disease among Japanese men based on their place of residence

Heart attack (per 1,000 men)

40 — 30 — 20 — 10 — 0

Japan **7.3**   Hawaii **13.2**   California **31.4**

Figure 6

Source: *Am. J. Epidemiol.* 1975; 102: 514-525

plant products such as fruits and vegetables or whole grain cereals.

More recently, the effect of the trade globalization that has picked up pace over the past 20 years probably provides the best illustration of the negative impact of our Western diet on health. During this period, inhabitants of economically less developed countries have had greater access to large amounts of empty-calorie foods, or high-sugar and high-fat products that lack essential nutrients. Whether soft drinks or processed foods rich in sugar, fat, and refined flour, all these mass-processed, lower-priced products have replaced many traditional dietary constituents in countries around the world and now comprise a significant proportion of the total caloric intake of these populations.

Such dietary changes have had a rapid, disastrous impact on health. For example, in 1989 barely 10% of Mexicans were overweight or obese; today the figure is 60%, an increase due, among other things, to a spike in the consumption of soft drinks, which have reached an average of 155 litres per person annually (Figure 8). At the same time, Type-2 diabetes – almost non-existent in this country just fifteen years ago – now afflicts 15% of the population. It is feared that incidences of other diseases linked to obesity such as cancer and cardiovascular disease will increase similarly over the next few years. The Mexican

Breast cancer mortality by age group (1995)

Figure 7A   Source: WHO statistics

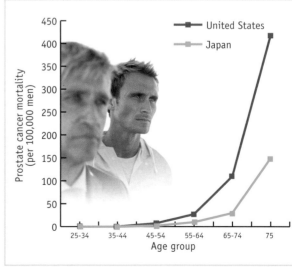

Prostate cancer mortality by age group (1995)

Figure 7B   Source: WHO statistics

15

example is not an isolated one. On the contrary, all countries that adopt this type of diet, whether in South America, the Middle East, or urban regions of India and China, soon witness a rapid deterioration in the health of their inhabitants. This "globalization" of chronic diseases is both a tragic and clear example of the adverse effects of Western processed food and the major role this type of food plays in the development of serious diseases.

A question of balance

The negative impact of modern processed food on health is largely due to its excessive nature, both in terms of quantity and nutrient deficiencies. On one hand, the rapid development of a wide selection of processed foods rich in both sugar and fats (potato chips, soft drinks, fast foods) has profoundly changed eating habits and caused an increased caloric intake, along with the inevitable problems of weight gain and obesity. On the other hand, this over-consumption of empty calories generally occurs at the expense of the consumption of plant foods, thereby depriving the body of

valuable sources of vitamins, minerals, fibre, and phytochemical compounds that play key roles in disease prevention (Figure 9).

The combined effect of these two extreme factors can be devastating: While being overweight due to excessive consumption of calories creates a pro-oxidant, pro-inflammatory, and pro-angiogenic environment that disturbs internal balance, deficiency in phytoprotective plant molecules removes one of the major forms of body cell defence against chronic inflammation. These two factors simultaneously produce an environment favourable to the progression of chronic diseases (Figure 9). Understanding this phenomenon is very important in seeing the degree to which a poor diet is harmful to health: in fact, despite differences in their effects on the human body, most cases of cancer, Type-2 diabetes, cardiovascular disease, and neurodegenerative diseases are direct consequences of our internal environment's imbalance. Re-establishing this balance by reducing the intake of high-calorie foods while increasing consumption of plant products rich in phytoprotective compounds can only have extraordinary repercussions on the prevention of these chronic diseases.

Don't bury your head in the sand

We've all heard family stories about an uncle, aunt, or other *bon vivant* who lived to an advanced age without ever giving up smoking, while some other unfortunate with no bad habits died from a devastating illness before reaching the age of forty. Such isolated examples, often the central argument of people who do not believe in the importance of taking care of their health, are very handy for justifying bad habits since they suggest that fate is predetermined at birth and cannot be altered regardless of what we do. However, as real as they may be, these extreme examples do not reflect reality as experienced by the vast majority of people, and despite their appeal to the imagination, they are in fact exceptions. In practice, these cases are marginal and something similar can always be found in any study involving a large number of people. For example, before even correcting an exam, a teacher knows that a small number of students will get an A and another small group a D. The majority, situated between these two extremes, will pass the exam with marks ranging from a B, often reflecting hard work and serious preparation for the exam, to a C or satisfactory. This is exactly the same phenomenon that comes into play when we examine the longevity of individuals in a population. There will always be a small group of lucky people who live to an advanced age regardless of what they do, and another more unfortunate group who will die at a young age. For most of the population, however, lifespan will fall between these two extremes; like the well-prepared students, these people can improve their chances considerably for increasing life expectancy by adopting healthier lifestyles (Figure 10).

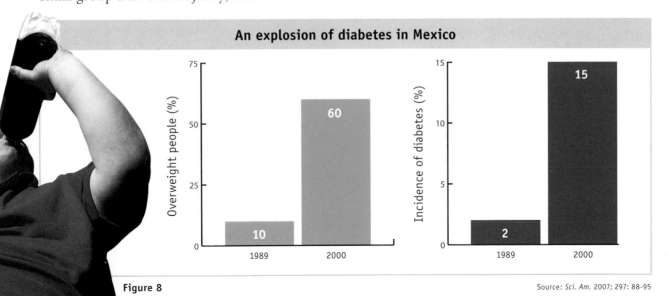

An explosion of diabetes in Mexico

Figure 8

Source: *Sci. Am.* 2007; 297: 88-95

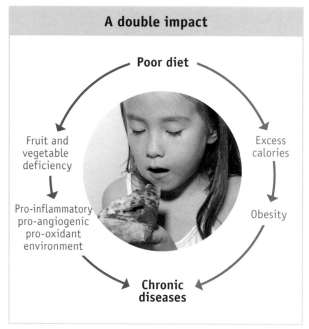

A double impact

Poor diet

Fruit and vegetable deficiency

Excess calories

Pro-inflammatory pro-angiogenic pro-oxidant environment

Obesity

Chronic diseases

Figure 9

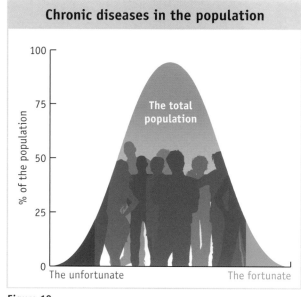

Chronic diseases in the population

The total population

% of the population

The unfortunate   The fortunate

Figure 10

Complex problems, simple solutions

Given the above, we can say that despite the high rate of chronic diseases today, the situation is far from irreversible and can be rapidly improved by adopting simple practices to correct our major lifestyle excesses (Figure 11). The potential to prevent the most common chronic diseases by applying these five principles is quite phenomenal. An estimated 90% of Type-2 diabetes, 82% of cardiovascular disease, and 70% of cancer cases could be prevented by adopting a better lifestyle, and the most recent research shows that applying these principles may even prevent the onset of a large number of neurodegenerative diseases such as Alzheimer's. It is therefore not surprising that these recommendations are made by all public health authorities such as the WHO, medical associations combating heart disease and diabetes, and various organizations fighting cancer. This preventive approach can have an extraordinary impact on our quality of life by delaying for several years the onset of diseases associated with ageing and by dramatically increasing the quality of life of the years gained (Figure 12). If we add to this the unprecedented progress made by

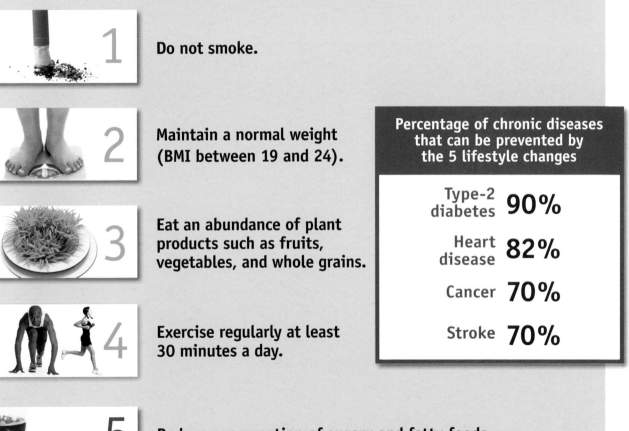

The 5 golden rules
of chronic disease prevention

1 **Do not smoke.**

2 **Maintain a normal weight (BMI between 19 and 24).**

3 **Eat an abundance of plant products such as fruits, vegetables, and whole grains.**

4 **Exercise regularly at least 30 minutes a day.**

5 **Reduce consumption of sugary and fatty foods, particularly those from the fast food industry.**

Percentage of chronic diseases that can be prevented by the 5 lifestyle changes

Type-2 diabetes	**90%**
Heart disease	**82%**
Cancer	**70%**
Stroke	**70%**

Figure 11

Living in good health for a long time

Poor lifestyle choices

Deaths (%)

50

Good health

Onset of chronic diseases

25   50   75

Years

Good lifestyle choices

Deaths (%)

50

Good health

25   50   75

Years

Figure 12

SMOKING KILLS

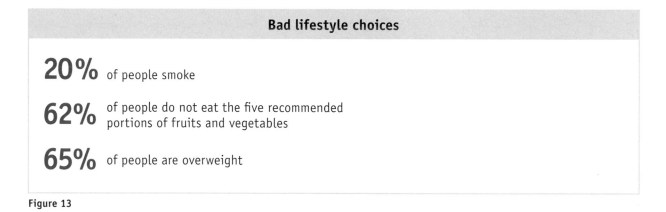

Bad lifestyle choices

20% of people smoke

62% of people do not eat the five recommended portions of fruits and vegetables

65% of people are overweight

Figure 13

curative medicines, such forms of prevention are without a doubt the best means at our disposal to achieve the full potential of human life.

Despite its apparent simplicity, applying these preventive principles is often seen as something difficult to achieve in our society, since a significant proportion of the population insists on pursuing a lifestyle that increases disease risk (Figure 13). In practice, an estimated 5% of the population applies the five key principles daily and therefore is maintaining an optimal lifestyle for effectively preventing the development of chronic diseases. This does not mean that most people are indifferent to the possibility of being struck by a serious disease, but rather it underlines how our society exerts pressures that are incompatible with a preventive approach and even encourages lifestyle habits that are totally opposed to the maintenance of good health. This is undoubtedly one of the great paradoxes of present-day Western societies. Collectively we constantly seek "all-risks insurance" by demanding that our leaders (over)protect us from difficult-to-control external factors (food contamination, accidents, natural disasters) that in fact cause only a small proportion of deaths (Figure 4). But individually we adopt a high-risk lifestyle that invites the development of serious diseases that are directly responsible for thousands of premature deaths annually.

Be informed, take charge

Taking a proper approach to preventive medicine requires, more than ever, serious thought about our lifestyles and more specifically about our eating habits. In this sense we must take full advantage of the tremendous progress made by research over the past few decades, which has identified options we can adopt to radically reduce the risk of squandering years of active life. This fount of information is unfortunately rarely used and has moreover been diluted by information overload and contradictory opinions that can needlessly complicate the situation, discouraging many people from initiating concrete actions to improve their health and life expectancy (see box, p. 22).

This book aims to present as simply as possible a summary of knowledge accumulated over the last few years about specific ways to prevent four major chronic diseases currently affecting our society: cardiovascular disease, Type-2 diabetes, cancer, and Alzheimer's. The strategies for countering most of these diseases are surprisingly simple and economical, but they may appear difficult for some people because they seriously call into question the place that diet occupies in our daily lives. The first step must be to identify the factors responsible for the increased risk of developing these diseases and also the reasons that lead us, often unconsciously, to adopt potentially unhealthy lifestyles.

(continued p. 24)

How to get information

Few subjects (outside of sexuality, of course) arouse as much interest in the population as the effect of diet on health. This concern is perfectly understandable: since the dawn of time we have known intuitively that what we eat exerts a major influence on our health and well-being. However, the volume of news items, articles, and publications on this subject makes it very difficult to distinguish what is true from what is not, especially since the advent of the Internet. This medium has brought about a veritable revolution by permitting huge numbers of people, regardless of where they are on the planet, to quickly obtain information on a subject of interest. Such accessibility can, however, become problematic when the information conveyed is incomplete, or worse, inaccurate.

To cope with this information overload, we must first avoid overreacting to every new study that comes along. We often have an idealistic vision of science, as if each new discovery expresses an absolute truth that must immediately be taken at face value. However, the way science works is quite the opposite: like bricks in a wall, individual studies have little intrinsic value; it is sequences of discoveries that bring coherence to a given subject. Therefore, the idea that promoting healthy lifestyles can prevent disease is not an act of faith or a personal opinion; it is an indisputable fact. Thousands of scientific studies conducted over the last fifty years with isolated molecules and animal models as well as large human population samples have made it possible to show that addiction to smoking increases the risk of lung cancer more than thirty times (3,000%), that obesity can cause many chronic diseases, and that a high consumption of fruits and vegetables significantly reduces the risk of several cancers. Consequently, there is a scientific consensus about the fact that lifestyles are responsible for a large number of diseases currently affecting the population.

On the other hand, we are often confronted by information that is essentially founded on opinion and not fact. An opinion, by definition, is something subjective, an interpretation of facts based on a belief or personal vision, which of course is not scientific. For example, asserting that pollution is a major cause of cancer is not a scientific claim, but is an expression of a personal opinion. Even if pollution definitely has a major negative impact on our environment, and indirectly, on our health, hundreds of studies have shown that it is alone responsible for barely 2% of all cancers. The concentration of carcinogenic molecules is much higher in cigarette smoke and certain foods we currently eat (deli meats, smoked meats) than in the air we breathe or the water we drink. It is nonetheless easier and less troubling to blame the pollution of others than to change one's lifestyle.

We must above all use our critical faculty when exposed to information that is promoting products – supplements, natural extracts, etc. – that allegedly prevent or even cure diseases as serious as cancer. These products may be very attractive, coming from faraway lands where they have apparently been used for thousands of years to cure a raft of diseases. But we must be mindful that there is no such thing as a miracle product and the aim of these companies is to make sales, not save humanity. Another prime example is the overconsumption of vitamins in North America, a direct consequence of the promotional efforts of the companies that aggressively market these products. With very few exceptions (vitamin D and folate for pregnant women), medical data does not show any benefit to using vitamin supplements in the prevention of chronic diseases. Rather it explains that these supplements validate the poor eating habits of those who consume them.

We must therefore value the more reliable information that comes from recognized health professionals such as doctors, researchers, or nutritionists. In the case of cancer, for example, there are many websites that contain very pertinent information about the disease in general, in addition to providing links that can answer the more specific questions of patients. In particular, websites of cancer organizations, universities, and internationally renowned hospital centres contain a wealth of information for the general public.

Some useful links:

Alzheimer Society of Canada: www.alzheimer.ca
American Institute for Cancer Research: www.aicr.org
Canadian Cancer Society: www.cancer.ca
Cancer Research Society: www.src-crs.ca
Diabète Québec: www.diabete.qc.ca
Fondation québécoise du cancer: www.fqc.qc.ca
Harvard Center for Cancer Prevention: www.hsph.harvard.edu/cancer
Heart and Stroke Foundation of Canada: www.heartandstroke.ca
McGill Program in Cancer Prevention: www.mcgill.ca/cancerprev

We believe the only way to really change our dietary habits and thereby reduce the scourge of chronic diseases is to look at the overall history of human diet and the biological processes involved in our eating behaviours. In this spirit, we provide an overview of the major evolutionary stages in the human search for foods that best suit our metabolism. We will discuss the complexity of taste and the mechanisms involved in controlling appetite to better understand what is driving the current obesity epidemic, while examining the degree to which the pleasure of eating represents an essential aspect of human existence. Better health from eating well? Why not? Prevention really can taste good!

Summary

- The spectacular increase in life expectancy that occurred in the twentieth century is associated with a dramatic increase in the incidence of several serious chronic diseases that considerably reduce the benefits associated with this increased longevity.
- These chronic diseases are not an inevitable consequence of ageing, but rather the result of poor lifestyle choices, particularly the type of diet that encourages their onset.
- The vast majority of these diseases could be prevented or significantly delayed with five major lifestyle changes: not smoking, maintaining a normal weight, getting regular physical exercise, adopting a healthy diet rich in plant foods, and reducing the consumption of mass-produced processed foods.

If you don't know where you're going,
look at where you've come from.

African proverb

Chapter 2

Cavemen Walking on the Moon

A diet poor in plant products, combined with the overconsumption of processed foods rich in refined sugar, salt, and saturated fats, certainly plays a major role in the development of the various chronic diseases currently afflicting most industrialized countries. While there are many explanations for our diet's disastrous effects on health – a topic addressed in the following chapters – it is fascinating to observe how closely these negative influences are related to the general development of our digestive system and metabolism throughout the evolution of our species. To better understand the repercussions of our modern diet on the development of chronic diseases, we need to examine how these foods affect our bodies, and also to go back in time to search for clues about the type of diet our bodies adapted to over millions of years of evolution. We are what we eat; but we are also what we *used to* eat!

Apes unlike others

While many human achievements over the centuries clearly attest to the brain's exceptional abilities and creative potential, it must be recognized that our beginnings were far more modest. Human beings, as we know them today, did not appear on Earth overnight. Remarkable discoveries during this past century have made it possible to establish a timeline of our ancestry, that is, its main evolutionary stages. This begins with *Proconsul*, a common ancestor of all hominids (man and the great apes), who lived in Africa about 20 million years ago (Figure 1). Orangutans first branched off from the evolutionary tree about 16 million years ago, then gorillas some 7 million years later. It has been just six million years since humans took a different evolutionary path from chimpanzees, our closest cousins among the species living today on our planet (see box, p. 29). As Darwin suspected, we are a very particular species of great ape, the extraordinary and improbable result of an evolution from "a

hairy, tailed quadruped, probably arboreal in its habits, and an inhabitant of the Old World" (*The Descent of Man*, 1871).

Wild for plants!

This close kinship between humans and the great apes has significant repercussions in understanding the type of diet we have adopted to meet our needs. Most of our basic physiological mechanisms, especially those involved in the digestion and metabolism of the essential elements of food, developed during this common evolution.

While it is difficult to determine the exact composition of our ancestors' diets during this period, many studies conducted on present-day great apes show that plant foods formed their principal means of sustenance. In fact, plants can form up to 98% of the apes' diet, and this abundant intake enables the absorption of large amounts of vitamins, minerals, fibre, and phytochemical compounds essential to health, and in far higher quantities than those most of us consume on a daily basis. This omnipresence of plants in the diet of great apes does not mean, however, that they laze about on tree branches, indiscriminately eating everything in sight. On the contrary, they are generally very particular and show a clear preference for certain fruits or young shoots, and can identify as many as 150 different plants! Great apes can assess the nutritional potential of their immediate environment

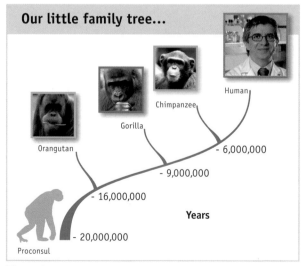

Our little family tree...

Human

Chimpanzee

Gorilla

Orangutan

- 6,000,000

- 9,000,000

- 16,000,000

Years

- 20,000,000

Proconsul

Figure 1   Source: adapted from *Sc. Am.* 2003; 289: 74-83

Our cousins the apes

We cannot help but be fascinated by the intelligent appearance of the great apes, as well as by their manual dexterity and highly developed social behaviours. At times they really do look like us! These similarities were first noted in 1641 by the famous Dutch anatomist Nicolaas Tulp (immortalized by Rembrandt), who published in his *Observationum Medicarum* the first detailed description of a great ape's anatomy. Tulp's general observations were confirmed in 1699 by English physician Edward Tyson, who dissected a young chimpanzee's brain and was astounded at the resemblance of its morphology to that of the human brain. While we can understand the surprised reaction of these physicians, we now know the reason for these similarities: human beings share almost 98% of their genetic makeup with chimpanzees!

As far as diet goes, one consequence of this genetic similarity between the great apes and humans is the shared need for a significant intake of plant foods. Humans and apes are among the few animals (with the notable exception of guinea pigs and some bats) that cannot produce vitamin C on their own and must therefore obtain it from dietary plant sources. Over the course of evolution, humans and apes lost the gene coding for L-gulonolactone oxidase, an enzyme involved in the production of vitamin C from sugar. However, this "genetic disorder" has had little effect on the survival and evolution of apes. Because they consume large quantities of fruits, it is believed their bodies can produce from 10 to 20 times the amount of vitamin C required!

The acquisition of this plant food was also facilitated by another genetic mutation that occurred more or less simultaneously, making humans and apes the only mammals that have trichromatic vision (perception of the colours blue, green, and red). This adaptation played a particularly important role in our evolution, permitting our ancestors to discern ripened red fruits in a predominantly green environment, thereby gaining access to an important food source.

This ability to identify fruits using trichromatic vision explains women's legendary attraction to the colour pink. Since women were responsible for gathering fruits throughout evolution, the female brain specialized in identifying colours ranging from pink to red, thereby developing a cultural preference for the colours that were synonymous with survival. This sensitivity to pink was hugely important for women in assessing the emotional and health states of family members and friends, by noticing the subtle facial vasodilations that are associated with emotions. It also helped develop women's heightened sensitivity to the feelings of others, which is today considered a basic characteristic of the female psyche.

Although the great apes are first and foremost herbivores, this does not mean they cannot tolerate animal foods. Chimpanzees in particular digest meat very well and show great ingenuity in catching insects and even small animals to meet their protein and fat requirements. However, these foods do not play a dominant role in their daily diet, as capturing animals and insects is difficult and involves an energy expenditure that is neither necessary nor viable for the survival of the species. In other words, even though great apes can be considered omnivores capable of eating plant or animal foods, they draw their basic sustenance from plants and are therefore primarily herbivores. But, as we shall see later, this potential for an omnivorous diet played a crucial role in the appearance of humans on Earth.

and select foods that best meet their needs, a very useful ability considering that only about 30,000 of the 300,000 existing plant species are edible.

This plant selection process serves not only dietary purposes. We now know that among certain species of great apes, sick animals can identify plant species that have specific medicinal properties and thereby succeed in effectively fighting diseases (see box, p. 31). So our knowledge of the nutritional and therapeutic effects of plants is actually ancient in origin, dating back several million years. During that period, humans took advantage of the exceptional amount of antioxidant, anti-inflammatory, and anticancer molecules in plants and chose those beneficial to health, particularly the fruits and vegetables that today form part of our diet.

It is neither original nor revolutionary to state how crucial plants are for the maintenance of good health. In practice, these foods have been part of our diet for 20 million years! Seen from this perspective, it is not surprising that an insufficient intake of plant foods, typical of the current diet of Western countries, can have such a harmful effect on health.

Ace in the hole

Although we share several traits with the great apes, our brain's phenomenal development during evolution is unquestionably what sets us apart from our cousins. For example, while the first bipedal hominid had a brain volume of about 400 cc (like the modern chimpanzee), the space it occupied gradually increased to achieve a final volume four times greater in modern man, or almost 1,600 cc. This increase in grey matter is extraordinary given the considerable energy required to maintain brain functions. The brain is a very demanding organ and by itself uses

Chimpanzee pharmacists

Not only can herbivorous animals identify toxic plants and avoid eating them, but some animals, especially chimpanzees, are able to choose specific families of plants to treat infections. For example, during the season when parasites are most active, some chimpanzees in Africa wrap the hairy leaves of a plant around their tongue and swallow them without chewing. Analysis of the stools of these monkeys has revealed the presence of the leaves, undigested but containing worms trapped in the hairs. An effective treatment!

In Tanzania, researchers observed profound changes in the behaviour of chimpanzees that were showing signs of intestinal discomfort. These animals ate almost nothing, with the notable exception of the stem of a small tree, which they normally avoid due to its bitterness. Chimpanzees with intestinal diseases would select the young shoots, remove the bark, and chew the stems for a long time to extract the juice. After 24 hours on this diet, they would become active and start eating again. Their choice was judicious: a biochemical analysis of this plant revealed the presence of several anti-parasitical compounds that had never been isolated before.

Furthermore, it was noted that certain chimpanzees that had been injured, as a result of fighting for example, changed their diet for a week by consuming the stems of a thorny plant (*Acanthus pubescens*) as well as the fruits and leaves of a certain species of *Ficus*. These choices would certainly be approved by the medicine men of the region, as the plants are used in local medicine to treat injuries and ulcers. Researchers have also observed that several of the plants selected by great apes are used in the traditional medicines of these regions, suggesting that close human observation of animal behaviour probably played a crucial role in the development of these treatments. The pharmaceutical industry is working to establish a profile of these plant molecules to help in developing new drugs.

almost 20% to 25% of a human's entire energy at rest, even though it represents just 3% of body weight. We may not always be aware of it, but thinking consumes a great many calories!

It is believed that the human brain's astonishing growth was largely made possible by major dietary changes over the course of evolution, the most significant certainly being the adoption of an omnivorous diet. By combining ample plant consumption with animal foods, our ancestors created a high-quality diet, blending the important elements essential to health (from plants) with meat's rich caloric content. Their increased exploitation of environmental resources, both plant and animal, required a long adaptation period to resolve the dilemma specific to all omnivores, that is, the difficulty of distinguishing foods beneficial to health from toxic foods. So it is not surprising that the major stages of human evolution have been marked by this constant quest for the benefits associated with food. These

include: the creation of various tools essential for acquiring new hard-to-obtain food sources (like big game); the use of fire to improve food digestibility (and taste!); and even the earliest forms of social organization permitting successful hunting and gathering. All of these typically human "inventions" made it possible to resolve the major issues of this dilemma and acquire a diversified diet that would provide enough calories to support the growth of the brain and the elements essential for the entire body to function. These efforts, starting with ordinary herbivorous great apes seeking to improve their fate by walking upright, led to the appearance of *Homo sapiens* – the most extraordinary omnivore to have ever inhabited this planet – about 200,000 years ago (see box, p. 35).

The caveman's pantry

The first representatives of our species were "hunter-gatherers," that is versatile omnivores who benefited from both animal and plant resources in their environment. The proportions of these two food categories in the daily diet of hunter-gatherers obviously varied depending on latitude, with more meat in the north and more plants in the temperate regions. However, overall it is believed that their daily subsistence diet consisted of two-thirds plant food and one-third animal food. It is striking to note that the combination of foods typical of the hunter-gatherer diet, specifically higher quantities of vitamin C, fibre, and certain minerals such as iron (Fe) and calcium (Ca) (Figure 2), provided far more essential elements than the diet currently popular in industrialized countries. The proportions of sodium (Na+) and potassium (K+) in the diet have also undergone extraordinary changes during evolution: While the amount of potassium we ingest is three times lower than it was during the prehistoric period, the amount of sodium is almost ten times higher. The result is that human beings today are the only animals that consume more sodium than potassium, an imbalance with major repercussions on our risk levels for cardiovascular disease (Chapter 5). The modern diet also contains lower levels of essential omega-3 fatty acids, a deficiency that causes a state of chronic inflammation, which promotes the development of several diseases (Chapter 4). On the other hand, we currently eat far more saturated fats and refined sugars than during the prehistoric age and these excesses are often implicated in the current obesity epidemic.

Of course it is not possible (or desirable) to return to the traditional hunter-gatherer lifestyle, but it is important to bear in mind that, despite all of our progress, most of our genetic makeup is identical to that of Paleolithic Age humans. We inherited a diet rich in fibre, vitamins, and omega-3 fatty acids in which sodium, refined sugar, and saturated fats used to occupy only a minor role. Yet our current diet is diametrically opposed to that established during human evolution, and these differences are clearly critical in the propagation of chronic diseases afflicting modern societies.

Comforts of home

The expertise acquired in gathering plants and hunting animals enabled hunter-gatherers to create a high-quality diet, yet this type of sustenance altered completely about 10,000 to 12,000 years ago with the advent of farming. The reasons for such a fundamental lifestyle change remain obscure, but it is believed that climate change in this period (the end of the first glacial age) reduced the availability of "traditional" food resources, forcing humans to seek other

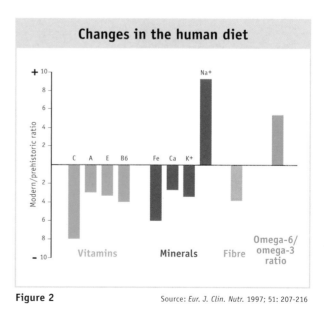

Figure 2

Source: *Eur. J. Clin. Nutr.* 1997; 51: 207-216

food sources. While the magnificent frescoes of the Lascaux and Altamira caves show abundant fauna at the end of the Paleolithic Age, a significant temperature increase caused the disappearance of these animals, in particular the reindeer – Europe's most prized game. It is also possible that humans acquired a considerable amount of knowledge about the plants and animals in their environment, which allowed them to control these resources better and ensure a sufficient food supply. Regardless, this transition to agriculture seems to have been inevitable, since it occurred independently and almost simultaneously in at least seven regions of the world (Figure 3), spreading rapidly into the majority of territories inhabited by hunter-gatherers. In some regions (Great Britain, for example), this transition happened very quickly (in less than 700 years), indicating that the agricultural "revolution" either truly satisfied a human need or that humans were naturally attracted to this lifestyle.

The advent of farming profoundly changed human life, in terms of both diet and cultivation. For one thing, control of plant and animal

(continued p. 37)

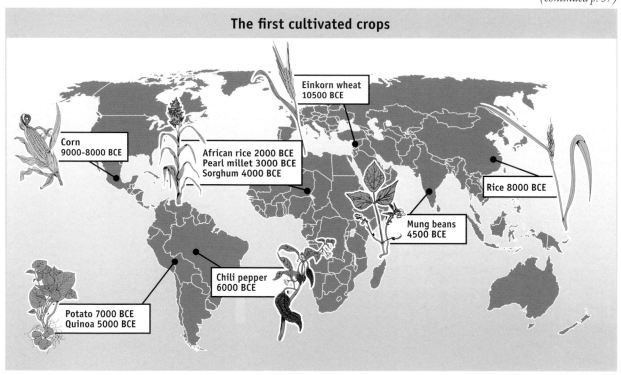

The first cultivated crops

Einkorn wheat 10500 BCE

Corn 9000-8000 BCE

African rice 2000 BCE
Pearl millet 3000 BCE
Sorghum 4000 BCE

Rice 8000 BCE

Mung beans 4500 BCE

Chili pepper 6000 BCE

Potato 7000 BCE
Quinoa 5000 BCE

Figure 3

Source: adapted from *Science* 2007; 316: 1830-1835

Prehistoric diets

It is believed that major climatic changes that swept through Africa about five million years ago played a crucial role in the emergence of humans. Notably, at the beginning of a glacial period, the climate became very dry and caused major upheavals in the habitat of the great apes. It transformed tropical forests, previously "supermarkets" abounding in plant foods, into savannas where such food is rarer and more dispersed. The achievement of bipedal locomotion probably represents the first adaptation to these changes: walking upright made it possible to cover more efficiently the great distances that were now necessary for acquiring food. That is aside from the fact that a vertical position frees up the hands, making it easier to reach food sources and facilitating carrying.

Australopithecus (about 4 million years ago) – The discovery of the skeleton of the most famous of these primitive hominids, Lucy, shows that *Australopithecus* were among the first great apes to have indisputably adopted bipedal locomotion. Lucy and her fellow creatures had a diet very similar to that of great apes, mainly consisting of plant foods. Certain species that were related to *Australopithecus*, but were more robust (*Parathropus robustus*) and lived at the same time, had such impressive jaws that paleontologists have affectionately nicknamed them "nutcrackers." While it is likely that these various *Australopithecus* species could also eat small animals, their skull injuries show they were probably more prey for leopards and hyenas than predators themselves!

Homo habilis (about 2 million years ago) – The first true member of the human genus, *Homo habilis* derives his name from the ability to make rudimentary tools, particularly from flint, which were probably used to remove meat from animal carcasses. It is believed that the transition to an omnivorous diet is largely attributable to *Homo habilis*. Changes observed in molar size and incisor shape suggest that these hominids steadily increased their consumption of meat, indicating a shift towards less fibrous food requiring less grinding. However, these hunters probably had modest beginnings; in several cases, the marks left by their tools had been made after other predators (hyenas) had consumed their prey, suggesting that the first humans largely ate carrion. Given their small size and brain capacity (400 cc in volume), which was much closer to apes than modern humans, *Homo habilis* probably had to work hard to compete with other ferocious predators and therefore must have preferred food sources very rich in energy and quickly accessible (bone marrow, brains, etc.). This preference marked the true beginnings of the human attraction to calorie-rich foods.

Homo erectus (about 1.5 million years ago) – *Homo habilis*'s innovations were largely perfected by his successor, *Homo erectus* or "upright man," the first of our ancestors to truly resemble modern-day humans in both stature and brain volume (850 cc or about 70% of ours). They used their increased cerebral capacity to make sophisticated tools for hunting and to control fire, an innovation that appeared some 500,000 years ago. The development of these first "cooking tools" had extraordinary consequences for the future of humanity. They considerably increased the digestibility (and nutritional value) of meat and made it possible to consume certain toxin-containing plants (mushrooms and some roots like manioc), thereby enabling these primitive peoples to exploit food resources more efficiently in their environment and support brain development. Skeletons of *Homo erectus,* great travellers always in search of new hunting territories, have been found in several regions of the world: in Europe, of course, but also in China.

Homo sapiens (about 200,000 years ago) – The first representatives of our species appeared in Africa only 200,000 years ago. However, the most obvious traces of their existence can be placed between 35,000 and 10,000 BCE, or the Upper Paleolithic Age, roughly corresponding to our image of the cave-dwelling Cro-Magnon man. These nomads, whose appearance and genetic makeup were almost identical to ours, had a diet largely derived from the gathering of plants, which was supplemented with meat obtained through increasingly sophisticated hunting strategies. Although their omnivorous diet required a considerable amount of work (hunter-gatherers would apparently cover about 10 km a day to acquire food), it was clearly worth their while: Analyses conducted on skeletons dating from this period show that prehistoric man was almost as tall as modern-day humans and showed no signs of serious dietary deficiencies. These hunter-gatherers enjoyed a good-quality diet, which is also suggested by studies of the dietary habits of some isolated communities that have preserved this lifestyle to the present day, particularly the !Kung San of the Kalahari Desert in southern Africa. These people eat a diversified diet, often made up of more than 100 different plant species and several distinct types of animal sources (and sometimes insects). It delivers a significant amount of vitamins, minerals, and fibre while providing enough calories to sustain a high level of physical activity. Their diet certainly seems well adapted to the functioning of the human body, given that the general health of these populations is excellent, and they are only rarely affected by "diseases of civilization" such as cardiovascular disease, Type-2 diabetes, and cancer.

reproduction made food accessible and also reduced the uncertainty inherent in hunting and gathering. This consistent food supply was greatly facilitated by the selection and cultivation of foods rich in calories, especially cereals (see box, p. 39) and certain tubers, which made it possible for the first time in history to store food surpluses for times of scarcity.

On the other hand, numerous cross-fertilizations and selections carried out over generations produced a wide assortment of new plant varieties – "genetically modified organisms." At the very least, their appearance, taste, and caloric content were improved (Figure 4)! For

example, corn, as we know it today, comes from domesticated teosinte, a grass that grows wild in Southern Mexico. Its appearance, however, in no way suggests it could have undergone such a metamorphosis: One ear of teosinte contains a maximum of 12 grains; modern corn contains 500 or more! While human intervention caused multiple dramatic changes in the morphology and properties of the plants and animals we domesticated, the opposite is also true: Certain modern characteristics, such as the consumption of milk in adulthood, are direct consequences of the advent of farming (see box, p. 42).

The transition of hunter-gatherers into farmers represented a fundamental change in the nature of human nutrition, causing a shift from a diet essentially dictated by the availability of food sources in the environment to an existence based on large-scale food production, permitting a steady supply of calories.

The blossoming of civilizations

Although this transition did not occur smoothly, the abandonment of a nomadic lifestyle completely revolutionized human existence by allowing a significant population increase and the appearance of the first socially organized communities. This was a key step in the development of farming and the emergence of complex civilizations. For example, the accumulation of accountable wealth such as grains stored in

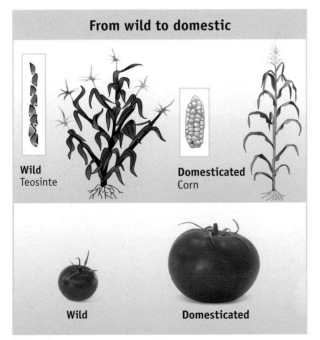

From wild to domestic

Wild
Teosinte

Domesticated
Corn

Wild

Domesticated

Figure 4

amphoras or granaries led to the appearance of calculus and writing in Sumer, Mesopotamia, and Egypt more than 5,000 years ago. These food surpluses also enabled certain categories of people to devote themselves to other tasks, encouraging the development of new trades and the appearance of hierarchical social classes subject to the authority of kings, priests, and warriors. Despite the wars, inequalities, and injustices that often resulted from the flowering of civilizations, it was thanks to agriculture that language, writing, religion, trade, and even different art forms – everything that constitutes the essence of our world – were able to see the light of day.

The need to extract from one's environment the food that is essential for survival and propagation of the species has been the driving force of the evolution of living species, and human beings are no exception. Our evolution required a very long period of adaptation during which we gradually changed from herbivorous great apes, taking their basic sustenance from plants, to versatile and curious omnivores, constantly hunting for food sources to improve their chances of survival (Figure 5). While herbivores devote much of their time to consuming large quantities of food to compensate for the weak caloric content of plants, and carnivores constantly risk failure

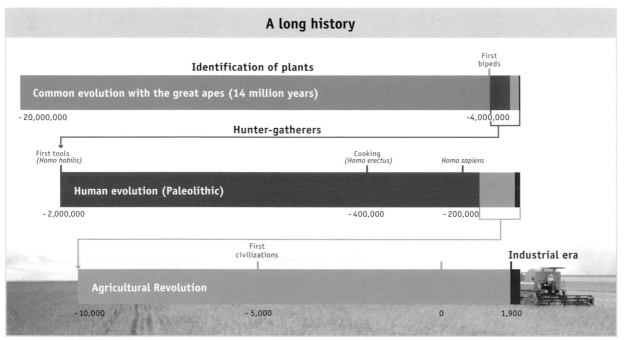

Figure 5

The original grain products

Wheat (*Triticum* spp.)

The first domesticated cereal grain product, wheat made its appearance around 10,000 years ago in the Fertile Crescent (a crescent-shaped region covering ancient Egypt, the Middle East, and Mesopotamia). Here we find the first traces of cultivation of two wild species, einkorn or small spelt (*Triticum monococcum*) and emmer (*Triticum turgidum dicoccoides*). Like most cultivated species, domesticated varieties probably emerged after humans selected plants with larger grains, which quickly improved crop yields. Domesticated emmer (*Triticum turgidum dicoccum*) is very rich in starch and was particularly enjoyed for several millennia.

Domesticated emmer is also the source of two very important types of dietary wheat. Durum wheat (*Triticum turgidum durum*), widespread in the Mediterranean basin as of 5,000 BCE, is rich in gluten and used to produce semolina (couscous, bulgur wheat) and pasta. Wheat (*Triticum æstivum*) derives from a combination of the genetic material of cultivated durum and *Aegilops tauschii,* which was produced about 9,000 to 12,000 years ago and used to make flour for bread. This wheat, along with its close relative spelt, has 42 chromosomes compared to 14 chromosomes in primitive types of wheat, showing once again the enormous work of selection and hybridization conducted since the beginning of farming. These wheats feed 35% of the world's population today, an impressive contribution.

Rice (*Oryza sativa*)

A cereal that provides 21% of the total calories currently consumed by the human race, rice was first cultivated on the banks of the Yangtze River in China about 8,000 years ago. It is believed that heavy summer rains and floods characteristic of this region provided ideal conditions for domesticating a wild rice species (probably *Oryza rufipogon*). Unlike other cereals, most rice varieties typically grow in flooded regions where the water level can sometimes reach 50 cm. In many Asiatic languages, the words for designating rice and food or even agriculture and cultivation are identical, indicating that rice already formed the basis of Chinese food while these languages were developing. Even today, rice remains unquestionably the staple of the Asian diet: in Myanmar, the population eats an average of almost 250 kg of rice per capita per year!

Maize (*Zea mays*)

An ancestor of corn, teosinte (*Zea mays* ssp. *parviglumis*) was domesticated around 9,000 years ago near the area around the Balsas River in Southern Mexico. While this "Corn Mother" is a grass that barely resembles the corn we know today (Figure 4), it is believed that a spontaneous genetic mutation considerably modified its appearance and promoted its domestication. Corn cultivation spread equally to the south (Central America) and the north (as far as the Great Lakes) over the next few centuries, and this food gradually became a dietary staple for most people in the Americas. Corn was so important that Mayans believed their bodies were fashioned by the gods out of *masa,* a corn dough. Few plants can produce as much organic material (and therefore calories) as corn, and its intensive cultivation makes it possible to feed large populations. This plant would never have become so important if Aztecs and Mayans had not first soaked the grains in alkaline substances such as lime or ashes before making *tortillas, pozole, tamale*, and other daily dishes. We know today that this procedure, called nixtamalization, enables the extraction of niacin from corn and prevents pellagra, a disease characterized by dermatitis, diarrhea, and dementia, and causing death within four or five years. Europeans who exported corn to Europe (Christopher Columbus, among others) unfortunately did not pay much attention to this technique and therefore pellagra hit hard those populations whose diet was based mainly on the consumption of this cereal grain, particularly in regions of Italy and France. This demonstrates why it is important to preserve culinary traditions developed over time!

in their hunting, the combination of these two diets allowed humans to acquire a high-quality diet that was crucial in our brain's phenomenal growth. And while food scarcity is a reality faced by the vast majority of living species, the intelligence and creativity of human beings allowed us to solve this problem effectively and devote the time saved to activities that are typically human, such as art and culture.

The aim of this overview of our dietary history is to help us better understand the reasons why the modern diet can be so harmful in the development of chronic diseases. In fact, while our metabolism has, over 20 million years, adapted to a diet primarily based on plants, meat was added to it only about 2 million years ago. The arrival of modern mass-produced foods, overloaded with sugar and fat, dates from barely 100 years ago, an infinitesimal fraction (0.0005%) of our evolutionary history (Figure 6). These radical changes clearly run counter to the type of diet we originally inherited. Over the course of our evolution, human beings have become the most intelligent animal species, the species that has accomplished most due to our prodigious development of the faculties of learning, reasoning, and understanding. But it is essential to recognize that we flourished primarily because of the development of our brain and not because of our biology in general. The human body, particularly in its way of metabolizing food, did not evolve at the same rate and has remained in a prehistoric state, subject to limitations on the type of food that must be eaten to promote health and well-being. Although we have built pyramids, walked on the Moon, and created great literary and musical works, these achievements should not blind us to the fact that most of our basic functions, particularly our way of assimilating food, stem from our caveman past, and in many respects from the great apes.

To effectively prevent the development of diseases, we must therefore become "hunter-gatherers of the twenty-first century," not by going back and sacrificing humanity's phenomenal progress, but rather by reviving the idea of what food has always been: a special source of

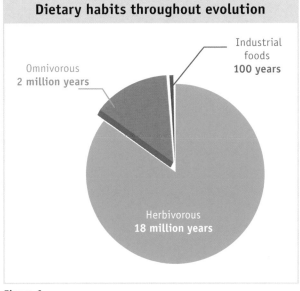

Dietary habits throughout evolution

Industrial foods
100 years

Omnivorous
2 million years

Herbivorous
18 million years

Figure 6

elements essential for the human body to function properly. In this sense, we must take full advantage of the enormous privilege we enjoy in having access to an extraordinary abundance of quality foods, the result of thousands of years of human exploration in identifying new food sources beneficial to health. And more important, we must enjoy one of the greatest gifts bequeathed by our evolution: the pleasure of eating.

Drinking milk: A recent habit!

Milking wild animals was an undertaking only for the fearless. Female aurochs, ancestors of the cow, grew to nearly two metres in height at the shoulder and were jealously guarded by male aurochs who had a reputation for being extremely ferocious. It was only after sheep, goats, and especially cows were domesticated, about 9,000 years ago, that milk became accessible as a food. The first cattle breeders who tried to exploit this new resource had to face a major obstacle: Humans, like most mammals, lose their ability to digest milk once they have reached adulthood due to the loss of the enzyme that breaks down the lactose, the sugar naturally present in milk. In the absence of this enzyme (lactase), the lactose is fermented by the bacteria present in the intestines, causing discomfort characterized by bloating and flatulence and in some cases leading to diarrhea and dehydration. In an age when finding enough food was a constant challenge, the ability to digest milk to benefit from its caloric content without suffering any side effects could be an enormous advantage in terms of survival.

That is exactly what happened. Pastoral peoples adopted the drinking of milk during the millennium that followed the domestication of cows. This was due to a genetic mutation that made sustained lactase production possible, even in adulthood. The mutation spread like wildfire among these populations, and today most adults who drink milk are descendants of populations that traditionally raised cattle. Therefore, sustained lactase production is present in more than 90% of adult populations of northern Europe (Sweden, Denmark), less so in the populations of southern Europe and the Middle East (50% in France, Spain, and the Arab countries), and practically non-existent in countries with no history of raising cattle (1% in China and 5% in western Africa). Worldwide, about 50% of the planet's population does not have this mutation and therefore cannot effectively digest milk in adulthood.

It is also interesting to note that other pastoral populations living in East Africa (the Tutsis and Fulanis of Tanzania, Kenya, and Sudan) also produce lactase in adulthood; the phenomenon, however, is due to a different genetic mutation than that seen among Europeans. This convergent evolution in which two distinct populations living in different parts of the world have managed to acquire the same ability to digest milk following the adoption of a pastoral lifestyle is a striking example of the influence that farming can have on our genes. In the same vein, those populations that have adopted a diet very rich in cereal products, like the Europeans and the Japanese, produce greater amounts of the enzyme amylase in their saliva. By improving digestion of the starch contained in cereals, this increase in amylase makes it possible to maximize the absorption of calories from these foods and therefore represents another example of the evolution resulting from humans adopting an agricultural lifestyle.

Summary

- Plants constituted the principal element of the human diet throughout human evolution, starting with the great apes.
- The phenomenal development of the human brain enabled the refinement of a high-quality diet combining essential plant elements with the significant caloric content of meats.
- The modern mass-produced diet, based largely on the consumption of processed foods rich in sugar and fat, is completely opposed to the diet to which our bodies adapted throughout our evolution. It is these differences that are contributing to the development of chronic diseases.

Appetite comes with eating;
thirst goes away when you drink.

François Rabelais, *Gargantua* (1542)

Chapter 3

What Makes Your Mouth Water?

Of all the senses that nature has granted us, it is taste, when all things are considered, that brings us the most enjoyment:

1) Because eating is the one pleasure that, when enjoyed in moderation, is not followed by fatigue;

2) Because it applies to people of all ages, anywhere, anytime;

3) Because it necessarily returns once a day, and may be repeated two or three times in the same day without unpleasant consequences;

4) Because it blends with all other pleasures, and even offers consolation in the absence of those others;

5) Because the impressions it makes are both more enduring and more the product of our will;

6) Because when we eat, we experience a certain indefinable feeling of well-being that is instinctive and personal. And when we eat, we are both compensating for what we have lost and helping prolong our lives.

Jean-Anthelme Brillat-Savarin, *The Physiology of Taste* (1826)

The many historical references and countless works of art that celebrate the pleasure of eating clearly illustrate the importance food holds in our daily lives. More than a simple act essential for survival and reproduction, the constant quest for new food experiences has driven the development of many different culinary traditions, all of which attach great importance to both taste and the benefits to the human body. The emphasis on herbs, spices, and condiments, the great diversity of culinary techniques, and the crafting of fine china all testify eloquently to the importance of eating as pleasure and its profound influence on our lives. We eat to live, of course, but we also live to eat. Food is first and foremost essential to our existence, and the pleasure we derive from it has gradually become a basic characteristic of the human spirit.

A nose for eating

The tongue and the nose are the main taste organs, and any person with a cold can attest to what degree the smells released into the mouth by chewing enhance the flavour of food. In fact, 85% of taste perception is due to smell! In humans, the detection of odours is limited to a small area in the nasal membrane (about the size of a postage stamp), which contains more than ten million nerve endings capable of transmitting to the brain information picked up by cell-surface *receptors*. The latter are a kind of molecular antenna designed to detect specific biochemical messages present in the environment (Figure 1). Just as a lock needs a particular key, each receptor has in its structure an area that recognizes only very specific messages. When a molecule (the key) corresponding to the lock is present, the receptor is activated, triggering a response that enables the cell to react appropriately to its presence by activating a series of complex molecular events. These may involve hundreds of distinct molecules that stimulate very specific areas of the brain involved in interpreting odours. The receptors are so vital that an estimated 1% of all mammal genes are involved in producing special receptors to detect smells, more than the number of cells responsible for producing antibodies!

Our sense of smell, through evolution, has become less sensitive than that of other species: a dog's, for instance, is one million times more sensitive than ours. Yet we have still preserved an olfactory repertoire made up of many hundreds of receptors capable of recognizing almost three thousand distinct odours, ranging from the pleasurable to the revolting. Certain smell specialists, such as perfume makers and wine masters, can

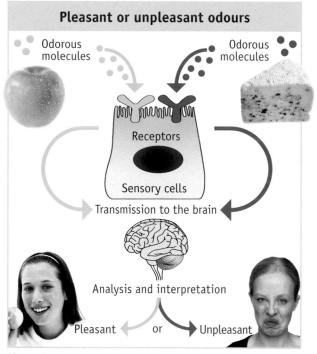

Figure 1

accurately identify some ten thousand different smells!

However, the brain's active participation in the olfactory process makes smell a very mysterious sense, strongly influenced by our experiences, our recall, and our visual perception of the external environment. For example, the simple act of closing your eyes and thinking about your favourite dish or a recently visited restaurant where you had a great time is enough to increase saliva production and literally make your mouth water! This psychological aspect is so decisive in smell perception that even the judgment of specialists is subject to these external influences, with consequences that are, at the very least, surprising (see box, p. 49).

Although it can be challenging to identify accurately certain subtle smells, others are easy to recognize, as they can quickly convey the quality of a given food. Bad odours, for example, are repugnant as they often signal the presence of rotting and inedible food, or unhygienic conditions incompatible with health. Recognizing these smells was particularly useful to our ancestors when they adopted an omnivorous diet, for it enabled them to identify meat carcasses contaminated by micro-organisms – a life-saver.

Conversely, pleasant odours are generally agreeable and often positively interpreted by our brain for the upbeat feelings they bring (perfumes, for example) and for their potential health benefits. It is interesting to note that the smell of certain foods can derive from molecules of substances that are essential to the proper functioning of the body. For example, tomatoes as they ripen produce pleasant volatile substances from essential molecules such as fatty acids or proteins. Upon detecting these smells, our senses encourage us to eat the fruit, resulting in the absorption of these molecules (Figure 2).

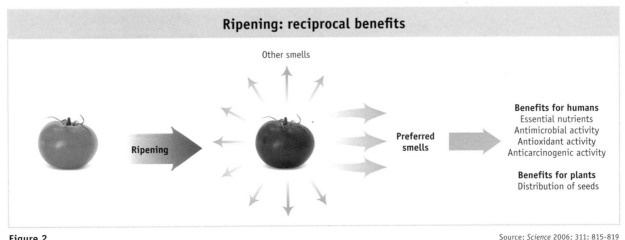

Ripening: reciprocal benefits

Other smells

Ripening

Preferred smells

Benefits for humans
Essential nutrients
Antimicrobial activity
Antioxidant activity
Anticarcinogenic activity

Benefits for plants
Distribution of seeds

Figure 2

Source: *Science* 2006; 311: 815-819

Although at first sight we emerge as the big winners in this relationship, we should not forget that the process is also crucial to the existence of the tomato itself. Most grains remain intact when passing through the digestive tract; since these smells entice animals (especially birds) to eat the grains, they enable the DNA present in the tomato to spread over great distances and find new ecological niches.

However, what smells good is not always edible. While a flower's scent may be irresistible, it does not make the flower a food! Conversely, fermented products and certain aged cheeses can emit a powerful smell that is not very appealing at first, but very often masks a great delicacy. Therefore, while smell may be essential to taste (and to the pleasure of eating), there are additional mechanisms helping us to decide whether or not a food is edible.

Taste and distaste

The word "taste" comes from the Old French *taster,* meaning to taste, feel, or touch, and from the Latin *tastare,* meaning to handle, evaluate. From a biological perspective, taste's primary function is to identify foods that contain substances essential to our body's good functioning and to detect the presence of toxic products that can threaten the body's integrity. This detection function is crucial: By selecting from the external environment only those substances that are compatible with health, it helps maintain the body's *homeostasis,* that is, the internal balance enabling various organs to work harmoniously. Maintaining homeostasis is a characteristic that is fundamental to all living beings. Even a single-cell bacterium can "taste" its environment and find its way, through chemotaxis, to a nutritional substance essential to its growth, like sugar. Conversely, it can flee from substances threatening its survival, such as antibiotics.

Among more evolved animals like humans, taste detection taps into a sophisticated system located in areas around the tongue, and organized into calciform, fungiform, or foliate structures. These optimize contact between our taste cells and the food molecules released through chewing (Figure 3). The taste cells look like buds, each possessing on their surface specific receptors for five main types of distinct tastes: sweet, salty, sour (acidic), bitter, and umami (see box, p. 51).

Our tongue does not work alone in detecting these five types of flavour; a number of other systems found in the oral cavity play an active part in taste detection. For example, orosensory perceptions of dietary fat are potent stimulators of the cerebral areas involved with the sensation of pleasure. This effect is related to their significance as a source of energy or of essential fats that our body cannot synthesize by itself (Figure 7). The simple presence of fats in the mouth is enough to activate a number of metabolic enzymes that can anticipate the calorie intake to come! The presence of a fat-specific receptor on the tongue

False nose

While taste and smell are first and foremost physical sensations, they nonetheless involve a cognitive aspect (linked to thought) that is vital to appreciating a given food. A good example of how thought can influence taste, even among connoisseurs, is the label (and price!) of a bottle of wine. In a study, oenology students were asked to taste the same wine served from two different bottles a few days apart. One bottle bore a well-known vintage label, and the other just had the words "table wine." Most of the future oenologists (50 out of 57) gave lower marks to the wine from the "table wine" bottle, and higher marks to the "vintage." Some went so far as to mention a woody note – although the wine in question had never been in contact with wood.

In another revealing experience, researchers asked students to describe the taste of a white wine and of a red wine. These were in fact the same white wine, with one coloured red using a natural colouring agent, devoid of taste or smell. The students used olfactory terms normally reserved for red wine (cassis, raspberry) to describe the fake red wine, and terms associated with white wine (apricot, honey) to describe the true white. These conclusions are certainly not meant to denigrate the talents of professional oenologists, but to show how one's perception of wine (and foods in general) is largely shaped in our brain. It is part of a process during which the chemical signal detected by the nose interacts with other perceptions (sight, memory) to create an "image." Professional oenologists can, of course, take into account nuances and their tremendous olfactory sensitivity generally protects them from distractions in the "tasting environment."

However, for most people, mentally constructing a positive or negative food image is fundamental to finding a food appealing or repugnant. It is disturbing to see today's children construct positive images largely around industrial foods laden with sugar and fat – foods that are "cool" and in vogue – rather than "boring" foods like fruits and vegetables or home-cooked meals.

called CD36 probably plays a major role in our physiological attraction to fat.

It is also fascinating to note that spices and seasonings, which have become essential ingredients for enhancing the taste of our foods, can all stimulate certain nerve endings specializing in the detection of pain, heat, or cold (see box, p. 57).

A complex sense

Whether or not we experience pleasure in eating a given food is the end result of a very complex biological process involving our physical senses and memory. Stimulation from eating food – the smell, taste felt by the tongue, aroma released by chewing, and the tactile and heat sensations produced in the mouth – are all decoded by our senses and sent to the brain. Then, based on the nature of these signals and on former experiences, the brain becomes the ultimate judge in determining whether the food is a likely source of pleasure, or something to be avoided. In other words, while each person's senses detect more or less the same flavours, our brain's interpretations can produce diametrically opposite effects in individuls, ranging from boundless pleasure to profound dislike. For example, *natto,* a dish of fermented soybeans with a very strong smell and texture, has for millennia been considered a

(continued p. 56)

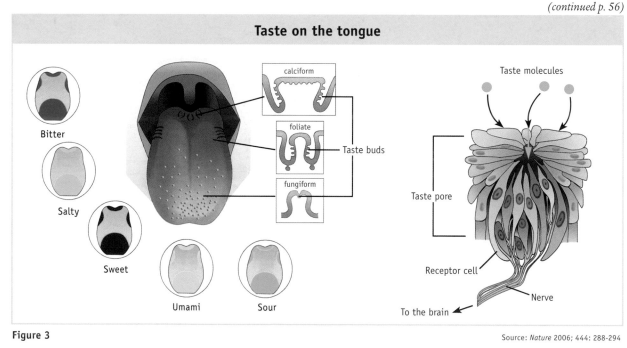

Taste on the tongue

Bitter

Salty

Sweet

Umami

Sour

calciform

foliate — Taste buds

fungiform

Taste molecules

Taste pore

Receptor cell

Nerve

To the brain

Figure 3

Source: *Nature* 2006; 444: 288-294

A matter of taste

When mixed with saliva, foods release taste molecules (sapids) that bind to receptors found on the surface of taste bud cells. Contrary to popular belief, taste detection does not depend on specific areas of the tongue. We now know that each taste bud has a large repertoire of specific receptors that recognize each of the following tastes:

Umami

Identified in 1908 by Professor Kikumore Ikeda of Tokyo Imperial University, *umami* (旨味), which is the basis of a kombu algae broth called *dashi*, literally means "very delicious" in Japanese. For many years considered the most mysterious flavour, the umami taste is now known to be due to glutamate, a constituent (10-25%) abundant in plant and animal proteins. Umami can therefore be regarded as a true "protein detector," a primary taste, considering the crucial role played by these molecules in the functioning of the human body. In addition, the receptors involved in detecting the umami taste on the tongue are very similar to those involved in recognizing sweetness, as

Some foods with umami taste

Foods	Glutamic acid (mg/100 g)
Cheeses	
Parmesan:	1680
Roquefort:	1280
Seaweed (kombu):	1608
Sauces	
Fish sauce: *(nuoc nam)*	1370
Soy sauce: *(shoyu)*	782
Vegetables	
Tomato:	246
Green peas:	106
Mushroom: *(shiitake)*	71
Green vegetables: (cabbage, asparagus, spinach)	50
Avocado:	18
Seafood	
Scallops:	140
King crab:	72
Meat	
Chicken:	22
Beef:	10

Figure 4

Source: *J. Nutr.* 2000; 130: 921S-926S

both systems share a common receptor (T1R3). This similarity suggests that these mechanisms, which make substances essential to life palatable, share a common evolutionary origin.

Glutamate is released in large amounts during the prolonged cooking of meat and during the fermentation process. For this reason, aged cheeses, fermented sauces (soy, fish), and meat broths are among the primary elements possessing an umami flavour (Figure 4). Certain vegetables like tomatoes also contain significant amounts of glutamate, a property long known to give flavour to many dishes, including pizza (especially with parmesan cheese!). Umami can also enhance the taste of dishes in the form of monosodium glutamate (MSG), a seasoning of which Asians are particularly fond. Although MSG was suspected of causing the "Chinese restaurant syndrome" in the 1970s, we now know that the discomforts (headache, numbness, chest pain) experienced by certain people were not due to MSG. Blind studies conducted among people who claimed they were sensitive to this substance showed that MSG quantities higher than those found in Chinese restaurant meals did not have any effect! This is hardly surprising when we consider that from a molecular point of view there is no difference between natural glutamate and MSG.

Sugar

The sensation of pleasure associated with the presence of sugar in foods is a good example of the crucial role played by taste in detecting substances essential to life (Figure 5). Sugar is a preferred energy source, which our body cells can utilize quickly, particularly in the brain – this organ alone consumes almost 80% of daily sugar intake. When present in sufficiently high concentrations in the saliva, sugar molecules interact with two receptors located in the taste buds: T1R2 and T1R3. This activates a nerve impulse, signalling to the brain the presence of a food with a good caloric value. The association of T1R2 and T1R3 is absolutely essential in tasting sugar. For example, although cats have the T1R3 receptor on their tongue, they lack the T1R2 receptor, which explains their total indifference to sweet foods. However, combining the T1R2 and T1R3 receptors does not make it possible to accurately determine the substance responsible for the sweet taste, and it is possible to "trick" the brain into using molecules that will interact with these receptors, yet contain no source of energy. This physiological reality has led to the development of aspartame and sucralose (Splenda), two agents used abundantly by the food industry to mimic sweetness without adding calories. Even

so, it seems that the brain, disappointed by the lack of sugar intake, stimulates the appetite to compensate for the absence of calories in the sweetening agents. Many studies suggest that consuming so-called "diet," or no-calorie, soft drinks does not contribute to reducing body weight as expected, and in certain cases can even contribute to increasing it.

Salty

From a chemical point of view, what we call salt is sodium chloride (NaCl). The taste of salt is important as sodium is an element absolutely essential to life and its concentration must be strictly controlled by living organisms. (While it has no energy value, sodium is responsible for, among other things, the transmission of nerve impulses.) Saltiness is produced by the large-scale entry of sodium into certain taste bud cells, triggering a nerve impulse that informs the brain of the food's salty content. Although actual sodium needs are relatively modest (a few grams a day are enough to ensure the body functions properly), it seems the brain is particularly fond of the salty taste. To illustrate: In the 1950s, researchers offered sweet potatoes to a group of Japanese macaque monkeys, depositing the vegetables on a sandy seashore. Instead of simply rubbing the potato with its paw to remove the sand, one of the monkeys decided to wash it in seawater, a technique that was picked up by his mates. From that moment on, the monkeys fell into the habit of dipping their food in salt water and even passed on this practice to their descendants over many generations. The taste for salt seems to be cultural, strongly influenced by our environment. However, this habit can in the long run result in a sodium intake that is much higher than our body's actual needs, an excess that can lead to certain cardiovascular pathologies.

Sour (acidic)

Recognizing sour taste is instrumental in detecting the degree of acidity in foods, a trait often associated with food deterioration caused by the presence of micro-organisms (bacteria, mould). To verify this system's effectiveness, all you have to do is drink a glass of milk after its expiry date has passed! This defence mechanism makes it possible to avoid the damage such foods can cause to various body tissues and to our acid-base balance (the maintenance of a neutral pH level in the blood). In small doses, sour substances blend beautifully with sugar or fat, a property long exploited in both Asian cuisine (sweet and sour) and European cuisine (salad dressings, etc.).

Bitter

While babies will happily eat sugar, remain neutral to salt, and grimace slightly when tasting something sour, they completely reject anything bitter. This instinctive dislike of the bitter taste is due to the predominant place that plants have held throughout our evolution. Toxic molecules found in certain types of plants have the common characteristic of being bitter, and detecting this bitterness has been fundamental to identifying edible plant species without endangering the survival of the human race (Figure 6). The importance of this instinct is well illustrated by the significant number of receptors that can detect bitterness and their great sensitivity to minuscule amounts of toxic

molecules. While only two receptors detect the sugar sensation, at least 50 distinct receptors detect bitterness, and these are at least 1,000 times more sensitive!

But that is one of the great paradoxes of the human diet. Many bitter compounds found in plants have multiple health benefits and they are one of the main weapons at our disposal for preventing chronic diseases. The complex polyphenols in fruits like cranberries, the isothiocyanates in cruciferous vegetables, or the sulfur compounds in vegetables of the garlic family are all recognized by our receptors as bitter. And it is this property that prevents many people from eating these foods. The dislike of bitter substances can be so strong that inter-individual genetic variations may make certain people particularly sensitive to bitterness. For example, an estimated 25% of people have a modified version of certain bitter receptors (called TAS2R16) that make them hypersensitive to bitterness, thereby discouraging them from consuming bitter foods.

However, bitter taste has a real gastronomic value and can introduce a good contrast into food tastes when combined with other flavours, producing a complex harmony impossible to achieve when it is not there. Acquiring a taste for bitterness represents a victory over our primeval instincts. It is a form of cultural evolution that allows us to overcome a major obstacle in our quest for new tastes and health benefits that were formerly inaccessible. It is therefore not surprising that all culinary traditions in the world have developed a blend of flavours in order to exploit the benefits of bitter taste. For example, the umami flavour is often used by Asians to enhance the taste of cruciferous vegetable dishes (soy sauce or fish, seaweed, shiitake mushrooms).

A passion for sugar

Sensory pleasure
- Colourful, ripe, and flavourful fruits
- Innate (mother's milk)

Evolutionary selection
- Brain fuel
- Quick source of energy

Figure 5

A dislike of bitterness

Evolutionary selection
- Identification of toxic substances
- Heightened awareness of these substances

Figure 6

A taste for fat

Sensory pleasure
- Roundness of flavours
- Rich texture
- Enhanced taste

Evolutionary selection
- Better source of energy
- Source of essential fatty acids
- Source of liposoluble vitamins

Figure 7

delicacy in Japan, but runs completely counter to the food preferences of most Westerners. Taste is therefore a relative sense, strongly influenced by culture and era, which consequently varies enormously according to the individual.

Control points

While taste and smell play crucial roles in the process of determining food *quality,* appetite control and body weight mechanisms are essential to determining the *quantity* of food necessary for our needs. Even if a food tastes delicious, there are still limits to how much of it we can eat!

Appetite control requires that many body organs work closely together. This process is supervised by the brain, the "supreme commander" that integrates information about the energy received from these organs and dictates appropriate behaviours to maintain an energy balance. The control unit is located in the hypothalamus, a tiny area at the base of the brain and possessing two control centres. One of these is for hunger, the other for satiety, and both are constantly listening for information about body energy. For example, blood sugar level (glycemia) is measured continuously by the hunger centre; any decrease, however slight, immediately triggers an alert, stimulating the appetite. A decreased-energy signal can come from the stomach, which produces a hormone called ghrelin (from the Indo-European *ghre,* meaning "growth"). This

acts as a potent appetite stimulator through its action on the nerve cells of the hunger centre. When you feel an energy drop, or irritation, or stomach rumblings, it means these mechanisms are working and telling you it is time to eat!

While the signals of hunger are easy to recognize, those responsible for halting the ingestion of food are much more complex and can sometimes be more difficult to interpret. The first control point is in the stomach lining, where nerve fibres detect how much the stomach has expanded, enabling the brain to estimate the volume of food to be brought into the body. In normal conditions, these nerve fibres are activated well before the stomach is filled to capacity, so as to avoid the negative effects on the digestive process of excessive eating. But as any food lover knows, we can bypass these signals and eat more than the amount our brain allows! While occasional overeating at certain festive times may be acceptable, if we overindulge repeatedly, our stomach can get used to a high level of distension, compromising the effectiveness of the satiety signals.

A Japanese man called Takeru "Tsunami" Kobayashi undoubtedly represents an extreme example of the potential of desensitizing satiety. As a result of intensive training to distend his stomach, in 2006 he managed the incredible feat of swallowing 54 hot dogs in 12 minutes! Now that this dubious record stands at 66 hot dogs (also in 12 minutes), we can only be astounded by the incredible adaptability of the human body,

When eating can make you hot or cold

The piquant taste of many spices and seasonings used in cooking is due to the high content in these plants of a molecule that stimulates pain detection systems. This property plays a major role in protecting the plants from predators.

The best-documented effect of spices is undoubtedly the activation of the pain system by capsaicin, a molecule responsible for the spiciness of hot peppers. This spicy sensation is due to the capsaicin binding with the vanilloid receptor TRPV1, a protein involved in detecting unpleasant stimuli such as temperatures over 43° C. By interacting with this receptor, the capsaicin mimics the sensation of heat or burning – the reason why some particularly spicy dishes can feel like they are setting your mouth on fire! The hotness of the peppers depends on their capsaicin content, a property often evaluated by measuring the amount of dilution required for the pepper's spicy sensation to no longer be detectable by the tongue. For example, while *jalapeno* peppers need to be diluted 5,000 times to remove the taste of their spiciness, the *Bhut Jolokia* variety, cultivated in the northwest of India, is still spicy even when diluted one million times, making it the hottest pepper in

the world! The capsaicin content of these peppers is so high that the inhabitants of this region use it to protect themselves against damage caused by elephants in their area by coating fences with the oil extracted from these peppers!

Some people can eat very spicy dishes. This ability is made possible by capsaicin's desensitizing of the nerve endings, which comes with regular consumption of spicy meals. For the non-initiated, however, the best way to alleviate the burning sensation caused by an overly spicy dish is to consume milk or yogurt instead of water. Although capsaicin is insoluble in water and binds with its receptor, it can be "coated" by the casein in milk, enabling the receptors to return to their normal state. In India, *raita*, a yogurt-based sauce, often accompanies hot curries.

Recent research has shown that similar mechanisms are responsible for the sensation caused by most substances that "spice up" our daily diet. Whether it is the piperin responsible for the hot taste of black pepper, the isothiocyanates of mustard, the horseradish that goes up your nose, the sulfur compounds of garlic, the eugenol of cloves, the cinnamaldehyde of cinnamon, the gingerol of ginger, or odorous molecules of many seasonings (thyme, oregano . . .), the sensations of these molecules are all due to their interaction with heat-sensitive receptors. Conversely, it is worth noting that the menthol found in mint interacts with a cold-sensitive receptor (TRPV8). This linkage is responsible for the sensation of freshness so characteristic of this spice.

The reason for humans' attraction to substances that stimulate the senses that are normally employed to detect pain is still not understood, but it may be connected to the release of pleasure molecules (endorphins). Regardless, these molecules are now important in our diet, which suggests that we have learned to come to terms with the supposed "dangers" associated with consuming spices and seasonings.

but mostly by the foolishness of abusing these capabilities.

When the brain says enough!

Besides the mechanical aspects of the satiety phenomenon, various hormonal mechanisms are also instrumental in signalling to the brain that food is being assimilated and the meal should be ended to avoid system overload. Too often we forget that our body's organs are not isolated compartments functioning independently of each other. On the contrary, each organ sends messages to its partners about the existing situation in various areas of the body and the measures to be taken if there are disruptions incompatible with vital functions. In the case of regulating appetite, these messages take the form of various satiety hormones produced in different parts of the intestine, liver, pancreas, and adipose tissue (Figure 8). For example, when food digested by the stomach reaches the intestine, specialized cells secrete into the neighbouring bloodstream a hormone called cholecystokinin (CCK). This is transported to the cerebellum where it activates a satiety centre. At the same time, other hormones such as PYY (intestine), insulin (pancreas), or signals sent by nutrient detectors in the liver act on the neurons of the hypothalamus to curb appetite. As we can see, while there are only a few appetite stimulators (the ghrelin secreted by the stomach is the only orexic hormone identified until now), there are many mechanisms involved in appetite suppression, illustrating how vital it is for the body to avoid excess food.

Other regulating mechanisms are also very important for appetite control. Leptin (from the Greek *leptos,* meaning slender) secreted by adipose tissue cells is particularly noteworthy as this hormone acts as an adipostat, indicating to the brain the state of energy reserves stored in the form of fat. Since this hormone's production is proportional to the fatty mass, a significant quantity of leptin in the blood indicates an energy surplus, leading to appetite loss and decreased energy intake. The hormone is absolutely essential to appetite control: It has been observed that mice that do not produce leptin (ob/ob mice) can ingest enormous amounts of food and grow excessively (Figure 9). Among humans, leptin deficiency also has dramatic consequences on body weight. Some rare clinical cases are known such as the young woman who could not produce this hormone due to a genetic mutation and weighed almost 90 kg by the age of nine. Some 57% of her weight was in the form of fat. However, such a leptin loss is very rare and is responsible for only a tiny percentage of obesity cases. The vast majority of obese people have normal (and often very high) leptin levels, but it is the brain's ability to manage these hormone signals that seems impaired. In fact, despite the energy surplus stored in their adipose tissues, these people maintain their appetite, making weight loss very difficult.

When your eyes are bigger than your stomach

From a biological perspective, appetite control is a well-regulated process in which a decrease in energy reserves automatically leads to hunger

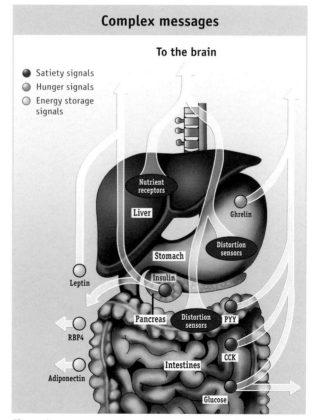

Figure 8   Source: adapted from *Sc. Am.* 2007; 297: 72-81

and demands for food intake to meet these needs (Figure 10). When energy levels return to normal, a range of regulating mechanisms kick in, preventing an energy overload. These mechanisms for controlling appetite and maintaining homeostasis seem to function wonderfully in most animals. In nature, excess fat is almost non-existent, except to protect against cold or compensate for prolonged periods of inactivity such as hibernation.

Unfortunately, the obesity epidemic now observed around the world is clear proof that these regulating mechanisms are less effective in humans. This ineffectiveness is due to the enormous influence exerted by our surroundings and our emotions regarding the perception of food. Due to the development of our cerebral cortex, attraction to food is not only a matter of biological need but also desire (Figure 10). In normal conditions, anticipating the pleasure of food is truly wonderful, allowing us to turn eating into a unique, typically human experience. The complexity of flavours and textures can generate incredible sensations while remaining in harmony with our physiological needs. However, when poorly controlled, these urges can short-circuit the hunger control mechanisms, leading to food intake that exceeds the body's energy needs (Figure 11).

Another major factor in excessive food consumption is undoubtedly the undeniable attraction of foods containing large amounts of the substances necessary for life – particularly sugar,

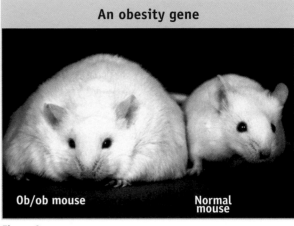

An obesity gene

Ob/ob mouse   Normal mouse

Figure 9   Source: Science Photo Library

fat, and salt. While a taste for spices and refined foods derives from a cultural dimension that has evolved relatively late in our history, we are biologically programmed to like sugar, fat, and salt. It is completely normal that we are very attracted to these basic substances. We should not be surprised, therefore, if a large amount of food produced by the junk food industry possesses this very characteristic: It is exceptionally rich in sugar, fat, and/or salt (and often all three at the same time). In meeting our primary needs, these products become very attractive.

However, our innate attraction to sugar, fat, and salt, and the intense pleasure associated with eating foods containing these substances, are so powerful that they can disrupt the internal appetite-control mechanisms. For example, we now know that sugar and fat release chemical messengers into the brain, particularly dopamine,

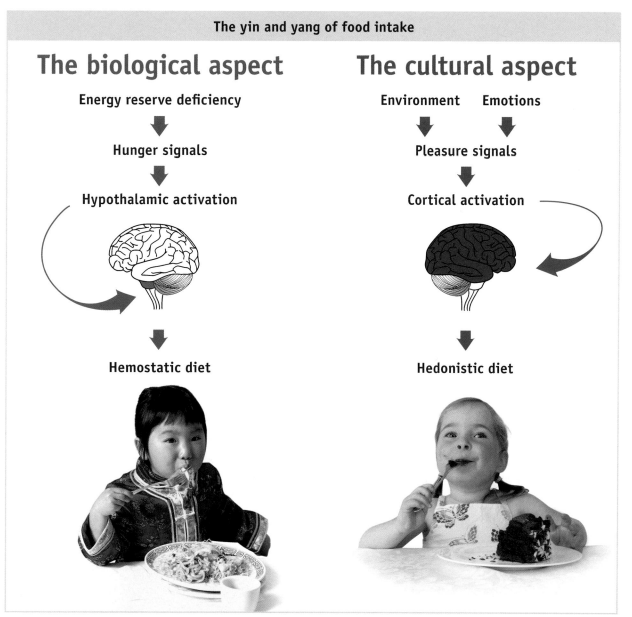

Figure 10

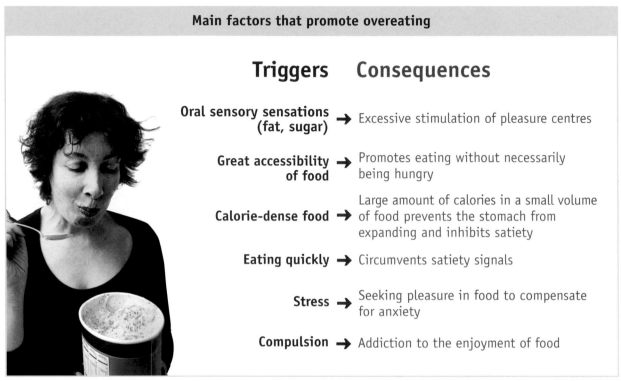

Main factors that promote overeating

Triggers		Consequences
Oral sensory sensations (fat, sugar)	→	Excessive stimulation of pleasure centres
Great accessibility of food	→	Promotes eating without necessarily being hungry
Calorie-dense food	→	Large amount of calories in a small volume of food prevents the stomach from expanding and inhibits satiety
Eating quickly	→	Circumvents satiety signals
Stress	→	Seeking pleasure in food to compensate for anxiety
Compulsion	→	Addiction to the enjoyment of food

Figure 11

activating compensatory and pleasure systems similar to the effects of drugs such as nicotine, alcohol, or cocaine! Like any form of addiction, the over-stimulation of pleasure centres by high-energy foods can generate a dependence that in the medium- and long-term will cause us to over-eat and accumulate excess energy in the form of fat. Unfortunately, nothing encourages such eating habits more than the environment in which we live.

Summary

- Taste is a very complex sense involving our physical senses, memory, and culture.

- The brain's active participation adds a hedonistic dimension to the act of eating, an essential characteristic of the human spirit.

- Excessive stimulation of the pleasure centres caused by calorie-rich foods disrupts the body's appetite-control mechanisms, an imbalance that contributes to the accumulation of calorie reserves in the form of fat.

Overindulgence kills
more than the sword.

Chinese proverb

Chapter 4

In the Land of Giant Appetites

According to the WHO, there are now more than one billion people in the world who must be considered overweight, in addition to 300 million people considered obese, of which 20 million are children under five. This epidemic of being overweight, which is evident both in industrialized countries and nations in economic transition, contrasts sharply with the situation of developing countries whose inhabitants suffer chronic shortages of basic foods, leading to hunger and malnutrition (Figure 1). As well as underlining the gross injustices of our world and the enormous amount of work to be done in the redistribution of wealth, these statistics highlight our complex relationship with food and the extreme forms it can take.

Critical mass

The measurement of excess weight is not based on aesthetic considerations, but rather on

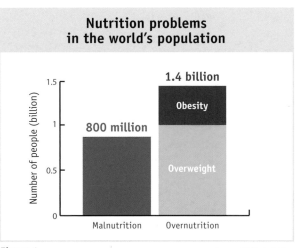

Figure 1   Source: WHO statistics

Are you overweight? Check the index

We owe to the Belgian statistician Adolphe Quetelet the formula that states that body weight, in adults age 20 and over, increases proportionally to height squared. Quetelet's index, better known as "body mass index" (BMI), can be easily calculated using this mathematical formula:

$$BMI = \frac{\text{weight in kg}}{(\text{height in metres})^2}$$

Although not perfect, this index has become the standard over the years for determining whether a person is carrying excess weight. According to WHO criteria, a BMI between 19 and 24 represents a normal weight; a BMI between 25 and 29 is considered overweight; and a BMI over 30 counts as obesity.

This index gained currency in the 1930s when American insurance companies noted that of all calculations measuring excess weight, a BMI of more than 30 was the best indicator of the risk of a policyholder dying. As we can see, the dangers associated with obesity have been known for a long time!

To calculate your BMI, use the formula below or the grid on the opposite page (Figure 2). For example, a man who is 1.75 m tall and weighs 75 kg has the following BMI:

$$75 \div (1.75 \times 1.75) = 24$$

Since our height does not change after reaching adulthood, a weight gain always increases the BMI. For example, this man's BMI would be 27 if he weighed 85 kg, and 32 if he weighed 100 kg. While 75 kg is a healthy weight for him, an additional 10 kg would make him overweight, and an extra 25 kg would mean he was obese.

We must be especially careful about excess weight in the abdomen. A waist measurement greater than 102 cm (40 inches) in men and 88 cm (35 inches) in women is generally a sign of health problems linked to overweight. The correct way to measure your waist is by putting a measuring tape around your abdomen between the navel and the bottom of the ribs. As we will see in Chapter 5, if your body mass index is around 30 and your waist measurement is also high, you should do something about it quickly. If serious heart disease is present, you are in a very high risk group.

well-defined criteria, validated by the scientific and medical community. Among the measures that can be used, body mass index (BMI) has been established in recent years as a simple and effective way to determine the incidence of overweight and obesity within populations (see box p. 66).

In North America as in many industrialized countries in Europe and Asia, the percentage of obese people dramatically increased in the early 1980s and has continued to rise since then. For example, in 1995 between 10% and 20% of the U.S. population was obese. The percentage rose considerably over the next ten years throughout the entire country, particularly in certain southern states, specifically Louisiana and Mississippi, where the proportion of obese people now exceeds

30% (Figure 3). This growth is so startling that if the pace continues, almost all American adults will be overweight by 2040!

A similar trend has been observed in Canada, especially among children. Twenty-five years ago, 3% of Canadian boys ages two to 17 were obese; this percentage rose to 9% in 2004, an increase that makes Canada a world leader in childhood obesity (Figure 4). If overweight children were added to these statistics, a little over one-quarter of young people would currently be overweight, a very disturbing situation considering that 70% of obese adolescents carry this excess weight into adulthood.

As mentioned earlier, overweight is no longer a problem limited to inhabitants of industrialized

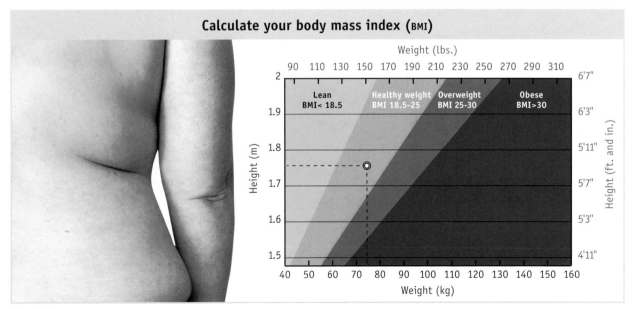

Figure 2

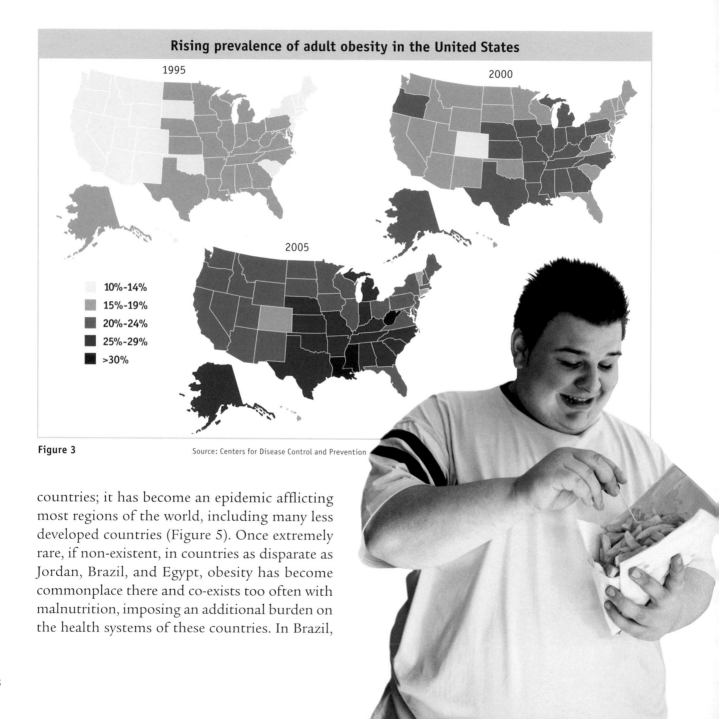

Rising prevalence of adult obesity in the United States

1995

2000

2005

10%-14%
15%-19%
20%-24%
25%-29%
>30%

Figure 3

Source: Centers for Disease Control and Prevention

countries; it has become an epidemic afflicting most regions of the world, including many less developed countries (Figure 5). Once extremely rare, if non-existent, in countries as disparate as Jordan, Brazil, and Egypt, obesity has become commonplace there and co-exists too often with malnutrition, imposing an additional burden on the health systems of these countries. In Brazil, for example, the heavy consumption of mass-produced calorie-laden foods lacking in essential nutrients is causing serious deficiencies and retarding growth among children. At the same time, consumption of these foods by adults is resulting in excessive caloric intake, promoting obesity. The simultaneous presence of these two extremes creates very painful social conditions, unimaginable even a few years ago: In an estimated 10% of Brazilian homes, children suffer from major nutritional deficiencies and live with a mother who is overweight.

Tipping the scales

These dramatic increases in excess weight and obesity are especially remarkable given that we have assumed, since time immemorial, that

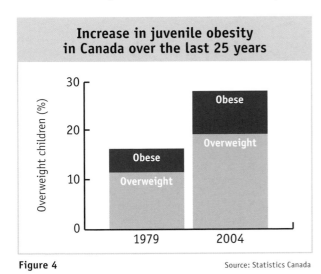

Increase in juvenile obesity in Canada over the last 25 years

Overweight children (%)

Figure 4   Source: Statistics Canada

natural environmental limitations imposed on our food intake will prevent us from becoming overweight. Despite the skill and efficiency of hunter-gatherers, they still had to expend considerable effort to obtain the amount of food necessary for survival; this kept them from being overweight. Statuettes of corpulent women created by humans at this time, such as the Venus of Willendorf (picture), symbolized our ancestors' fascination with an inaccessible world of abundance and fertility. (Paradoxically, we now know that obesity is a major cause of infertility.) Later, the development of cities and complex social, economic, and political structures improved food production, but the increasing number of mouths to be fed exerted tremendous pressures on the availability of resources. Excess weight denoted a great power's wealth in the same way as luxurious clothing or jewellery. In some cultures, obesity took on such a special quality that it was central to the development of complex religious rituals (see box, p. 71).

How to explain such a turnaround? Obviously, since excess weight and obesity are by definition problems associated with an accumulation of excess energy in the form of fat, the weight gain is clearly due to an imbalance between energy intake and energy expenditure. When energy intake through food is counter-balanced by equivalent energy expenditure, the weight remains stable. But when caloric intake from overconsumption of food is accompanied by reduced energy expenditure due to a more sedentary lifestyle, the energy surplus is stored as fat (Figure 6).

Balancing this equilibrium can be very delicate: For example, a 10% difference between energy intake and energy expenditure can lead to a weight gain of 14 kg in one year alone! Similarly, a surplus of just five calories a day,

equivalent to less than one tablespoon of sugar, can result in a 10 kg gain if continued over 40 years.

This kind of weight gain is very likely to occur today, given that most people in the industrialized world have easy and almost unlimited access to a great abundance of food without having to expend much effort to acquire it. While hunter-gatherers used up considerable stores of energy to obtain food, and the first farmers worked relentlessly to ensure successful harvests, today the only physical effort needed to obtain food may be pushing a grocery cart! As a result, it is

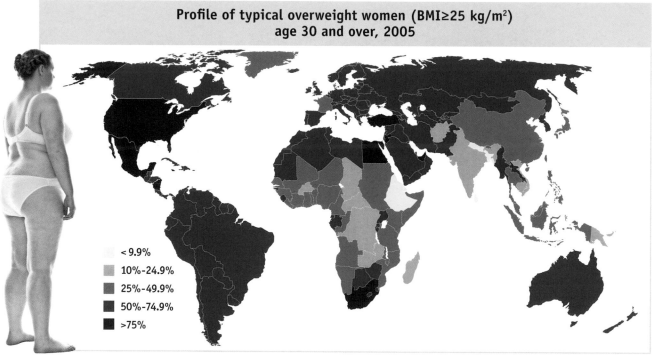

Profile of typical overweight women (BMI≥25 kg/m^2) age 30 and over, 2005

< 9.9%
10%–24.9%
25%–49.9%
50%–74.9%
>75%

Figure 5

Source: WHO statistics

A mass-appeal sport!

Sumo, a word derived from *sumsi* (wrestling), is a typically Japanese form of wrestling probably inspired by the *kaku-tegi* practised in China during the Han dynasty (202 BCE). According to the Japanese mythology described in *Kojiki (Records of Ancient Matters,* 712), the *kami* (god) Takemi-kazuchi defeated Takeminakata during a sumo match, thereby allowing his people to take possession of the Japanese islands. The origins of sumo thereby paralleled the emergence of Japan.

Besides the match itself, the most spectacular aspect of sumo is undoubtedly the impressive size of the *rikishis,* who combine formidable weight (generally around 150 kg) with great flexibility and agility. The wrestlers achieve this condition by following intensive training, combining fighting fitness with a very rich diet to encourage weight gain. The *rikishi*'s main dish is *chanko-nabe,* a protein- and fat-rich stew, containing (among other things) fish, chicken, seafood, eggs, and vegetables, all blended in a thick sauce. They eat this meal twice a day, with rice and several accompanying dishes, each time followed by a siesta to encourage storage in the form of fat. This "diet" contains between 5,000 and 10,000 calories. Konishiki, who at 285 kg was the heaviest sumo wrestler in history, could eat in a single meal 10 portions of *chanko-nabe,* eight bowls of rice, 25 portions of grilled beef, and 130 pieces of sushi!

Idolized by a society that paradoxically values a healthy and moderate diet, sumo wrestlers represent the exceptional and marginal nature of obesity, which is borne out by the lifestyle's negative impact on the health of these wrestlers. Excess weight considerably increases the development of diabetes and heart disease, not to mention the stress it puts on weight-bearing joints, which can promote the onset of arthritis. Sumo wrestlers have a life expectancy of about 65 years, or 10 years less than Japan's male population.

very easy to accumulate a surplus of energy, with all the inherent risks of being overweight.

However, as simple as it may appear to be, this balance hides a much more complex reality, one that most people trying to lose a little weight will understand well: It is much easier to gain weight than to lose it! This is not due to laziness or a lack of willpower, but rather reflects a basic characteristic of our metabolism: It is always trying to tip the scales towards storing calories for times of scarcity. Inherited from our long evolution and deeply rooted in our physiology, this metabolic property is a fundamental factor in the current obesity epidemic.

A history predisposed to obesity

As we saw earlier, food scarcity and the concomitant threat of famine represented the main challenge for survival throughout human history. During periods of serious food shortages throughout our existence, famines exposed populations to appalling ordeals, the extent of which we can hardly imagine (see box, p. 76). These famines had a devastating impact: Recent data show that 70,000 years ago, or just before the migration of the first *Homo sapiens* from Africa to Europe, humanity faced extinction after a major drought and only an estimated 2,000 people survived. While humanity fortunately lived through this ordeal, famines devastated a number of populations over the millennia that followed, posing a serious threat

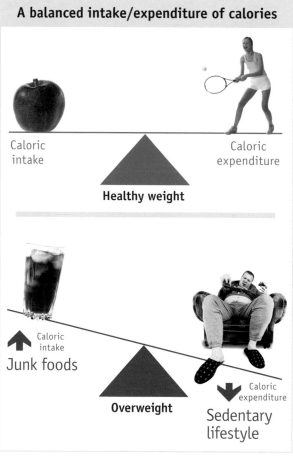

A balanced intake/expenditure of calories

Caloric intake

Caloric expenditure

Healthy weight

Junk foods

Caloric intake

Overweight

Caloric expenditure

Sedentary lifestyle

Figure 6

to their survival (Figure 7). This ongoing struggle to obtain the food essential for life is still a reality today: More than one billion people face a chronic shortage of basic food every day and some 100,000 die each day from hunger or a malnutrition-related disease. The contrast between these people's lives and the lifestyle excesses of industrialized societies is simply shocking.

Our constant struggle against food scarcity and famine has had a profound influence on our attraction to food and the means to assimilate the energy in it. When the availability of food is limited, people whose metabolism can adapt to these shortages have a greater chance of survival and can pass on this trait to their descendants. For example, if one of our ancestors (let's call him Igor) has genes facilitating the storage of energy contained in food, he and his descendants will have a greater chance of surviving repeated famines. Conversely, another person, Jurg, who does not have such genes will be much more disadvantaged when faced with such an ordeal and his chances of enduring prolonged food shortages are far less (Figure 8). Since most peoples of the world have suffered from famine during their history, the "high-performing" genes that can store the maximum amount of energy have become widespread and are now an integral part of our genetic heritage.

Genetically not adapted to abundance

Our ability to adjust to food scarcity and store energy as fat has undoubtedly been an important trait that has helped us survive periods of food shortages. However, this mechanism

Historic famines (in percentage or number of deaths)		
Rome	(400-800)	**90%** of the population
Russia	(1601-1603)	**33%** of the population
India	(1630)	**2,000,000**
France	(1693-1694)	**2,000,000**
Prussia	(1708-1711)	**41%** of the population
Bengal	(1770)	**10,000,000**
Cape Verde	(1830)	**50%** of the population
Ireland	(1845-1849)	**1,000,000**
China	(1876-1879)	**13,000,000**
India	(1876-1879)	**5,250,000**
Ethiopia	(1888-1892)	**33%** of the population
Persia	(1917-1921)	**25%** of the population
Russia	(1921)	**5,000,000**
China	(1959-1961)	**20,000,000**
Uganda	(1980)	**21%** of the population
North Korea	(1996-1999)	**600,000**

Figure 7   Source: Wikipedia

paradoxically *over*performs in an environment in which food is abundant and energy expenditure is often minimal. In such conditions, the level of excellence achieved by our genes in storing food can work against us: The irresistible attraction of omnipresent food combined with our great efficiency in maximally extracting the energy contained in it, then storing it as fat, very often leads to overconsumption and excessive fat accumulation (Figure 8).

Over 100 genes have been associated with obesity, 22 of which appear to predominate. These are associated with specific biological or behavioural traits: increased caloric storage in the form of fat; poor appetite control; sedentary lifestyles; metabolism-altering fats; slow metabolism and inadequate thermogenesis.

The significance of these genetic factors in extra weight gain is illustrated by a number of studies showing that BMI is closely linked to heredity. For example, adopted children have obesity levels similar to those of their biological parents, but not of their adoptive family. Similarly, we know that concurrent obesity in identical twins (boys and girls) is much more pronounced than in non-identical twins, thus

(continued p. 77)

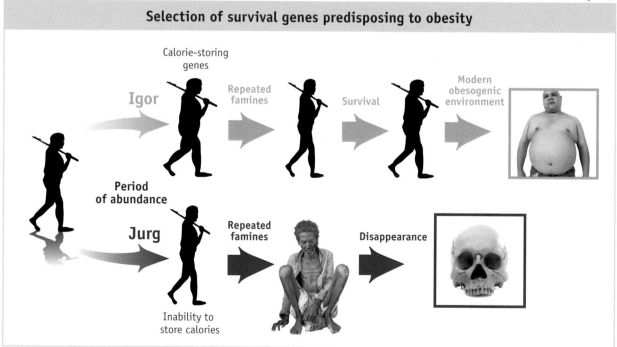

Selection of survival genes predisposing to obesity

Calorie-storing genes

Igor

Repeated famines

Survival

Modern obesogenic environment

Period of abundance

Jurg

Repeated famines

Disappearance

Inability to store calories

Figure 8

In the throes of hunger

There are countless stories of the tragic consequences of famines endured by humans throughout our history. In 585, "almost all of Gaul suffered from famine [. . .] many others who had no flour at all, collected grasses, ate them and swelled up and died; many died consumed with hunger" (Gregory of Tours, *History of the Franks,* Book VII). A few centuries later, in 1033, "atmospheric conditions changed the normal course of the seasons to the point that it was never favourable to sowing, and especially because of the flooding it was never favourable to harvesting [. . .]. The food shortage tightened its grip on the entire population: The affluent and well-to-do suffered from hunger as much as the poor [. . .]. However, after eating the birds and animals, and driven by tremendous hunger, people quarrelled over carrion and other unmentionables. In their desperation, people were reduced to eating human flesh. Travellers were kidnapped by people stronger than they, and their body parts cut up, cooked over a fire and devoured. Many people who travelled from place to place to flee the famine encountered hospitality along the way, and during the night had their throats slit and were used as food by those who had welcomed them. Many, by showing a piece of fruit or an egg to children, lured them to isolated places, butchered them, and ate them up. Dead bodies were in many places snatched from the ground and also used to assuage hunger" (Raoul Glaber, *Histoires, 1030-1047).*

Far from being limited to Europe, such desperation caused by famine affected all regions of the world, particularly China where, during the Chu army's siege of the Song Fortress in 594 BCE, the inhabitants had recourse to *yizi er shi* or "exchanging each other's children to eat them" (Sima Qian, *Historical Records,* 91 BCE).

Even more recently (1693), France "endured the greatest and most widespread famine that we had ever known [. . .]. We heard the dismal cries of poor children abandoned by their parents, scream- ing day and night, begging for bread . . . . Families were so poor, abandoned and in such misery that they were reduced to eating the grass like animals and eating things that vile animals would never have touched (Louis XIV, *Memoirs and Other Writings*). A little over a century later, in January 1789, when Mirabeau wrote upon his return from a trip to Aix-en-Provence that "the Exterminating Angel struck down the human race from one end of the kingdom to the other. All the scourges have been unleashed; I have found people dead from cold and hunger everywhere." He described an untenable situation in which extreme deprivation of food, especially bread, would lead a few months later to one of the greatest political revolutions in history.

These horrible ordeals illustrate just how deeply rooted in our biology are the survival instinct and the need to eat.

confirming the presence of a strong inherited genetic component. In other words, there is an obese person lying dormant in all of us! However, with very few exceptions, not one of these factors can cause overweight on its own; this vulnerability requires an environment that encourages the genes to express their full potential for accumulating energy.

Excess weight and obesity are very complex problems resulting from the interaction of a broad range of genetic, environmental, and cultural factors. We must never underestimate the influence of our social and cultural environment. For example, we know that people have a higher risk of becoming obese if others in their circle, particularly friends and family members, are overweight. Our social network has an astonishing impact on our weight: Close friendships with obese people increase the risk of becoming obese by almost 200% (Figure 10)! It appears that the presence of obese people in our immediate environment makes excess weight "contagious." This may affect our perception of what is normal weight so that we tend to surround ourselves with obese people.

However, regardless of the major role played by the social environment, obesity is first and foremost an eating problem. The rapid increase in obesity worldwide means that significant dietary changes have occurred and are having dramatic consequences in the accumulation of surplus energy as fat. Among these factors, nothing plays as great a role as the consumption of calorie-dense food produced and distributed by the junk food industry.

Refining without refinement

Blinded by the technological innovations that today form an integral part of our lives, we forget that our creature comforts and most of the objects around us were unimaginable barely three generations ago. However, it is not only our telephones, computers, and television sets that are the products of such progress: A large proportion of our food in the last few years is also of recent invention, part of a panoply of processed foods that increasingly replace traditional home-cooked meals.

Processed foods commonly contain huge amounts of at least one of this diet's four staples: sugar, fat, refined flour, and salt. The food industry's systematic and intensive use of these ingredients has radically transformed our daily diet by encouraging the production of fast food products in which caloric content takes precedence over nutritive value. Candies, potato chips, cereals, snacks, desserts, and frozen foods – all these foods that occupy an increasingly

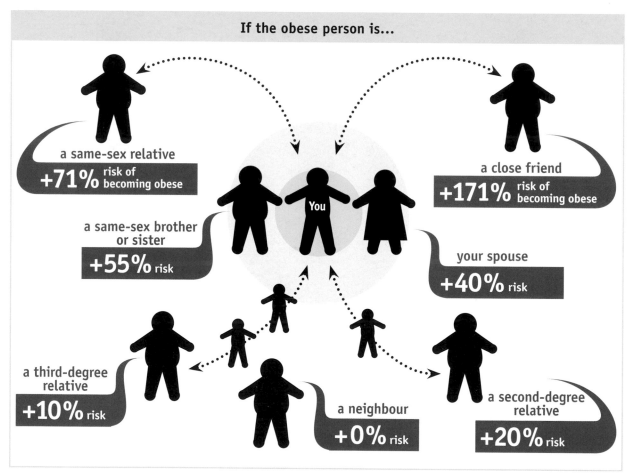

If the obese person is...

a same-sex relative
+71% risk of becoming obese

a close friend
+171% risk of becoming obese

a same-sex brother or sister
+55% risk

You

your spouse
+40% risk

a third-degree relative
+10% risk

a neighbour
+0% risk

a second-degree relative
+20% risk

Figure 9

Source: *NEJM* 2007; 357: 370-379

important place on our supermarket shelves are a direct consequence of this new diet "philosophy" that has completely changed the composition of most people's grocery baskets.

Diverging goals

Every year, about 10,000 new food products try to claim a piece of a market that already includes some 300,000 items (Figure 10). This profusion illustrates the vitality and enormous innovativeness of the modern food industry. As in any sector of business, food manufacturers are constantly on the lookout for new trends and production technologies that will give them a larger share of the market and generate more profits. While some of these products are of excellent quality and provide us with a wide assortment of foods from around the world, many, unfortunately, are overprocessed. They may contain a surprising list of ingredients whose names are often incomprehensible to anyone without an advanced degree in chemistry.

The main factors contributing to the excessive production of these processed foods are economic in nature. The food industry is evolving in a relatively closed financial sector and its growth is largely limited by the amount of food that people can consume. Therefore, the best way to increase profits generally is to reduce production costs. This involves using cheaper and poorer-quality products as well as developing production processes that improve product shelf life to reduce losses. Unfortunately, such a strategy is often used to the detriment of consumer health. Although recent studies suggest we should encourage the consumption of omega-3 fats due to their many beneficial health effects, one of the easiest ways to extend a food product's shelf life is to destroy these fats by hydrogenation, as they quickly turn rancid. This causes the products containing them to deteriorate rapidly. However, not only does this hydrogenation reaction eliminate beneficial fats, it also creates trans fats, substances now known to be instrumental in the development of heart disease (see Chapter 5).

An abundance of choices

- **300,000** food products are available in the United States with an average of 35,000 products per supermarket

- Every year the food industry introduces **10,000** new grocery products, including:

3,000 candies

3,000 snacks

2,000 soft drinks

1,000 bakery products

Figure 10

This reduced flexibility in generating profits also favours food production that reflects the tastes of the largest number of people, in order to grab the largest market share possible. Adding significant amounts of sugar and fat to processed foods certainly is the best way to achieve such goals. These substances come from plants whose production is largely subsidized (sugar from corn and fat from soy) and inexpensive; but, more significantly, everybody likes them, which is why people continue to eat them.

While the junk food industry does not set out to make people sick, we must nonetheless remember that processed foods rich in fat and sugar derive from economic principles that have no regard for the impact of such food on health. As we will see, while this policy may be good for the food industry, sustained profit growth based on the sale of such highly processed products is clearly incompatible with consumer health.

(continued p. 83)

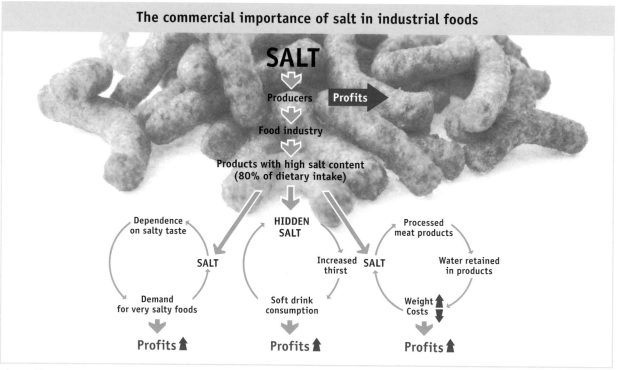

The commercial importance of salt in industrial foods

SALT

Producers → Profits

Food industry

Products with high salt content
(80% of dietary intake)

HIDDEN SALT

Dependence on salty taste

SALT

Demand for very salty foods

Profits ↑

Increased thirst

SALT

Soft drink consumption

Profits ↑

Processed meat products

Water retained in products

Weight ↑
Costs ↓

Profits ↑

Figure 11

Source: *Int. J. Epidemiol.* 2002; 31: 320-327

Sugar

While consumption of refined sugar was almost non-existent before the industrial era, being limited to sugars like honey or maple sugar, the development of processes for extracting sugar from cane and then from sugar beets resulted in wider dietary use of this sweetener. In 1815, inhabitants of industrialized countries consumed on average six kg of refined sugar a year; today inhabitants of countries like the United States consume almost 70 kg. Soft drinks represent one of the main sources of added sugar; just one beverage can contain 42 g or the equivalent of nine teaspoons of sugar! On average, Canadians drink 120 litres of soft drinks a year (or almost the equivalent of a 355-mL can per day), which means they consume 15 kg of sugar from this "liquid candy" alone. That can translate into a weight gain of seven kg in one year if it is not compensated for by an increase in physical activity!

Fats

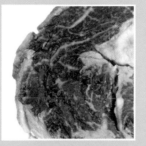

The industrialization of food has also completely changed the nature of dietary fats. For example, meat as we know it today has very little in common with the meat eaten before the industrial era. While traditionally cattle ate grass and reached a size sufficient for slaughter only after four or five years, most of today's meat comes from animals that are force-fed cereals (particularly corn) and may be slaughtered at only 14 months. This improved productivity, however, has consequences on the composition of the meat: Animals raised the modern way may contain up to 30% fat, most of which is saturated, while traditional breeding produced a leaner meat, containing less saturated and more polyunsaturated fat (including healthful omega-3 fats). The contrast between the meat we eat today and the wild meat consumed by our prehistoric ancestors is even greater; game contained three times more unsaturated fat and a fifth of the saturated fat.

Refined flour

Before the industrial revolution, the flour obtained by grinding cereal with stone-mills was "complete"; that is, in addition to starch, it contained all the original grain components (fibre, vitamins, bran). Its composition was radically altered in the late nineteenth century with the invention of metal mills and mechanized processes. Grinding the grain more finely made the flour more sensitive to rancidification, and only by eliminating the surface components of grains could this refined flour be preserved for long periods. Unfortunately, this process eliminates all the beneficial components of cereals from the outset! Refined flour is therefore a good example of the problems that can arise from excessive food processing.

Salt

The food industry loves salt because this inexpensive condiment adds taste to foods that would normally not have any, while increasing their shelf life (Figure 11). An estimated 90% of salt consumed by the population comes from processed foods, which shows how important salt is for the industry! Its omnipresence means that we consume too much salt: an average of 3,000 mg a day, which considerably exceeds our needs (about 1,500 mg). As mentioned earlier, this systematic use of salt by the food industry has very serious repercussions on the development of heart disease.

David and Goliath

One of the most obvious consequences of the excessive industrialization of food is the increasing amount of space these products occupy in our everyday surroundings. Besides the weekly supermarket visit, we can encounter a wide variety of processed food products almost anywhere: at service stations, rest stops, pharmacies, big-box stores, and even hospitals. In some places, getting around displays of potato chips, cookies, soft drinks, and other snacks can be a feat in itself! We are constantly being tempted by these products, which are often sold cheaply, especially when our food budget is tight.

Such fare becomes even more appealing when pushed at us by mass advertising campaigns. In the United States, fast-food restaurants spent over $2 billion on advertising in 2004, including about $500 million to promote the leading soft drink brands (Figure 12). These campaigns are often directed at very young audiences in the hope of instilling the consumption habit as early as possible, creating loyal customers for years. The other side of the coin is that only about $5 million, or 1/500th of the money invested by the fast-food industry, was spent promoting the benefits of fruit and vegetable consumption – however essential to good health it may be. To put this in relative terms, children are exposed daily to advertising that extols junk food products, but will have to wait the equivalent of a year and a half before hearing the message that regular consumption of fruits and vegetables has a

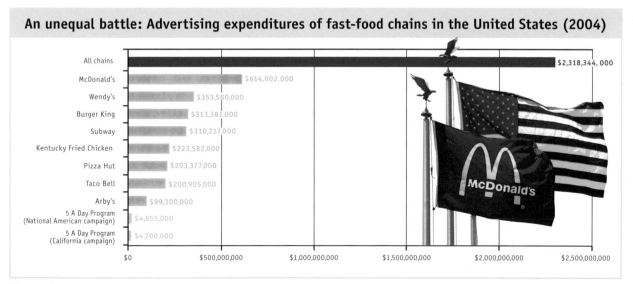

An unequal battle: Advertising expenditures of fast-food chains in the United States (2004)

All chains	$2,318,344,000
McDonald's	$614,002,000
Wendy's	$353,580,000
Burger King	$313,381,000
Subway	$310,217,000
Kentucky Fried Chicken	$223,582,000
Pizza Hut	$203,377,000
Taco Bell	$200,905,000
Arby's	$99,300,000
5 A Day Program (National American campaign)	$4,855,000
5 A Day Program (California campaign)	$4,700,000

Figure 12

Source: www.consumersunion.org

positive impact on health. This really is a battle between David and Goliath. The difference is even more pronounced as the message conveyed by these ads is generally very appealing, often featuring active young people in good health who can perform "extreme" athletic feats as part of an attractive and trendy peer group.

We should not underestimate the impact of advertising on eating habits, particularly among children who are vulnerable to outside influences. Many studies have shown that aggressive marketing by the junk food industry directed at children results in their being able to recognize company logos by the age of two. This obviously has major repercussions on their attraction to these products.

The junk food industry's enormous influence on the eating behaviours of children is well illustrated by the remarkable changes in the type of food they consume (Figure 13). In just 25 years, consumption of candy, snacks, and other processed products by children ages six to 11 has skyrocketed. These changes are especially worrisome because they are accompanied by a significantly decreased intake of foods essential to good health, such as fruits and vegetables.

A similar phenomenon is being observed all over the world, even in societies considered benchmarks for quality eating. For example, despite the outstanding quality of the Japanese diet, the massive influx of leading fast food restaurant chains is revolutionizing Japanese eating

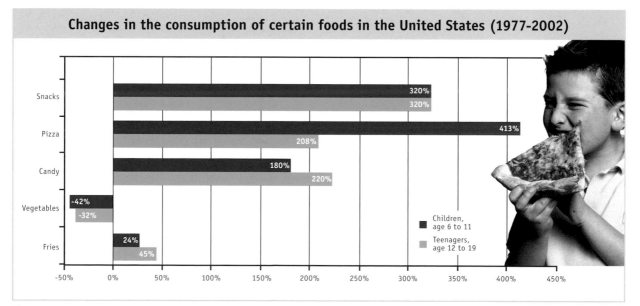

Changes in the consumption of certain foods in the United States (1977-2002)

- Snacks: Children 320%, Teenagers 320%
- Pizza: Children 413%, Teenagers 208%
- Candy: Children 180%, Teenagers 220%
- Vegetables: Children -42%, Teenagers -32%
- Fries: Children 24%, Teenagers 45%

Children, age 6 to 11
Teenagers, age 12 to 19

Figure 13

Source: www.consumersunion.org

habits. Today children in Japan prefer hamburgers and fries to traditional dishes such as sushi or soy-based products.

Obesogenic environment

By reducing foods to basic consumer products, the industry has created a culture that trivializes the act of eating or drinking foods that are nutrient-deficient and whose sole attribute is high energy. What was unimaginable behaviour only a few decades ago, such as seeing a toddler eating fries and drinking a soft drink, has now become so common that it goes unnoticed. Preparing and sharing food has, since time immemorial, been the glue that binds families and societies together. But the increased consumption of prepared or fast-food meals has completely marginalized these practices and given rise to such antisocial behaviour as eating in cars, or in front of the television or walking on the street. Far from being an exception, this type of behaviour is becoming more widespread: An estimated 17% of meals in the U.S. are consumed in a vehicle.

As profitable as they may be for the food industry, such basic lifestyle changes inflict enormous costs on a society by promoting the overconsumption of these foods and the obesity that inevitably follows from it.

Domino effect

Overweight and obesity are often regarded as an aesthetic problem whose consequences are primarily psychological rather than physical. This perception is absolutely false: On the contrary, obesity is a serious medical condition that dramatically increases the risk of contracting a large number of serious chronic diseases. As we will see in the next chapters, Type-2 diabetes, heart disease, many types of cancer, and certain neurodegenerative diseases are very often the consequences of obesity and the direct result of profound imbalances caused by excess weight. Rather than merely being regarded as weight gain, obesity should be seen as the equivalent of an additional organ transplant: It is like a reservoir of very powerful molecules disturbing the normal functions of many organs and creating chronic inflammatory conditions that can foster disease. And while accumulating excess fat is a relatively slow process that generally takes many years, the consequences from it can occur quickly and, by a domino effect, bring on very serious pathologies.

In short, we can see that the industrialization of food has completely redefined the relationship between humans and food. We have created an environment of overconsumption based exclusively on the high intake of calorie-laden foods without considering whether they contain elements essential to health. Optimized for millions of years to maximize the accumulation of energy in case of food scarcity, our genetic makeup has not adapted to today's environment. This can only promote obesity in a large segment of the population. Because of our great vulnerability, we must question our relationship with the present environment to escape the traps laid for us, which make us eat more food, often unconsciously. Such eating habits can have very negative consequences on our health.

Summary

- The many periods of famine that humans have endured throughout evolution have greatly influenced our metabolism by selecting traits that enable us to store the maximum energy from the minimum food.

- The growth of the food industry has profoundly altered the availability of food by enabling mass production of inexpensive food that contains calorie-rich ingredients and is made very appealing through big-budget advertising campaigns.

- All these factors encourage overeating, to which we are vulnerable, contributing to the development of obesity and diseases inevitably associated with excess weight.

The heart has its reasons,
of which reason knows nothing

Blaise Pascal, *Pensées* (1670)

Chapter 5

At the Heart of the Problem: Cardiovascular Disease

Since the dawn of time, the heart has been perceived as a special organ imbued with unique qualities that confer on human existence a particular status. More than 4,000 years ago, the heart was considered the centre of emotions and feelings in India, and in China and ancient Greece it was thought to be the seat of intelligence. This organ is undoubtedly the supreme symbol of life, not only because of its crucial physiological function, but also because we connect it so closely with our emotions. For Egyptians, the heart represented the very essence of human consciousness: According to *The Book of the Dead* from Ancient Egypt, it was the only organ that embalmers were required to leave in place to ensure eternal life after mummification. The symbolism of the heart is still omnipresent in our daily lives, as shown by the many popular idiomatic expressions that perpetuate its imagined role in love (my heart belongs to you), sympathy (my heart goes out to him), and even intelligence and memory (as in to learn something by heart).

Heartbeats

From a more pragmatic perspective, the heart's role is to beat regularly so that blood can flow through the body and deliver to its cells the oxygen and nutrients they need to function. A marvel of adaptation and regularity, the heart can adjust perfectly to the body's needs: It can beat very slowly in large mammals like the blue whale or very fast in birds like the hummingbird (Figure 1). In humans, the heart beats on average 70 times a minute, or about 100,000 times a day, making it possible to pump some 7,500 litres of blood per day. By the time a person has reached the age of 70, this continuous activity adds up to more than 2.5 billion beats and 200 million litres of blood pumped, or the equivalent of three full supertankers!

Ever since William Harvey's work in 1628 we have known that blood vessels also play a major role in blood flow, creating an extraordinarily complex network that distributes blood to all the cells in the body: If all of our body's blood vessels were connected end to end, they would stretch almost 100,000 km, or about two and a half times the circumference of the Earth! However, it is difficult to visualize this massive amount of blood vessels since more than 80% are capillaries,

vessels so tiny that 50 of them would make up the diameter of a single hair. Nevertheless, these capillaries play an essential role and their presence in all parts of the body (some 2,000 in an area covered by the head of a pin) makes it possible to deliver blood to every body cell.

Heart problems

Given the essential role of both the heart and the blood vessels in the functioning of the human body, it is not surprising that diseases of the heart and blood vessels can be very serious and lead to disastrous consequences. Unfortunately, these diseases are widespread, ravaging the human

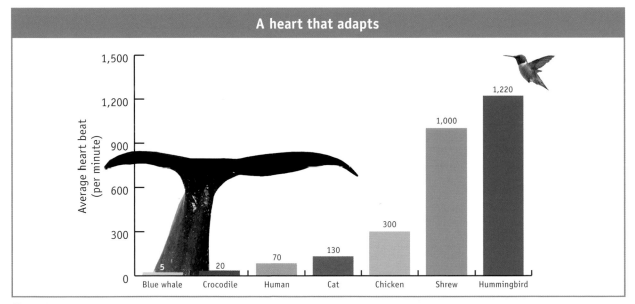

A heart that adapts

Average heart beat (per minute)

Blue whale	Crocodile	Human	Cat	Chicken	Shrew	Hummingbird
5	20	70	130	300	1,000	1,220

Figure 1

Source: *Cardiovasc. Pathol.* 2004; 13: 282-292

population on a staggering scale: In 2005 alone almost 20 million people died worldwide as a result of cardiovascular disease (see box, p. 92). For each year of the twentieth century, with the notable exception of 1918, the year of the Spanish Flu epidemic, heart disease was the world's leading cause of mortality. And while the treatment of cardiovascular disease has made massive progress over the past few years, both in the development of highly sophisticated surgical techniques (dilatation of arteries, coronary bypasses, stents, etc.) and the discovery of many drugs, the catas-

trophic impact of these illnesses remains deeply worrying, with one death every 30 seconds from heart disease in certain Western countries like the United States. Although the miracles of modern medicine are saving lives, the consequences of some of these conditions, particularly stroke, can be debilitating and lead to a dramatic decrease in the quality of life (Figure 2).

Heart pain

The high incidence of various cardiovascular diseases is indeed troubling. With the exception of some rare congenital cardiovascular disorders often responsible for infant death, we now know that the vast majority of cardiovascular diseases are not an inevitable consequence of ageing and can be prevented. An impressive number of studies conducted in the last few decades, particularly the Framingham study (see box, p. 98), have established that diseases as

(continued p. 95)

Strokes with serious consequences	
Percentage of people affected	**Reduced quality of life**
50%	Paralysis of at least one side of the body
35%	Depression
30%	Inability to walk without assistance
26%	Inability to perform familiar tasks (housework, eating alone, bathing, etc.)
26%	Institutionalization
19%	Aphasia (difficulty speaking and understanding others)

Figure 2
Source: National Heart, Lung, and Blood Institute's Framingham Heart Study

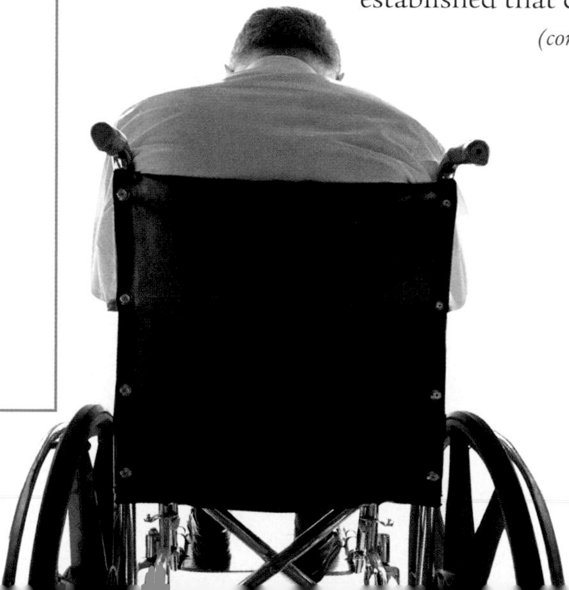

What is cardiovascular disease?

Cardiovascular disease covers all of the disorders affecting the heart and blood vessels, including:

1) coronary disease, which affects the blood vessels that feed blood to the heart;

2) stroke or cerebrovascular accident (CVA), which affects the blood vessels that feed blood to the brain;

3) rheumatic heart disease, which affects the heart muscle and is caused by certain bacteria of the streptococcus family;

4) deep leg vein thrombosis and pulmonary embolism associated with it (blood clots formed in veins that can migrate to the lungs);

5) peripheral artery disease, radiating to the arms and legs;

6) congenital heart defects.

In the West, the principal cardiovascular problems are (1) coronary disease and (2) stroke. These alone are responsible for about 75% of deaths due to heart and blood vessel disease. The most terrifying thing about these conditions is undoubtedly their enormous destructive potential even when there are no apparent symptoms: In about one-third of patients, the first manifestation of heart disease is sudden death. Despite its violent nature, the onset of cardiovascular disease nonetheless represents the end of a long process during which heart and blood vessel functions have gradually deteriorated following accumulated damage to the structure of their tissues.

One of the main causes of this damage is the presence of atheromatous plaque – deposits of fatty material in the lining of blood vessels. Initially described as "fatty tumours" containing "a humor resembling a gruel given to small children" (Ambroise Paré, *Complete Works,* 1575), this plaque in the blood vessels gradually causes hardening and obstruction, a phenomenon known as atherosclerosis, from the Greek *athere,* meaning gruel and *skleros* meaning hard. In some cases, sclerotic vessels were so rigid that the Englishman Caleb Hillier Parry, one of the first doctors to describe this phenomenon in 1799, thought that the coronary artery he was examining contained pieces of plaster that had fallen from the dilapidated ceiling of the autopsy room!

Atherosclerosis – Atherosclerosis is a highly complex process during which atheromatous plaque formed in the lining of blood vessels gradually gathers fat, sugar, blood cells (platelets), and minerals, forming increasingly larger deposits that cause the diameter of the vessel to narrow markedly and reduce blood circulation (Figure 3). In general, plaque rupture is responsible for the main damage caused by atherosclerosis; by rupturing, cells present in the plaque come into contact with blood proteins, causing coagulation and formation of blood clots that can completely block circulation. When atheromatous plaque ruptures in vessels feeding blood to the heart (coronary arteries), thrombosis occurs and the blood supply is immediately cut off in the area fed by these vessels, resulting in a heart attack. Similarly, when these thromboses occur inside vessels that transport blood to the brain, a stroke can occur, which may cause considerable brain damage by depriving the neurons of oxygen (Figure 4).

Cholesterol – Since the work of Russian pathologist Nikolai Nikolaevich Anichkov (1885-1964), we have known that cholesterol plays a significant role in the development of atherosclerosis. A substance absolutely essential to cell functioning, cholesterol is mainly manufactured in the liver and carried in the circulating blood by lipoproteins, a type of protein, which distribute it to the body cells. Under normal conditions, this mechanism is finely regulated so that the amount of cholesterol in the blood does not exceed physiological needs due to the concerted action of two main types of lipoprotein: LDL (low-density lipoprotein) or "bad cholesterol" and HDL (high-density lipoprotein) or "good cholesterol." The balance between these two types of protein is very important since a surplus of LDL cholesterol is stored in the lining of the blood vessels where it undergoes various chemical and enzyme changes that activate the immune system. An increased presence of certain components of the immune system, particularly macrophages, releases numerous messengers that promote the creation of inflammatory conditions in the vessel lining, accelerating the formation of atheromatous plaque and ultimately causing it to rupture, resulting in blood vessel occlusion (thrombosis). Atherosclerosis can therefore be considered a chronic inflammatory disease, as shown by the presence of high levels of certain inflammation markers, particularly C-reactive protein, in the blood of individuals presenting with cardiovascular disorders.

Blood pressure – In addition to obstructing blood vessels, extra pressure exerted by the blood on the lining of these vessels plays a very important role in the onset of cardiovascular disease. Hypertension is dangerous because the vessels are subjected to stress that, over a prolonged period of time, weakens the lining and considerably increases the risk of rupturing the atheromatous plaque, resulting in thromboses. This link between hypertension and thrombosis is particularly well documented in cases of stroke or high blood pressure and increases by four to five times the risk of being struck down by such an event.

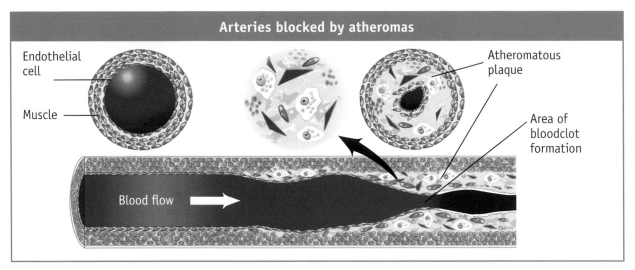

Arteries blocked by atheromas

Endothelial cell

Muscle

Atheromatous plaque

Area of bloodclot formation

Blood flow

Figure 3

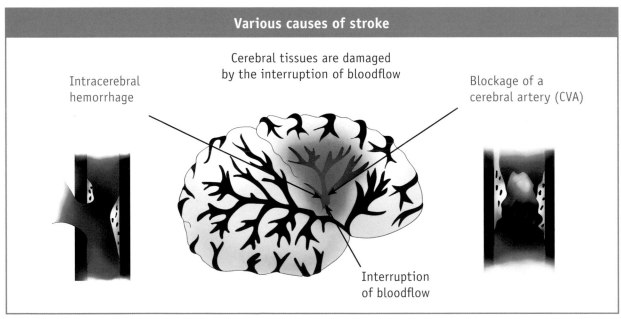

Various causes of stroke

Cerebral tissues are damaged by the interruption of bloodflow

Intracerebral hemorrhage

Blockage of a cerebral artery (CVA)

Interruption of bloodflow

Figure 4

Source: WHO

Many people will be surprised to learn that the kidney, and not the heart, is the main organ involved in regulating blood pressure; in fact, by subtly controlling water excretion through the urine, the renal system adjusts blood volume so that the pressure exerted on the vessel linings remains within normal limits. This is why a sodium-heavy diet promotes hypertension: In the presence of large quantities of salt, the kidneys must reduce water excretion in order to maintain the concentration of sodium within normal proportions, which increases blood volume and pressure. However, hypertension is a complex state that involves several processes, some of which remain little understood even today.

Besides control systems located in the kidney, an oddity associated with hypertension is the major role played by a gas: nitric oxide (NO). Although this molecule is very unstable and survives for only a few seconds, it causes blood vessels to expand and therefore improves blood circulation while reducing the pressure exerted on the vessel linings. The significance of the action of NO is well illustrated by the recent observation that populations living at high altitudes, such as Tibetans (average altitude in Tibet: 4,200 m), have up to 10 times higher levels of NO in their blood, allowing their bodies to increase the oxygen supply to tissues, thus compensating for the reduced oxygen content in the air. From a therapeutic perspective, the NO impact is illustrated by the effect of nitroglycerine, whose usefulness in dilating the vessels during angina attacks depends on its transformation into NO. The dilatation of blood vessels by NO has become very popular following the launch of sildenafil citrate, better known as Viagra. By increasing the effect of NO released into the hollow chambers of the penis, this molecule boosts the influx of blood into the tissue, and as a result stimulates an erection.

serious as myocardial infarction (affecting the heart muscle) and even strokes are very often the result of the close relationship between genetic makeup and lifestyle (Figure 5). While certain genes may predispose us to high levels of cholesterol, elevated blood pressure, or even diabetes, the influence of these hereditary factors on heart disease risk can be seriously aggravated by lifestyle factors. In addition to smoking (akin to a weapon of mass destruction in terms of its catastrophic effects on both the heart and cancer development), these studies have shown unequivocally that the main factors in the development of cardiovascular disease are diet and physical inactivity.

The type of diet plays a major role in the development of cardiovascular disease, since what we eat exerts a decisive influence on a range of factors that can, to various degrees, considerably increase the risk of contracting these diseases

(Figure 6). Whether it is high levels of blood lipids (triglycerides) and cholesterol, hypertension or the presence of chronic inflammation, all of these factors are directly modulated by our diet and can interact synergistically to accelerate the development of atherosclerosis or the formation of blood clots. This will promote the onset of cardiovascular disorders. Changing our eating habits to reduce the influence of certain foods on heart disease risk factors – while eating more foods that neutralize these factors – can have an extraordinary impact on disease prevention.

Aggravating factors

Types of fat in food

Given the major role that fats, particularly cholesterol, play in the formation of atheromatous plaque (see box, p. 92), fat-rich foods were the first to be identified as a reason for the high incidence of cardiovascular disease in the Western world. This "guilt by association" has demonized all dietary fats, even in foods as healthy and appealing as eggs, nuts, and avocados. We now know that it is not the *amount* of dietary fats that influences the risk of cardiovascular disease but their *quality*. Not all fats are created equal

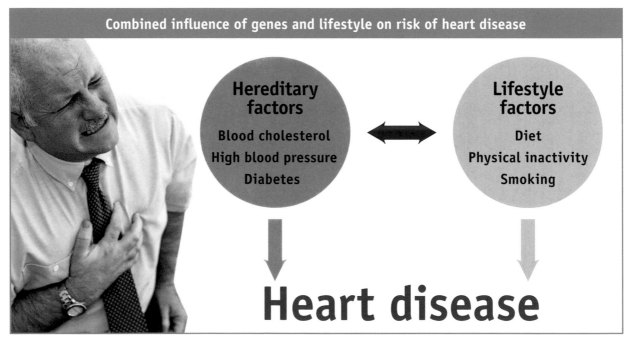

Figure 5

(see box, p. 101). For example, comparisons made among different countries demonstrate that people who consume large amounts of saturated fats, such as in Finland, are strongly affected by heart disease, while inhabitants of Crete, in southern Greece, who are great consumers of monounsaturated fat in the form of olive oil, have been virtually spared this disease (Figure 7).

This paradox is partly explained by the very different effects that various types of fat can have on the levels of bad (LDL) and good (HDL) cholesterol (Figure 8). As mentioned earlier, we now know that LDL cholesterol is a major risk factor

for cardiovascular disease: This observation has led to the discovery of statins, undoubtedly one of the drug classes that have had the greatest impact on public health in the last few decades (see box, p. 104). When present in very high quantities, LDL has a tendency to accumulate in the lining of blood vessels and can therefore promote the formation of atheromatous plaque that increases the risk of cardiovascular disease; conversely, high levels of HDL reduce these risks by containing the excess cholesterol present in these blood vessels. As a result, fats that increase LDL or reduce HDL are more likely to promote atherosclerosis and cardiovascular disease.

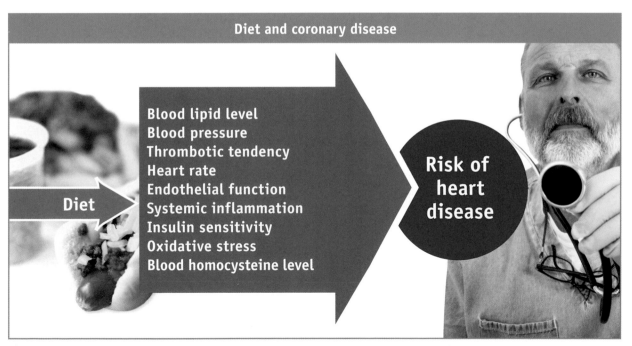

Diet and coronary disease

Diet →

Blood lipid level
Blood pressure
Thrombotic tendency
Heart rate
Endothelial function
Systemic inflammation
Insulin sensitivity
Oxidative stress
Blood homocysteine level

Risk of heart disease

Figure 6

Source: *JAMA* 2002; 288: 2569-2578

A community that takes its health to heart

We owe the identification of the main risk factors of heart disease to the residents of the small town of Framingham, Massachusetts, near Boston. After the community's enthusiastic reception of a tuberculosis study conducted at the beginning of the century, Framingham was selected in 1948 by the American National Institute of Health as the location of a study to examine the causes behind the high incidence of heart disease observed in the first half of the twentieth century. The first generation of volunteers – 5,209 volunteers aged 30 to 60 – were recruited at the beginning of the study and a second generation of subjects was added in 1971. The study continues today with a third generation of participants that was recruited in 2005 – a unique occurrence in the history of epidemiology! Among the many discoveries made as a result of this community's active participation, the following are noteworthy: risk of heart disease increases with smoking (1960), increases with high cholesterol levels (1961), and increases with hypertension (1970), but decreases with physical activity (1967) and high levels of HDL cholesterol (1988).

As can be seen in Figure 8, trans fats are undoubtedly the worst dietary fats, not only because they increase bad LDL cholesterol but also because they also reduce good HDL cholesterol. The impact of such changes is catastrophic: Trans fats are directly responsible for almost 100,000 deaths every year in the United States alone! In the same way, saturated fats, large quantities of which are present in dairy and meat products, also boost LDL levels, a harmful effect that is partly offset by an increase in HDL levels. Many studies show that people who consume large quantities of saturated fats have a higher cholesterol level and an increased risk of cardiovascular disease; however, it is likely that the increase in HDL may not completely neutralize the negative effects of an LDL increase. Conversely, substituting saturated fats with vegetable oils has a very positive impact on these two types of cholesterol levels: It reduces the LDL while increasing the HDL. As we can see, the contribution of fats to increased risk of cardiovascular disease is very complex: While some fats, such as trans fats or saturated fats, are truly harmful to health, other types of fats, particularly monounsaturated and polyunsaturated, can significantly help to prevent this disease.

Obesity: a weight on the heart

Despite cholesterol's involvement in the development of cardiovascular disease and the spectacular success of drugs that lower cholesterol in reducing the mortality of this disease, we must stop regarding cholesterol as uniquely responsible for the onset of cardiovascular disorders. Being overweight, especially obese, is also a very important risk factor for this disease.

As illustrated in Figure 9, an increase in body mass index (BMI) results in a corresponding increase in the incidence of hypertension and cardiovascular disorders. This effect is especially

pronounced in obese people (BMI over 30). The impact of BMI on hypertension is particularly troublesome since it plays a major role in the genesis of cardiovascular and cerebrovascular disorders; in the Framingham study, almost 80% of hypertension cases were linked with obesity. A high body mass index in childhood is strongly associated with an increased risk of cardiovascular disease in adulthood, especially among boys. Given the high proportion of children and adolescents presenting today with excess weight, the number of people with cardiovascular disease could increase by almost 15% from now until 2035, which unfortunately could jeopardize the declining incidence of this disease observed in the last few decades.

The way that excess weight is distributed in the body also plays a major role in the increase of this risk (Figure 10). Many studies have shown that excessive abdominal fat (apple-shaped, android) is a more significant risk factor for cardiovascular disease than when the extra fat is located lower, for example in the hips (pear-shaped, gynoid). Therefore, women with a waistline greater than 96 cm can expect their risk of cardiovascular disease to increase by 300%! This difference seems to be due to the fact that adipose cells specific to the abdomen have a very different metabolic function, increasing the cholesterol level and encouraging resistance to insulin (a precursor condition to diabetes) and the secretion of chemical messengers that foster inflammatory conditions.

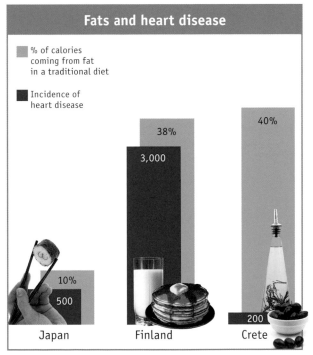

Fats and heart disease

% of calories coming from fat in a traditional diet

Incidence of heart disease

Japan — 10% / 500
Finland — 38% / 3,000
Crete — 40% / 200

Figure 7

Source: *Sc. Am.* 2003; 288: 64-71

(continued p. 102)

Fats with very different effects!

Type of fat	Main sources	Bad cholesterol	Good cholesterol	Assessment
Trans	Industrial foods, shortening, partly hydrogenated oils	LDL ⬆	HDL ⬇	☹ ☹
Saturated	Butter, cream, meat, coconut oil, palm oil, and lard	LDL ⬆	HDL ⬆	☹
Polyunsaturated (omega-3)	Vegetable oils (canola), flaxseed, chia seeds, fatty fish	LDL ⬇	HDL ⬆	☺
Mono-unsaturated	Olive oil, nuts	LDL ⬇	HDL ⬆	☺

Figure 8

Good and bad fats

Cholesterol, hydrogenated, trans, saturated, mono-unsaturated, polyunsaturated, omega-6, omega-3 . . . it's not easy to find your way around the world of fats! However, the subject merits special attention as these various fats all greatly influence – positively or negatively – how our body functions. Learning to distinguish between good and bad fats can therefore have major repercussions on our health.

Good fats

Monounsaturated – Monounsaturated fatty acids, found mainly in olive oil, nuts, and some fruits like avocados, have very positive effects on our health as they reduce bad cholesterol, which decreases the risk of heart disease. These positive effects are underlined by the finding that inhabitants of Crete and Sardinia, who use olive oil as their main source of fat, rarely contract heart disease and have a life expectancy above the world average.

Polyunsaturated – Polyunsaturated fats can be divided into two major classes called omega-3 and omega-6. These two types of fat are what we call essential fatty acids. They are indispensable to good body functioning, but we cannot produce them ourselves: they can only be obtained through food. Omega-6 fatty acids, which are found in several foods (meat, eggs, etc.) and particularly in some vegetable oils (corn and sunflower, for example), are readily available. Omega-3 fatty acids, on the other hand, are rarer and are derived mostly from vegetable sources such as flax and chia seeds and from some fatty fish such as salmon and sardines.

These differences in distribution must be taken into account because our bodies have adapted to function with a balanced diet of polyunsaturated fatty acids – that is, equal amounts of omega-3 and omega-6. Today, unfortunately, with major changes introduced by the industrialization of food, particularly the excessive use of vegetable oils rich in omega-6, this balance no longer exists and most of us consume about 25 times more omega-6 than omega-3. The health consequences of this imbalance are dramatic since excessive omega-6 generally fosters inflammation and prevents the production of some omega-3 derivatives essential for many physiological processes. While omega-6 must be considered primarily a good fat, it can become bad if consumed in far larger quantities than omega-3.

Bad fats

Saturated fats, present in red meat and some dairy products, increase blood cholesterol and multiply the risks of cardiovascular disease and some cancers, particularly of the prostate. Consumption of these fats must be closely monitored to reduce the risk of developing these serious diseases. That is why, for several years, margarine was proposed as a valuable alternative to butter since it is made from omega-6 polyunsaturated fats. However, when margarine is manufactured, these fats are altered to give them a solid consistency, which forms very harmful trans fats that promote the development of coronary disease. In addition to margarine, trans fats are also present in various processed foods (pastries, cookies, potato chips, snacks), which must be eaten in moderation. Completely eliminating these harmful fats – a relatively recent trend – can only be positive, as long as they are not replaced by fats with an equally negative impact on health!

To sum up, increased consumption of mono-unsaturated and omega-3 polyunsaturated fats, combined with a reduction in saturated fats and trans fats, is a simple way to improve the quality of dietary fats and also to help prevent cardiovascular disease.

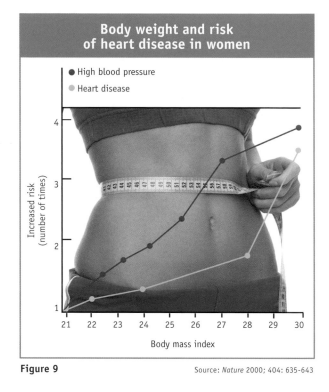

Body weight and risk of heart disease in women

● High blood pressure
● Heart disease

Increased risk (number of times)

Body mass index

Figure 9

Source: *Nature* 2000; 404: 635-643

Blood sugar level (diabetes)

As we will see in more detail in the next chapter, an increase in blood sugar associated with diabetes causes many destructive effects on the body. From a cardiovascular perspective, these high sugar levels are very damaging as they increase production of harmful oxygen derivatives (free radicals) that can attack the lining of blood vessels, causing inflammation and fostering atherosclerosis. Diabetics also tend to have significantly more fat in the blood, as well as higher levels of

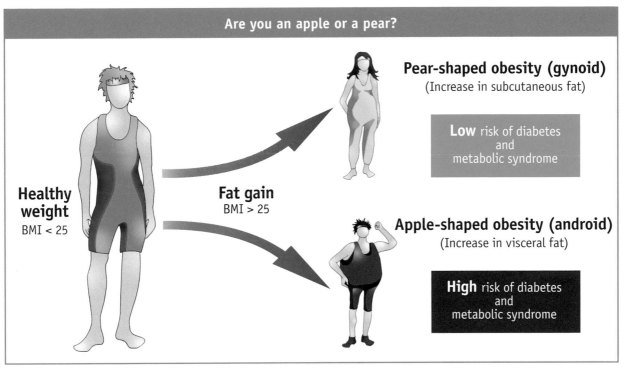

Are you an apple or a pear?

Healthy weight
BMI < 25

Fat gain
BMI > 25

Pear-shaped obesity (gynoid)
(Increase in subcutaneous fat)

Low risk of diabetes and metabolic syndrome

Apple-shaped obesity (android)
(Increase in visceral fat)

High risk of diabetes and metabolic syndrome

Figure 10

Source: *Cell* 2007; 131: 242-256

bad LDL cholesterol and lower levels of good HDL cholesterol. The combined influence of these factors puts diabetics at greater risk of developing cardiovascular disease.

In light of this, we can better understand how dietary excesses typical of industrialized societies, particularly heavy consumption of saturated fats, trans fats, and sugar, play a major role in the high incidence of cardiovascular disease found in these populations. The negative impact of this type of diet is even more pronounced since almost two-thirds of these populations is currently overweight, another factor contributing to increased risk of cardiovascular disease.

Stress

We often attribute the diseases we contract to the influence of external factors beyond our control: the environment, pollution, or psychological and emotional factors. This type of thinking reflects psychological distress stemming from a misunderstanding of the causes responsible for the serious diseases that overwhelm us and from trying to explain them rationally.

Statins to the rescue

Family hypercholesterolemia is certainly the most tragic example of LDL cholesterol's harmful effects on the risk of cardiovascular disease. Particularly common in communities consisting of a small number of people, notably in Quebec, this hereditary condition is characterized by the presence of enormous quantities of LDL cholesterol in the blood, causing the onset of heart disease before the age of 40, and in more serious cases during the first 10 years of life. We now know that these high levels of LDL cholesterol are caused by a genetic mutation that prevents the elimination of this type of cholesterol and leads to its accumulation in the blood. An understanding of cholesterol metabolism has led to the development of statins, a class of drugs that interfere with cholesterol production in the liver, thereby causing a pronounced decrease in LDL cholesterol. Statins have a remarkable impact: A 25% decrease in LDL cholesterol levels results in a 30%-40% reduction in mortality associated with heart disease. For most people, adopting a diet in which saturated fats are replaced by monounsaturated and polyunsaturated fats makes it possible to considerably reduce blood cholesterol levels and avoid taking drugs.

Of all these psychological factors, stress is undoubtedly the one most often cited as a direct cause of heart disease. This comes from the close link between heart rate and emotions. Actually, like any physical effort, intense stress releases adrenalin and other "fighting" hormones leading to an accelerated heartbeat and increased blood pressure. For healthy people, these effects are not sufficient to cause a heart attack. However, for a person whose arteries contain atheromatous plaques, an increase in cardiac effort caused by stress can act as a catalyst for plaque rupture and arterial thrombosis, resulting in a heart attack or a stroke. Stress can therefore be responsible for heart disease, but only in people predisposed to this disease because of lifestyle.

However, stress can significantly impair our quality of life, and lead to behaviours that significantly increase the risk of disease, especially smoking and bad diet. For this reason, learning to manage everyday stress must be considered vital to our physical and mental health.

The ways to appropriately manage tensions caused by the modern lifestyle can vary significantly based on a person's tastes, skills, or physical conditioning. Approaching life positively, focusing on pleasures rather than problems, treating the people around us with respect and courtesy, and regularly doing physical or intellectual activities we enjoy are all ways of bringing a calming dimension to our daily life. Regular physical activity is undoubtedly one of the best-documented ways of managing stress and making a very positive impact on our health in general.

Solutions: heart disease prevention

For people who are resistant to change, the idea of altering their dietary habits, which is necessary to prevent the development of cardiovascular disease (and all chronic diseases), is often perceived as a restriction, a sort of punishment incompatible with quality of life. According to their thinking, "You can live to be a hundred if you give up all the things that make you want to live to be a hundred" (Woody Allen). However, nothing could be further from the truth! In practice, heart disease prevention means we can enjoy a great variety of delicious foods that will diversify our culinary experiences and bring us extraordinary gastronomic pleasure.

Fruits and vegetables – Plant products are indisputably the foods that have the greatest potential to prevent cardiovascular disease. Not only does abundant consumption of plant foods help to reduce our consumption of foods rich in sugar, saturated fats, and trans fats, but it also allows you to benefit from the many preventive properties associated with the constituents of these exceptional foods.

An impressive number of studies have shown that abundant consumption of plant foods is associated with a reduced risk of coronary disorders. This effect is particularly significant for green vegetables, cruciferous vegetables (cabbage, broccoli, etc.), and those rich in vitamin C (green vegetables in general). Specifically, each daily portion of fruits and vegetables reduces by about 4% the risk of coronary diseases, which is an excellent reason to eat these foods as often as possible.

The mechanisms involved in the protective effect of fruits and vegetables are still only partly understood but probably have to do with several of the molecules contained in these foods. Plant foods contain high levels of phytochemical compounds, particularly certain polyphenols called flavonoids, that have very high antioxidant activity. These properties are significant as they make it possible to offset the harmful effects associated with some oxidation processes, particularly that of LDL cholesterol, a key factor in the formation of atheromatous plaque. While all plants have a positive impact on the risk of cardiovascular disease, some stand out. For example, recent studies suggest that the consumption of broccoli is associated with a marked reduction in the risk of heart disease. This result concurs with observations from a pilot study showing that consumption of young broccoli stems (100 g per day for a week) reduces LDL cholesterol (bad cholesterol) and increases HDL cholesterol (good cholesterol). More recently, another study has shown that broccoli's protective role could also be linked to its ability to improve the heart's muscle function and protect it from damage caused by free radicals. This is apart from the fact that a diet rich in green vegetables such as the cruciferous kind also helps increase the intake of folic acid, a very important vitamin (B9) in heart disease prevention. Regular consumption of vitamin B9-rich foods makes it possible to lower the concentration of homocysteine, an amino acid, high levels of which are often linked to an increased risk of coronary disease caused by damage to the lining of the arteries.

Our understanding of the mechanisms by which fruits and vegetables reduce the risk of heart disease is only in its early stages, regardless of the mechanism involved. These foods certainly constitute a first-line defence against the development of heart disease and must absolutely be part of any preventive strategy.

Whole grains – Who would believe that a change in lifestyle as simple as replacing everyday white bread with bread containing whole grains could reduce the risk of coronary disease and stroke by 40%? But it really can! Whole grains are one of those foods whose remarkable impact on the prevention of chronic diseases is greatly underestimated. We are so accustomed to the presence of refined flour in almost all of our cereal products that we forget just how much this refining eliminates most of the beneficial constituents of the grain. Whole grains contain an abundance of antioxidants, minerals, vitamins, phytochemical compounds, and fibres present in both the bran (outside layer) and the germ (layer inside the bran). It is becoming increasingly clear that all these constituents act synergistically to prevent the development of heart disease. In addition, as we will see in the next chapter, consumption of whole grains helps to prevent too great a variation in blood sugar levels, thereby reducing the risk of diabetes.

Nuts – We absolutely must rediscover nuts, too often dismissed because of their high fat content. They are a remarkable source of monounsaturated fats that are beneficial to the health of the cardiovascular system. Studies have shown that daily consumption of one portion of nuts reduces the risk of coronary disease by as much as 30%! This effect is even more pronounced if the nuts are replacing "processed" snacks rich in sugar, saturated fats, or trans fats.

Omega-3 – The first indication of the benefits associated with omega-3 fatty acids came from studies conducted among the Inuit of Greenland who, despite a diet almost exclusively based on the consumption of sea animal meat, are surprisingly unaffected by heart disease. The animals in their diet, and most fatty fish such as salmon,

sardines, and mackerel, contain large amounts of eicosapentaenoic acid (EPA), docosahexaenoic acid (DHA), two long-chain omega-3 fatty acids that play a major role in the prevention of certain coronary diseases. Other major consumers of fish like the Japanese, who absorb on average almost 1 g of EPA and DHA a day, have a coronary disease mortality rate almost 90% lower than that of inhabitants of regions where little fish is eaten such as in North America. The protective effects of these fats can even be observed in less significant quantities: Modest consumption of about 250 to 500 mg of EPA and DHA a day – barely equivalent to a half-portion (100 g) of salmon – reduces by about 40% the risk of mortality due to coronary disease. And this positive effect sets in quickly: Studies have shown that regular consumption of fatty fish causes positive effects on the heart within weeks by reducing episodes of arrhythmia, a pathology often responsible for sudden death.

Green tea – Recent studies show that people who drink at least two cups of green tea a day (about 500 mL) have a 16% lower mortality rate than those who drink less. This effect is especially pronounced in women: While the mortality rate of men who are regular tea drinkers is reduced by 12%, that of females is 23% lower, resulting in a protective effect two times greater! This protective effect seems mainly due to a major reduction in mortality rates associated with coronary disease (25%) and especially with stroke (60%).

Fish for health

Despite the well-documented positive effects of fish consumption on health, we often try to discredit this food source under the pretext that these aquatic species contain overly large amounts of toxic products, especially mercury and polychlorinated biphenyls (PCBs). Mercury is a heavy metal that can come from natural sources like volcanoes and from human activity like coal-burning power stations. In water, mercury is transformed into methyl mercury, a form allowing it to accumulate in aquatic species. However, the concentration of methyl mercury in fish varies greatly since it depends not only on environmental contamination but also on the life span of the fish and its place in the food chain. Throughout their lives, large predatory fish with a long life span, like sharks or swordfish, eat a great deal of aquatic species that may contain methyl mercury, which can lead to an accumulation of toxins over the years. Conversely, fish with a shorter life span, like salmon or sardines, do not have time to accumulate significant toxins and therefore contain very little. Mercury is mainly harmful to the fetus and it is recommended that pregnant women avoid eating shark or swordfish (two unpopular species in North America anyway) and replace them with fish that have low levels of contamination, like salmon. In this way, gestating fetuses may benefit from the positive effects of omega-3 on brain development, especially in the final three months of pregnancy, without having to be exposed to the potentially harmful effects of mercury.

Although PCBs have been banned since 1977, they have a long persistence and are still present in our environment. It is important to know that PCB levels in various fish are comparable to those we find in many other foods we eat daily. For example, farmed salmon contains about 30 nanograms of PCBs per gram (30 ng/g), an amount similar to that present in chicken (32 ng/g), beef (22 ng/g), butter (70 ng/g), and eggs (19 ng/g). These amounts are well below the limits set by government control organizations, equivalent to a maximum daily intake of 2,000 ng/g.

Given its effect on reducing mortality rates from coronary disease, the benefits of eating fish far outweigh the potential negative impact of any contaminants. So in fact it is more dangerous *not* to eat fish at all than to eat it regularly!

Chocolate – Numerous studies have shown that cocoa paste contains very high amounts of proanthocyanidin, a class of polyphenols that has many properties beneficial to health. For example, Kuna Indians, who live on islands near Panama, consume huge amounts of cacao and have normal blood pressure despite a high-salt diet. This is due to the positive effect of cacao polyphenols on the dilatation of arteries, and the decrease in platelet aggregation, two factors that play a major role in the development of hypertension and heart disease. A recent study shows that people who regularly consume 70% dark chocolate (about 20 g per day) show a marked improvement in blood flow, while no improvement is observed in those who eat "processed" chocolate, which contains very little cocoa paste. It seems that the positive effect of dark chocolate is linked to a property in its polyphenols that releases a chemical messenger, nitric oxide (see page 101), which increases arterial dilatation, at the same time improving blood flow and reducing platelet aggregation. However, it is important to note that previous studies have shown that milk prevents the absorption of dark chocolate's polyphenols, thereby neutralizing its beneficial effects. Milk contains large amounts of casein, a protein that interacts with polyphenols and prevents them from being efficiently absorbed by the intestine. It is therefore always preferable to consume dark chocolate unaccompanied by milk. A similar phenomenon is observed with tea: While consumption of tea leads to a significant improvement in the ability of arteries to dilate, which confirms that the polyphenols contained in tea have a positive effect on the cardiovascular system, adding milk completely reverses this effect and neutralizes its positive effects on the cardiovascular system.

Red wine – Red wine is a very complex product that contains several thousand chemical compounds, but it is generally acknowledged that the positive effects associated with moderate consumption of wine are mainly due to a molecule called resveratrol. This molecule, which is found in significant quantities only in red wine, has many positive effects on the cardiovascular system, including restricting the formation of blood clots that can block blood vessels, causing serious problems. Red wine's protective effect against heart disease has been well illustrated and is now called the "French paradox": People who regularly drink red wine have quite a low mortality rate for heart disease, despite the presence of many risk factors such as smoking, hypertension, and high levels of blood cholesterol.

Physical activity – Cars make it possible to get from place to place effortlessly; machines have considerably reduced the work of labourers; food is easily accessible; and television and computer use are now more popular pastimes among children than playing sports. While these innovations have considerably improved our quality of life, most of us would have to admit to being less physically active than our grandparents were. This decline in activity causes many negative effects on health.

We cannot overemphasize the importance of regular physical activity in preventing heart disease and maintaining good health in general. An impressive number of studies have shown that the simple act of walking at a good pace for two and a half hours a week (or 30 minutes a day) – not an enormous effort – reduces the risk of heart disease by 30% to 50%! This beneficial effect is due to the many positive effects of exercise, both on heart function and on metabolism in general (Figure 11). Regular physical activity is one of the major lifestyle factors associated with increased quality of life and life expectancy. For example, we have known for a long time that sedentary people are more likely to prematurely contract a chronic disease, particularly heart disease, even more so if this inactivity is combined with excess weight (Figure 12). On the other hand, people who adopt a lifestyle that incorporates regular physical activity can significantly delay the onset of these chronic diseases, and the effect can be more pronounced if the physical activity is intense. Exercise is not only an excellent way to maintain muscular function; it is even important as a preventive medicine that can delay the onset of heart disease and all other chronic diseases.

Multiple benefits of exercise	
Effects of exercise	**Consequences**
⇧ glucose absorption by tissues	Maintains normal glycemia
⇧ lipoprotein lipase activity	Improves blood cholesterol profile (HDL/LDL ratio)
⇧ heart muscle contractions	Improves heart functions
⇩ heart rate at rest	Lowers blood pressure
⇩ platelet aggregation	Decreases formation of blood clots

Figure 11

Strength in combination

Remember, it is the combination of foods mentioned above that reduces the risk of developing heart disease. The complexity of heart disease and the many factors contributing to its onset are such that only by drastically changing eating habits to incorporate the maximum beneficial elements while reducing ingestion of harmful elements can we effectively prevent this disease.

The most spectacular example of the extraordinary impact that a combination of dietary changes can make on cardiovascular health comes from a French study conducted in Lyon in the late 1980s on the benefits of a typical Mediterranean-style diet. While there are as many versions of the Mediterranean diet as there are countries located in this magnificent part of the world, the diets share some common elements. These are notably: an abundance of plant foods,

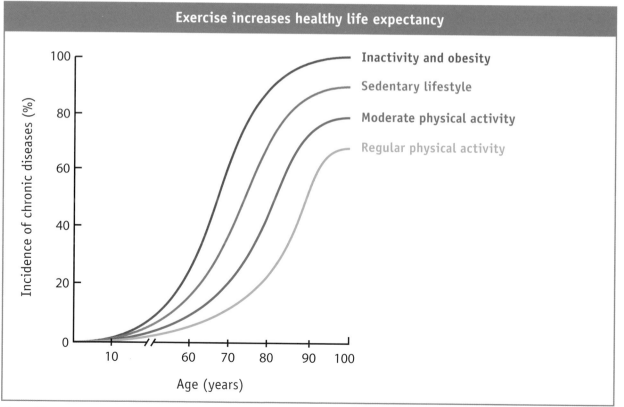

Figure 12

Source: adapted from *Nature* 2008; 454: 463-469

such as fruits, vegetables, and cereal products; systematic use of olive oil as a fat source; and low intake of red meat and products rich in saturated fats such as butter and cream. This is an exemplary diet, rich in phytochemical compounds, vitamins, minerals, monounsaturated and polyunsaturated omega-3 fats, in which complex sugars from fibres and cereals are the main sources of carbohydrates, with proteins coming mainly from fish and legumes instead of red meat. Not surprisingly, Mediterranean cuisine is among the best in the world!

The study in question aimed to establish the impact of the diet on the risk of recurrence among people who had survived a heart attack, compared to the low-fat diet that was then prescribed for such situations. The results were spectacular: A simple increase in the intake of plants (fruits, vegetables, and legumes) and monounsaturated and polyunsaturated omega-3 fats radically decreased the recurrence of heart attack and lowered the mortality rate among study participants (Figure 12). The benefits associated with a Mediterranean-type diet were so extraordinary that the study had to be stopped before its planned conclusion so as not to further disadvantage those patients on the low-fat diet!

The beneficial effects of the Mediterranean diet were recently confirmed by a large-scale study conducted in the United States involving 214,284 men and 166,012 women. The most dedicated followers of the Mediterranean diet saw their risk of heart disease mortality decline by 20% compared to those who never adopted it.

These results show just how possible it is to effectively fight the scourge of heart disease by changing our dietary habits. That means: increasing the intake of plant products such as fruits and vegetables and whole grains, as well as certain foods such as tea, red wine, and dark chocolate; and reducing consumption of junk foods laden with trans fats, saturated fats, and sugar. Combining the range and quality of this type of diet to prevent chronic diseases is the best illustration of the enormous potential of a preventive approach based on the goal of eating well.

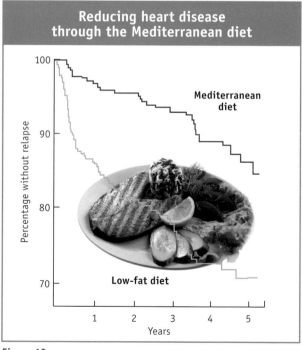

Figure 13 — Source: adapted from Willett (2001)

Summary

• A diet rich in plant products such as fruits, vegetables, and whole grains, combined with fewer saturated fats and more unsaturated and polyunsaturated fats, helps to considerably reduce the risk of heart disease.

• This protective effect increases if it is accompanied by not smoking, maintenance of normal body weight and regular physical activity – three major factors in preventing the disease.

• Given the number of deaths caused by heart disease, adopting this lifestyle could have extraordinary repercussions on the general population's quality of life and life expectancy.

Too much glue won't stick
and too much sugar doesn't
make things taste better.

Chinese proverb

Chapter 6

An Extra Spoonful of Sugar Leaves a Bitter Taste: Type-2 Diabetes

Of all the chronic diseases discussed in this book, Type-2 diabetes is undoubtedly the one whose negative health consequences are the most underestimated. We may all fear being struck down by a heart attack or stroke, or dying slowly from cancer, or placing an unbearable burden on our family due to a neurodegenerative disease like Alzheimer's, yet most people regard diabetes as a "minor" disease, without major consequences on our quality of life. This perception is false. On the contrary, diabetes is a serious disease with catastrophic health consequences: For diabetics, life expectancy may be reduced by an average of 12 years, similar to that of smokers. In addition, the health costs of this disease are astronomical. In the United States, annual treatment costs linked to diabetes are estimated at $175 billion. Diabetes prevention should therefore be a key object-ive when aiming to improve quality of life and longevity, and to reduce the enormous pressure this disease exerts on our health system.

From antiquity to the discovery of insulin

A description of the symptoms and dramatic consequence of diabetes appears among the most ancient observations in the history of medicine. The *Codex Ebers* – an Egyptian medical treatise dating back 3,500 years – mentions it as a disease causing "abundant urination." But it was the Greek doctor Aretaeus of Cappadocia who produced the first detailed study of this " . . . rare and very surprising disease. The sick have a terrible thirst; the abundant amount they drink does not compensate for the amount of urine they discharge, as it is prodigious [. . .] and it comes out like a siphon. When the disease reaches this degree, the sick can still live but for a short period of time" (*The Causes and Symptoms of Acute Disease,* circa 100). These observations, as well as those made by other doctors from antiquity such as Galen and Celsus, are behind the origins of the word "diabetes" (from the Greek *diabaino,* literally "siphon" or "passing through").

A specific characteristic of diabetic urine, other than the quantity, is its high sugar content. This characteristic had been mentioned a few centuries earlier by the Indian doctor Charaka, who noticed that ants were drawn to the urine of diabetic patients as if it contained sugar or honey. To describe this disease, Charaka proposed the term *madhumeha* (from *madhu,* meaning "sugar" and *meha,* "abundant urine"). Almost 2,000 years later, the Englishman Thomas Willis confirmed (courageously) the presence of sugar by directly tasting the urine of patients, discovering that it "was wonderfully sweet as if imbued with honey or sugar" (*Pharmaceutice rationalis,* 1674). He proposed the term *diabetes mellitus* (from the Latin *mel,* which means "honey") to describe this disease, and it is still used today in medical literature.

However, despite the knowledge accumulated over the centuries about the symptoms of diabetes, only in the early twentieth century were the underlying mechanisms of this disease understood, making it possible to work toward a treatment to save diabetics. This feat was accomplished by Canadian researchers Frederick Banting and Charles Best, who in 1921 observed that administering a pancreatic extract to diabetic dogs markedly lowered their blood glucose. This effect seemed to be associated with the presence in the pancreatic extract of a hormone called insulin (see box, p. 119). The two researchers injected an insulin preparation into Leonard Thompson, a dying 14-year-old diabetic patient, dramatically improving his state of health. Repeated daily injections prolonged his life for a number of years (he would die 13 years later in a car accident). The discovery of insulin by Banting and Best, for which they were awarded the Nobel Prize in Medicine a year later, is one of the great achievements in the history of medicine, contributing to the saving of numerous lives. An estimated 15 million people alive today would have died prematurely were it not for their daily administration of insulin.

Type-2 diabetes: A silent killer

High blood sugar levels associated with diabetes may be caused by two very different forms of the disease, known as Type-1 (insulin-dependent) and Type-2 (non-insulin-dependent). This classification reflects the major differences in the mechanisms involved in hyperglycemia and in the nature of the factors promoting the onset of these two diseases (see box, p. 124).

Insulin: Glycemic conductor

A hormone secreted by pancreatic cells in islet-like groups, insulin (from the Latin *insula,* or "island") plays an indispensable role in controlling blood glucose levels, as well as regulating metabolism in general. This function of insulin is critical because glucose brings to the cells the energy they need to function, and glucose concentration must be maintained at a stable level – about 1 g per litre. During a meal, the absorption of carbohydrates from food (sugars and starches) increases glycemia, which releases insulin through the pancreas. This increased insulin production has three main effects, all designed to derive maximum benefit from the energy in the sugar. These effects are:

- to help transport glucose into the cells, particularly in the muscles;
- to store glucose in the liver and muscles in the form of glycogen for future use;
- to help convert excess glucose into fat.

Diabetes symptoms and the incurable nature of this disease before the discovery of insulin are closely linked to the disruption of these functions.

In fact, without insulin, diabetics cannot effectively absorb sugar, resulting in the production of an abnormally high amount of glucose in their blood (hyperglycemia). The kidneys cannot retain all the sugar and thus eliminate most of it through the urine, a phenomenon inevitably accompanied (through osmosis) by the massive excretion of water. For this reason, the presence of abundant and sweet urine is a precursor of hyperglycemia, caused by diabetes.

However, being unable to use glucose as fuel has even more serious long-term effects: Deprived of glucose, the cells must draw on other types of energy substances (fats and proteins) to meet their needs, which leads to a depletion in the body's reserves and marked weight loss. Excessive use of these energy sources also increases the production of ketonic bodies, compounds that alter the blood pH and lead to metabolic acidosis, with disastrous consequences. Insulin's essential function is a striking example not only of the enormous complexity of human metabolism, but in particular of the dangers associated with any disruption to the system's equilibrium.

Over the past few years, Type-2 diabetes, which alone is responsible for 80% of diabetes cases, has become one of the major chronic diseases affecting the world population. The number of people afflicted by this disease worldwide is mind-boggling: In barely 25 years, or from 1985 to the present day, the number of diabetics has increased from about 30 million to about 200 million, or almost seven-fold (Figure 1)!

This trend is worrisome because diabetes considerably increases the risk of complications caused by hyperglycemia on blood vessel function (Figure 2). Chronic hyperglycemia caused by Type-2 diabetes is a condition that triples or quadruples the risk of cardiovascular diseases such as heart attack, stroke, and various pathologies such as kidney failure (progressive loss of kidney functions), retinopathy (major eye diseases causing blindness), and circulatory disorders in the lower extremities (arteritis). In the case of circulatory disorders, these can often lead to the onset of what is called diabetic foot, that is the development of a necrosis requiring amputation of the extremity, the only way to save the afflicted person's life. Every 30 seconds somewhere in the world, a leg is amputated due to vascular complications caused by diabetes.

Sugar: A substance to use cautiously!

Despite how fond or passionate we are about sweets, the damage associated with surplus glucose in the blood reminds us that sugar is not as harmless as we think. Its effects are not surprising: like all forms of energy, it must be used judiciously to avoid the onset of serious side effects. A parallel can be made with the fuel in a car: It is essential for the vehicle to function, but dangerous when its combustion is not carefully controlled by the engine. The same applies to sugar: Although our body – our brain in particular – constantly needs glucose to function, it has concurrently developed a very sophisticated control system to maintain the concentration of this molecule at levels just sufficient to meet its

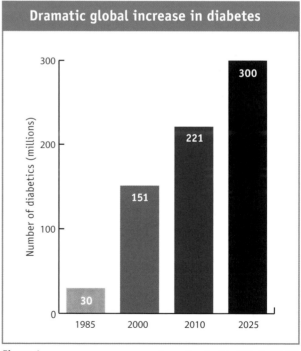

Figure 1 Source: *Ann. Rev. Nutr.* 2003; 23: 345-377

Diabetes-related diseases

Vascular pathologies associated with diabetes	Facts
Cardiovascular diseases	Triples or quadruples the risk of a heart attack or a stroke
Kidney failure	Diabetic nephropathy is the leading reason for dialysis in the West
Retinopathy	Affects one-third of diabetics and is one of the main causes of blindness
Angiopathy (arteritis)	Causes necrosis of the lower limbs, leading to amputation
Erectile dysfunction	Affects 35% to 45% of diabetic men
Dementia (e.g., Alzheimer's)	Diabetics have a 50% greater risk of cognitive decline

Figure 2

needs. And these levels are much lower than we may think: On average, a healthy person's blood contains a maximum of four to five grams of sugar, or barely the equivalent of one teaspoon! Sugar is therefore an invaluable source of energy, but it is used very cautiously by our body. From a dietary point of view, what we call table sugar is actually sucrose, a substance formed by combining glucose and fructose. In terms of energy, glucose is the preferred fuel of our cells, and its blood concentration is about 1,000 times higher than that of fructose.

It is important for the body to maintain an optimal level of blood glucose as illustrated by the complex nature of the mechanisms responsible for controlling glycemia. Although we may

eat three times a day, the sugar level remains constant due to the concerted action of many organs, constantly on the lookout for the smallest glycemic variations (Figure 3). The main source of sugar is of course food, but between meals, glucose levels remain constant thanks to the liver. This organ is like a sugar "warehouse" whose function is to release necessary amounts of glucose in order to maintain normal glycemic levels in response to commands from the brain. During a meal, the sugar contained in the food is rapidly absorbed by the intestine and transported into the blood, sharply raising the glycemic level. To respond to this sudden increase, the pancreas secretes insulin, which enables muscles and adipose cells to absorb the excess sugar and store it for future use. At the same time, the pancreas indicates to the liver that it must stop producing glucose since the amount of sugar in the blood is sufficient. The equilibrium maintained between these processes keeps the glycemic level constant and precisely matched to the needs of the body's cells.

As we will see later, certain lifestyle factors disturb the functioning of these regulatory mechanisms, preventing the muscles and adipose cells from adequately responding to the insulin's message. In such conditions, the blood sugar levels are much higher than the concentrations to which our system has adapted, a hyperglycemic state responsible for multiple complications associated with Type-2 diabetes.

A matter of "AGE"

The presence of elevated amounts of sugar in the blood is harmful, for it can react with the many components present inside and outside cells. The French chemist Louis-Camille Maillard (1878–1936) discovered that sugar has the ability to bind chemically with proteins, a reaction based on the caramelization process (Strecker degradation) so essential in cooking: Subjected to high temperatures, glucose interacts with proteins to form a complex responsible for (among other things) the golden hue characteristic of pie crusts or the browning of meat. At body temperature, the Maillard reaction is obviously slower, but when blood sugar levels are elevated for long periods, as is often the case in the stages preceding the onset of Type-2 diabetes, the reaction can occur, causing many deleterious effects on health.

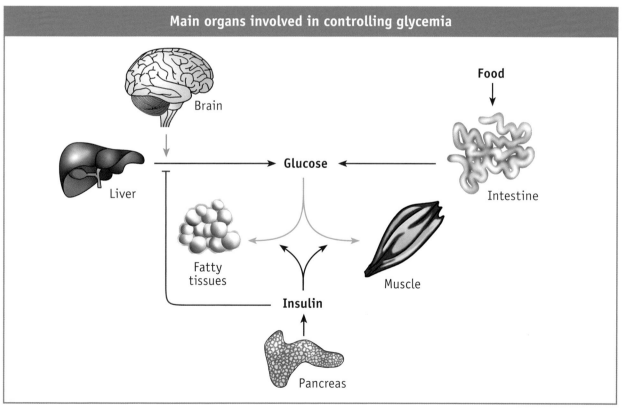

Main organs involved in controlling glycemia

Brain · Liver · Glucose · Food · Intestine · Fatty tissues · Muscle · Insulin · Pancreas

Figure 3

Source: *Nature* 2006; 444: 847-853

What is diabetes?

Diabetes is defined as a chronic hyperglycemic condition caused by loss of insulin production or the inability of the organs to absorb sugar in response to insulin. Based on the mechanisms involved, two major types of diabetes can be distinguished.

Type-1 diabetes – The hyperglycemia associated with this disease is due to the destruction of the pancreatic cells responsible for insulin production. It has been known for some time that this type of diabetes appears in childhood. However, the extremely complex factors responsible for this disease (genetics and lifestyle) are still poorly understood today.

Type-2 diabetes – Responsible for over 80% of diabetes cases, in the last few years it has become one of the major chronic diseases affecting the entire world population. Type-2 diabetes is characterized by the "insulin resistance" phenomenon; that is, a condition in which body organs (liver, muscles, adipose tissues) gradually lose their ability to absorb sugar in response to the insulin signal. By interfering with sugar absorption, this resistance leads to the pancreas "overheating," which increases insulin production in hope of the cells absorbing the sugar at any cost. When it occurs over prolonged periods, insulin resistance can wear out the pancreas, which ultimately loses its ability to secrete this hormone effectively.

Insulin resistance is often associated with a range of other physiological disorders such as hypertriglyceridemia (rise in blood fats), hypertension, a decrease in good HDL-cholesterol and obesity, especially in the abdomen. These symptoms, collectively called metabolic syndrome, represent a major risk factor for heart disease and Type-2 diabetes.

As we will see throughout this chapter, the Western lifestyle clearly contributes to the development of Type-2 diabetes. The best example is undoubtedly the alarming increase in Type-2 diabetes among certain aboriginal populations genetically predisposed to this disease. For example, the Pima Indian tribes living in the Arizona desert have one of the highest incidences of Type-2 diabetes and obesity in the world, which is directly linked to their adopting a Western diet rich in processed food. Conversely, the same Indians living in Mexico, by preserving a traditional diet, are largely spared these diseases and enjoy excellent health.

During this chemical reaction, called glycation, the glucose molecules bind to certain protein structures, gradually forming advanced glycation end-products, or AGE. The most typical example is a change in hemoglobin, the protein transporting oxygen in the blood: This "sweetened" form of the protein (HbA1c) acts as a marker to measure hyperglycemia and the development of diabetes.

In addition to the hemoglobin, AGE products are very dangerous for blood vessel functioning since they alter the normal functions of certain proteins present in the vessel walls (Figure 4). For example, the interaction of sugar with the collagen fibres in artery walls thickens the vessels, increasing the risk of thrombosis (formation of blood clots). Concurrently, glycation alters the structure of LDL cholesterol, enhancing its retention in the vessel walls, a factor that considerably increases the risk of atherosclerosis (see Chapter 5). This risk grows when the number of proteins altered by the glucose creates inflammatory conditions and a loss in vessel elasticity. For all these

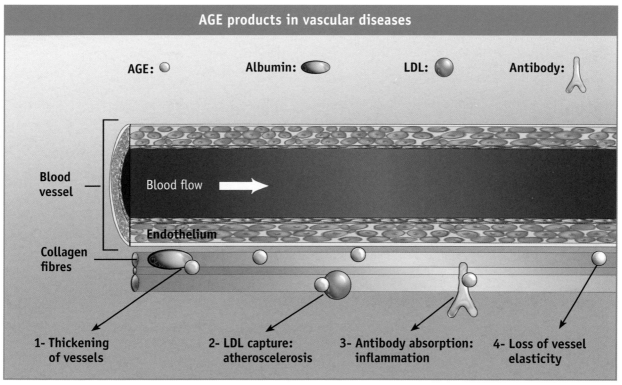

Figure 4

Source: http://209.209.34.25/webdocs/glycation

reasons, hyperglycemia promotes the development of cardiovascular diseases: By chemically changing the components of blood vessels, the prolonged excess of glucose in the blood ages these vessels prematurely, causing a pathological caramelization, with dramatic consequences.

Obesity: The main cause of diabetes

The profound metabolic imbalances caused by obesity have undoubtedly played a key role in the recent increase in the number of Type-2 diabetes cases. Almost 80% of diabetics are obese. This situation can be explained by the marked increase in the risk of Type-2 diabetes associated with high body mass index or BMI (Figure 5). Even for a BMI that is considered normal (below 25), the risk of contracting diabetes is already almost three times higher than among slim people (BMI below 23, roughly corresponding to a person 1.65 m tall and weighing 60 kg) and eight times higher for overweight people (BMI = 25 to 30). For the obese (BMI = 30 to 40) and the morbidly obese (BMI = 40),

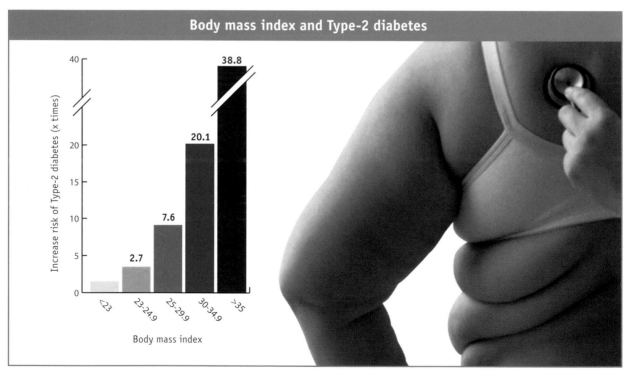

Figure 5

Source: *New Engl. J. Med.* 2001; 345: 790-797

the risk increases tremendously, in the order of 20 to 40 times. This relationship therefore indicates that Type-2 diabetes is one of the main types of collateral damage resulting from today's global obesity epidemic. In fact, the link between obesity and diabetes is so close that the term "diabesity" is often used to illustrate the point.

The mechanisms by which obesity promotes the onset of Type-2 diabetes are complex and certainly among the best illustrations of the negative effects of the enormous metabolic imbalances caused by excess weight. This bears repeating:

Obesity is not simply the accumulation of excess fat; on the contrary, it is a pathological condition caused by hypertrophy of the adipocytes, or fat cells. This profoundly alters the fundamental role played by these cells in the metabolic balance. The surplus of fat is toxic for the body as it actively promotes insulin resistance, a very serious condition ultimately leading to the development of diabetes.

Fat overload in the adipocytes releases excessive amounts of fat into the blood, causing the cells to prefer this source of energy to glucose. As

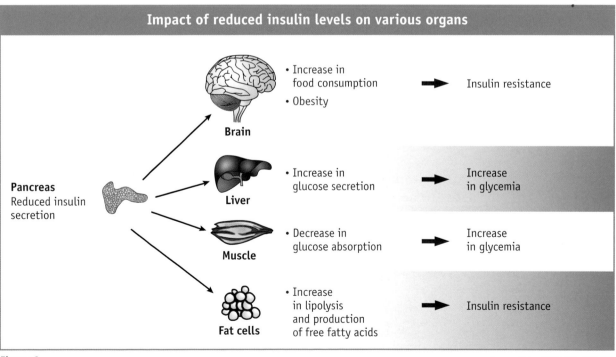

Impact of reduced insulin levels on various organs

Pancreas
Reduced insulin secretion

Brain
• Increase in food consumption
• Obesity
→ Insulin resistance

Liver
• Increase in glucose secretion
→ Increase in glycemia

Muscle
• Decrease in glucose absorption
→ Increase in glycemia

Fat cells
• Increase in lipolysis and production of free fatty acids
→ Insulin resistance

Figure 6

Source: *Nature* 2006; 444: 840-846

development of Type-2 diabetes, maintaining a normal body weight is an essential aspect of any preventive approach. The most spectacular illustration of how weight loss can influence the risk of diabetes is undoubtedly the effect of bariatric surgery (reducing stomach size) on morbidly obese people. Radically reducing the size of the stomach rapidly decreases obesity and almost completely eliminates Type-2 diabetes!

However, it is neither necessary nor desirable to undergo this type of surgery to reap the benefits of weight loss: Losing just 5 kg, even over several years, can reduce the risk of diabetes by 50%! At a time when overweight has become the norm rather than the exception, Type-2 diabetes undoubtedly illustrates the dangers of excess weight and the need to be as slim as possible in order to prevent this disease. As we will see in the conclusion of this book, maintaining a healthy weight requires major changes in our eating habits.

Controlling glycemia – You can also significantly reduce the risk of diabetes by paying particular attention to the amount and especially the type of carbohydrates: that is, the sugar in your diet. There are three main types of carbohydrates.

The first is **simple sugars** – like those in fruits, dairy products, maple syrup, or honey – and sugars added to various products sold in grocery stores. Added sugar is quite significant: In 2001, it represented more than 10% of the calories consumed by Canadians, or the equivalent of 60 g (12 teaspoons) of sugar a day! This sugar surplus is sometimes difficult to identify as the industry uses many sources of sugar in its preparation of food products. But make no mistake. When a product label uses terms like sucrose, dextrose, fructose-enriched corn syrup, glucose-fructose, malt syrup, etc., it can mean only one thing: sugar has been added! The closer these items are to the top of the ingredient list, the more of them the product contains.

The second main form of sugar is **starches**. These are created by combining a number of sugar molecules. Starch is found in cereals, potatoes, and certain vegetables and legumes. Generally, the sugar present in foods in starch form is digested more slowly than simple sugars. Conversely, all starches are not digested at the same rate: For example, potato starch has a structure that breaks down into sugar very quickly while legume starches are much more resistant.

The third main form is **dietary plant fibres**, found only in plant products such as vegetables, fruits, and whole grains. These fibres are so complex that our stomach cannot digest them and only the bacteria present in our intestines can extract a small amount of their sugar content.

The main difference between the various types of carbohydrates is how fast they are absorbed by the intestine and transported intestine breaks down these sugars much more slowly, causing sugar to appear gradually in the blood and produce less insulin. To distinguish the effects of carbohydrates on blood glucose, we use the concepts of glycemic index and glycemic load (see box, p. 129).

Ingesting a food with a high glycemic load, such as corn flakes, rapidly increases the blood glucose level, which is accompanied by a massive secretion of insulin striving to absorb all the sugar (Figure 8). However, it may happen that the amount of insulin produced by the pancreas in response to this sugar level is too great, which can result in excessive glucose absorption, and paradoxically, a hypoglycemic state a few hours after eating a meal. This is not a desirable outcome as

into the bloodstream.

In the case of simple sugars, their rapid assimilation forces the pancreas to react by secreting a large amount of insulin. Conversely, in the case of dietary plant fibres or complex starches, the

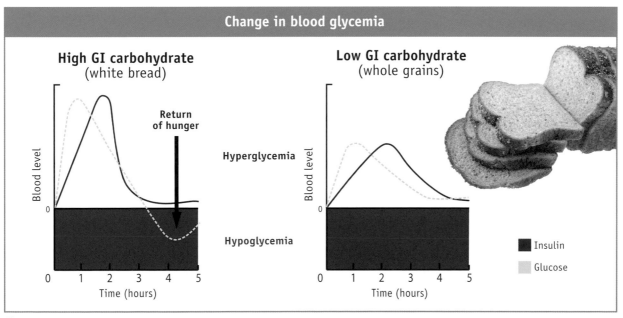

Figure 8

Source: adapted from Willett (2001)

Glycemic index and glycemic load

Glycemic index (GI) is calculated by comparing the increase in blood sugar produced by the absorption of a given food to that of pure glucose. For example, a food with a glycemic index of 50 produces half the amount of glycemia as glucose, which has a glycemic index of 100. The general rule is that values below 50 correspond to a low GI while those over 70 are high. Despite its theoretical usefulness, this index has fallen out of favour because it does not take into account the amount of carbohydrates present in foods. This can produce a poor estimate of their actual impact on glycemia.

The concept of glycemic load, in which the GI is multiplied by the amount of carbohydrates, resolves this problem (Figure 7). For example, although carrots and breakfast cereals have a high GI (85), the low carbohydrate content of carrots (6 g per 100 g) equals a glycemic load of 5 while the 85 g of carbohydrates in a breakfast cereal produces a load of 72, or 14 times greater! Carrots do not pose any threat in the control of blood glucose. Similarly, the GI of watermelon (GI = 72) and chocolate cake (GI = 38) may suggest that watermelon has a higher glycemic load; in reality, the 58 g of sugar in the cake produces a much higher glycemic load than that of the melon, or 22 and 4 respectively. And, yes, watermelon is a much healthier food than chocolate cake.

the lack of glucose in the blood greatly stimulates the centres involved in appetite control, causing a craving for more food to raise the glucose level. If repeated excessively, these fluctuations will not only wear out the pancreas but also promote obesity. Actually, insulin helps convert sugars into fats, as well as store them in the adipose tissues.

Conversely, consuming foods containing complex carbohydrates (with a low glycemic load, such as whole grain products and legumes) produces a much smaller amount of glucose and insulin in the blood. Under these conditions, the glycemia is stabilized over a longer period, without hypoglycemic episodes. By avoiding blood glucose fluctuations, this type of carbohydrate reduces insulin production and prevents overloading of the pancreas. In addition to being important for diabetics or pre-diabetics, who must maintain a stable glycemic level, consuming complex carbohydrates with a low glycemic load is a dietary change that can have a big impact on diabetes prevention in general (see box, p. 134).

Choosing dietary fats. The type of dietary fat can also exert a huge influence on the development of Type-2 diabetes. Certain saturated fats, for example, promote inflammation, indirectly causing insulin resistance. Conversely, oleic acid, the main fat in olive oil, has an anti-inflammatory action, thereby reducing the risk of insulin resistance. It is noteworthy that omega-3 fats can improve the insulin response of our organs. As for heart disease prevention, using olive oil as the main fat combined with sustained omega-3 intake is a key element in diabetes prevention.

Physical exercise. Besides its central role in preventing cardiovascular diseases, regular physical exercise is essential for Type-2 diabetes prevention. Muscles are the main organs involved in the absorption of glucose in response to insulin. Therefore regular physical exercise, by maintaining optimal muscular function, improves our sensitivity to insulin, thus ensuring stable blood glucose levels. A study of pre-diabetics who presented with, among other things, hyperglycemia upon fasting (over 1.1 g of glucose per litre) and high blood pressure, showed that regular exercise (150 minutes a week) over three years reduced glycemia considerably more than if they had taken a frequently used molecule (metformin) to reduce blood glucose levels (Figure 9). Regular exercise not only reduces glycemia but notably improves blood pressure, an extremely positive effect for heart disease prevention and one not seen in treatment with hypoglycemic drugs. In other words, while molecules like metformin are vital allies in fighting disorders responsible for diseases like Type-2 diabetes, we must never

underestimate the remarkable effect of lifestyle changes such as physical exercise on a number of processes induced by these diseases.

Adding a little spice to food! As incredible as it may seem, certain spices can be instrumental in diabetes Type-2 prevention. The most obvious one is undoubtedly cinnamon, an aromatic substance that improves glucose tolerance and has the ability to interfere with the creation of glycation products that damage blood vessel linings. This property appears to be widespread in the plant kingdom as spices and seasonings such as Jamaican allspice, black pepper, thyme, and many other herbs can also block glycation reactions. Turmeric

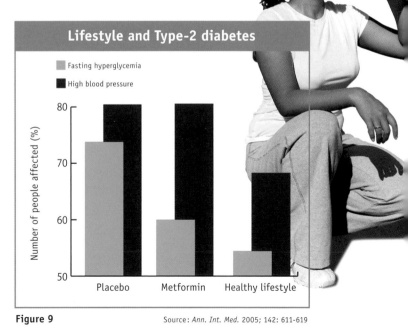

Lifestyle and Type-2 diabetes

■ Fasting hyperglycemia
■ High blood pressure

(Chart: Number of people affected (%), y-axis from 50 to 80; categories: Placebo, Metformin, Healthy lifestyle)

Figure 9

Source: *Ann. Int. Med.* 2005; 142: 611-619

133

Carbohydrates: How to use them

It is easy to avoid blood sugar overloads by simply modifying certain (bad) eating habits.

Drink water instead of sweet drinks and, above all, avoid soft drinks containing large amounts of sugar. Many recent studies indicate that consumption of these drinks is playing a key role in the obesity epidemic currently afflicting the population. In addition, beware of the many "energy" drinks flooding the market. The industry targets adolescents and young adults who don't understand the harmful consequences of these products. They are nothing but sweetened drinks containing an astronomical amount of caffeine (almost 100 mg per can) – the equivalent of a very strong double espresso. These drinks, which have nothing energizing in them, are just stimulants!

Pay particular attention to breakfast cereals. Most cereals contain too many simple sugars and not enough complex sugars in the form of fibre. Ideally, a good cereal should have a minimum of 2 g of fibre per portion.

Avoid eating too many products from refined cereals, such as those used to make white bread or other junk food products: These starches rapidly increase the blood sugar level, producing significant amounts of insulin. A growing number of quality products made from whole grains are available in grocery stores. Legumes, still little known, are the ideal replacement solution since they contain complex carbohydrates and are rich in essential nutrients.

Eliminate diet products! Regularly consuming diet or so-called low-fat foods containing artificial sweeteners such as aspartame or sucralose does nothing to alter our habits: On the contrary, research shows that regularly eating these products stimulates the appetite and can lead to weight gain! Recent studies indicate that consuming diet soft drinks increases the risk of metabolic syndrome in the same way that consuming the sweeter versions of these products does. On top of this, a sweet tooth also encourages people to reject more bitter foods (for example, green vegetables and green tea) that in fact offer major health benefits.

also seems to reduce blood glucose levels, which is why it is used in traditional Indian medicine (Ayurveda). In addition, turmeric's powerful anti-inflammatory activity is a very good preventive weapon for reducing the damage caused by a sugar surplus in the cardiovascular system. Spices continue to surprise us!

Summary

- Hyperglycemia leading to the development of Type-2 diabetes is caused by the inability of tissues to respond properly to insulin, which concurrently reduces the assimilation of sugar present in the blood.

- Overweight and obesity are two main risk factors for Type-2 diabetes, an effect linked to the toxicity of excess fats and the production of inflammatory molecules that interfere with the pancreas's ability to function properly.

- Weight control, combined with regular physical exercise and a diet rich in plants, like whole grains, may prevent over 90% of Type-2 diabetes cases.

Those who excel at solving problems
solve them before they arise.
Those who excel at defeating their enemies
triumph before the threats materialize.

Sun Tzu, *The Art of War*

Chapter 7

Cancer: Taming the Enemy Sleeping Within

According to the WHO, 25 million people in the world currently live with cancer, and 11 million new cases are diagnosed each year. Even more alarming is the fact that cancer causes 7 million deaths each year, and is alone responsible for 12.5% of all deaths recorded in the world. Cancer has a mortality rate higher than AIDS, tuberculosis, and malaria combined. The scourge of modern times, cancer has become a disease that arouses the most concern among people, as much for its dramatic effect on life expectancy as for the slow and inevitable deterioration in the quality of life accompanied by physical and psychological suffering.

In addition to cancer's incredibly destructive potential, we fear it mostly because we do not understand the factors responsible for its development. While most of us acknowledge that cardiovascular disease or Type-2 diabetes can be a direct consequence of bad living habits, we still tend to regard cancer as a matter of fate. We see it as a calamity that strikes indiscriminately and about which we can do nothing, except hope that it will spare us. This feeling of powerlessness is demoralizing as it only leads to despair, without bringing anything positive to our battle against the disease.

This false perception must be challenged: As formidable as it may be, cancer is still a chronic disease, like others, an enemy requiring very specific conditions in which to manifest its destructive potential. We can still keep it in a latent and harmless state by adopting a healthful lifestyle. And as is the case for other diseases, the best way to prevent cancer is to understand the mechanisms involved in its development.

Potentially costly errors

All cancers are caused by errors that occur in our genes, those small areas of our genetic material (DNA) that create proteins essential for cells to function properly (Figure 1). When some of these genes contain errors, which we call mutations, normal cell function changes, setting in motion a series of very complex events. This can lead to abnormal cells growing uncontrollably and ultimately forming a cancerous mass (see box, p. 139).

The main source of these genetic mutations is the renewal of cells – a phenomenon called cell division. During this process, some 3 billion of our DNA constituents must be copied fully; each copy is transmitted to the next generation of cells

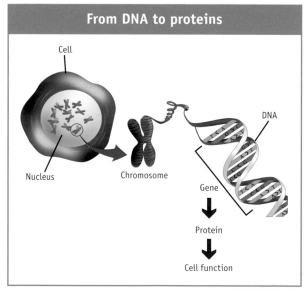

From DNA to proteins

Cell

Nucleus

Chromosome

Gene

DNA

Protein

Cell function

Figure 1

Source: www.bbc.co.uk

A high level of error in a human lifetime

Number of cell divisions in a human lifetime:
1,000,000,000,000,000,000,000

New cells per day:
100,000,000,000

Even if the mutation rate is very low,
the human body produces
1,000,000 mutated cells per day

Figure 2

so they can perform exactly the same functions as the parent cell from which they came.

In normal life, these cells divide at a frenetic pace and reach enormous proportions (Figure 2): Our cells divide about one thousand billion billion times during our lifetime, a number roughly equivalent to the number of grains of sand in all of the world's beaches! While this process is extremely reliable and subject to excellent quality control, the scope of the task is such that it is impossible to prevent errors from occurring. Some 100 billion new cells produced daily by cell division generate about 1 million abnormal cells daily, or almost 25 billion over 70 years! As these altered cells accumulate with age, the risk of developing cancer gradually increases; the likelihood of being diagnosed with cancer at age 70 is about 100 times greater than at age 20 (Figure 4).

What is cancer?

Cancer is an incredibly complex disease in which abnormal cells containing a mutation in their DNA gradually acquire the ability to grow indefinitely and invade body tissues. With very few exceptions, the initial mutation – whether hereditary in origin, linked to lifestyle (smoking), or appearing randomly (cell division) – cannot by itself form mature cancer cells. To do so, pre-cancerous mutant cells need numerous additional mutations that collectively will allow them to acquire certain characteristics essential for circumventing the body's natural defences. The acquisition of all these properties is a considerable challenge for pre-cancerous cells, and most cancers need several years, if not decades, to reach an advanced, clinically detectable stage (Figure 3). For example, a period of 20 years may be necessary for pre-cancerous lesions to appear in the colon (adenoma) or the prostate (intraepithelial neoplasia), and an additional 10

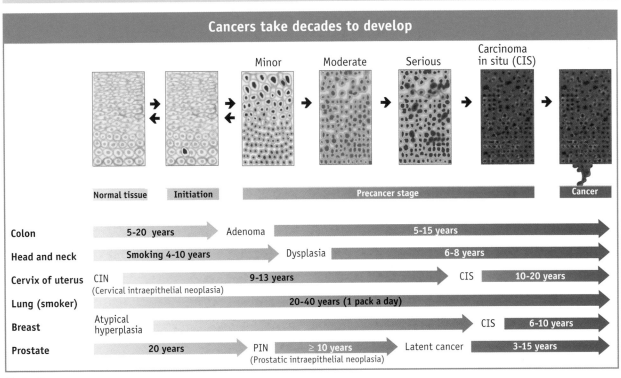

Figure 3

to 15 years for these lesions to develop into a mature cancer.

This long latency period is due to the resistance of the environment in which pre-cancerous cells are found; under normal conditions it is very resistant to their development and nips in the bud all their attempts to acquire the additional mutations necessary to develop. However, when the balance in this environment is altered, these defensive mechanisms are removed and the cancer cells are free to achieve their full potential. In other words, cancer development is not just the consequence of genetic mutations that occur in the pre-cancerous cells themselves, but also of factors in the cell environment that permit these changes.

Among the factors involved, inflammation undoubtedly plays a decisive role in creating a climate that promotes the onset of mutations and the development of cancer cells. Globally, one cancer in six is directly caused by chronic inflammatory conditions, so this is not a rare occurrence. Recent data show that the negative impact of inflammation is due to the catastrophic effects of free radicals on the DNA of pre-cancerous cells, as they greatly accelerate the onset of mutations promoting the growth of these cells, thus leading to cancer.

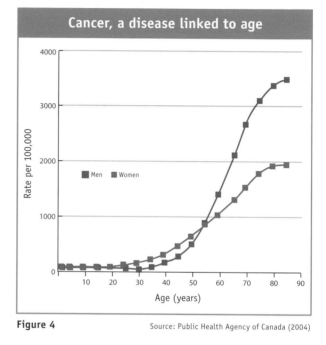

Figure 4 Source: Public Health Agency of Canada (2004)

A disease linked to lifestyle

It is important to understand that mutant cells that accumulate with age are a real cancer threat. These cells are not yet cancerous. They only have the potential to become cancerous if they can benefit from conditions favourable to their development.

Of all the factors contributing to pre-cancerous cells developing into a mature, clinically detectable cancer, none plays as significant a role as lifestyle. The first indication that lifestyle significantly influences cancer risk came from the observations of the Englishman Percivall Pott. In

The first study on cancer prevention

1775: a scrotal cancer epidemic strikes young chimney sweeps in Europe

Cause: polycyclic aromatic hydrocarbons in chimney soot

Preventive measure: daily bath

Figure 5

1775 he showed that the scrotal cancer epidemic afflicting chimney sweeps in Britain was due to their appalling working conditions (Figure 5). Chimney sweeps started working around the age of five; they had to clamber down narrow, still-burning chimney flues, which meant that their skin became permanently impregnated with the residue from coal combustion. More specifically, the rubbing of the scrotum against the sooty rope, which was used to descend into the chimneys, caused toxic particles to accumulate in this organ's wrinkled skin. Daily exposure to the particles, combined with deplorable hygienic conditions, resulted in these chimney sweeps developing cancer. This generally appeared at the end of their working lives, at around 30. The Chimney Sweeps' Guild recommended taking a bath daily instead of annually,

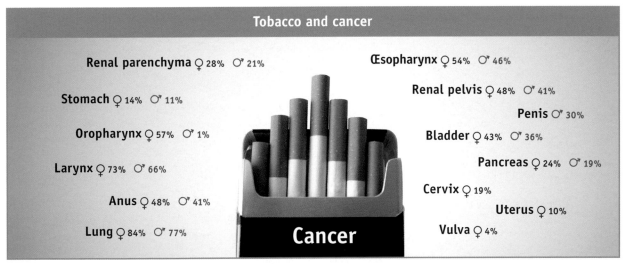

Tobacco and cancer

Renal parenchyma ♀ 28% ♂ 21%

Stomach ♀ 14% ♂ 11%

Oropharynx ♀ 57% ♂ 1%

Larynx ♀ 73% ♂ 66%

Anus ♀ 48% ♂ 41%

Lung ♀ 84% ♂ 77%

Œsopharynx ♀ 54% ♂ 46%

Renal pelvis ♀ 48% ♂ 41%

Penis ♂ 30%

Bladder ♀ 43% ♂ 36%

Pancreas ♀ 24% ♂ 19%

Cervix ♀ 19%

Uterus ♀ 10%

Vulva ♀ 4%

Cancer

Figure 6

Source: *Pharm. Res.* 2008; 25: 2097-2116

the standard at the time. That simple measure managed to contain this type of cancer.

While such conditions are unimaginable today, other aspects of our contemporary lifestyle exert a decisive influence on cancer risk. The best example is undoubtedly smoking, the main cause of lung cancer (80% of cases), and a major factor in deaths caused by at least 13 other types of cancer, particularly those of the throat and neck (larynx, oropharynx, oesopharynx), as well as the bladder, kidneys, and pancreas (Figure 6). Globally, smoking (30%) and factors associated with health practices – diet, obesity, and physical inactivity (35%) – are directly responsible for two-thirds of cancer cases. This is far more than heredity (15%), infections (10%) and many

other factors such as excessive exposure to UV rays (2%) or pollution (2%) (Figure 7). Cancer is for the most part not a hereditary disease as is too often believed (see box, p.146), but a pathology closely linked to our habits.

The influence of lifestyle on cancer development is well illustrated by the massive differences in the incidence of many types of cancer in different parts of the world (Figure 8). For example, while stomach cancer is relatively rare in North America, it is very common in Asia, where it is one of the major types of cancer affecting the population. Conversely, certain cancers that are widespread in the West, specifically breast and prostate, are rarer in the East and in Africa. The range of these differences is impressive: Five times as many North American women develop breast cancer than their Chinese counterparts (Figure 9), while for prostate cancer the difference can be 50 times greater (Figure 10). As mentioned in the introduction, these variations are not due to various genetic predispositions, since the incidence of these cancers among inhabitants of Asia who migrate to America becomes identical to those of their adoptive country. Lifestyle clearly is a determining factor in the risk of developing cancer.

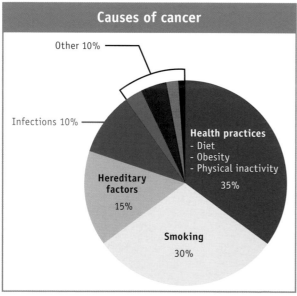

Causes of cancer

Other 10%

Infections 10%

Health practices
- Diet
- Obesity
- Physical inactivity
35%

Hereditary factors
15%

Smoking
30%

Figure 7

Causes of cancer: The role of health practices

The second report resulting from the collaboration of the American Institute for Cancer Research and France's Fonds Mondial de Recherche contre le Cancer, published in fall 2007, is undoubtedly the best synthesis to date of the influence of lifestyle on cancer risk. Over a period of five years, several hundred scientists scrutinized the results of more than 500,000 studies on the link between certain lifestyle habits, particularly diet and exercise, and the risk of developing several types of cancer (Figure 11). A committee of 21 internationally renowned experts rigorously evaluated these results and subsequently identified the major risk factors for cancer and the lifestyle changes that were most likely to

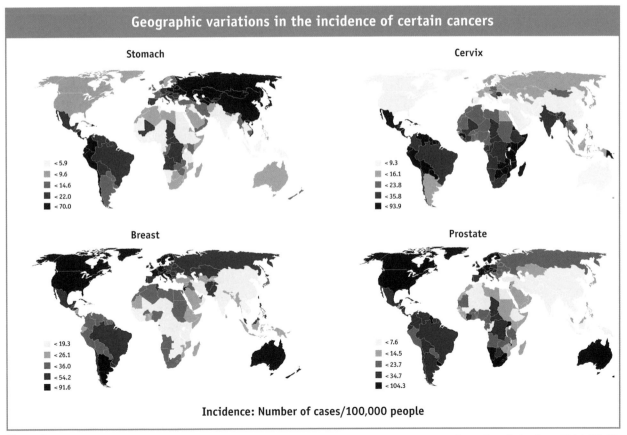

Geographic variations in the incidence of certain cancers

Stomach

< 5.9
< 9.6
< 14.6
< 22.0
< 70.0

Cervix

< 9.3
< 16.1
< 23.8
< 35.8
< 93.9

Breast

< 19.3
< 26.1
< 36.0
< 54.2
< 91.6

Prostate

< 7.6
< 14.5
< 23.7
< 34.7
< 104.3

Incidence: Number of cases/100,000 people

Figure 8

Source: *Nature Reviews Cancer* 2004; 4: 909-917

significantly decrease its incidence. This report must therefore be considered an authority and its 10 recommendations a particular source of inspiration in improving the general health of populations[1] (Figure 12). The report is especially useful for cancer survivors as it sets out for the first time specific ways of minimizing the risks of recurrence.

Among the report's recommendations, two points related to today's eating habits are particularly important for cancer prevention: maintaining a normal body weight and consuming plant products instead of processed food, especially junk food. As discussed earlier, overweight and

1. The FMRC report called *Food, Nutrition, Physical Activity and the Prevention of Cancer: A Global Perspective* can be consulted at: http://www.dietandcancerreport.org

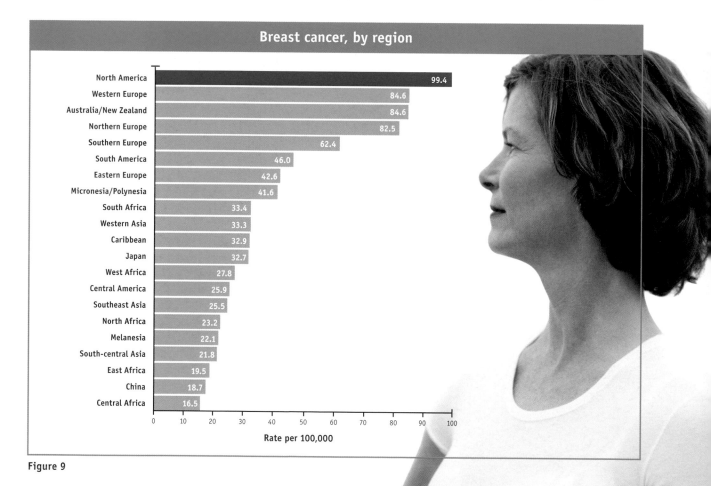

Breast cancer, by region

Region	Rate per 100,000
North America	99.4
Western Europe	84.6
Australia/New Zealand	84.6
Northern Europe	82.5
Southern Europe	62.4
South America	46.0
Eastern Europe	42.6
Micronesia/Polynesia	41.6
South Africa	33.4
Western Asia	33.3
Caribbean	32.9
Japan	32.7
West Africa	27.8
Central America	25.9
Southeast Asia	25.5
North Africa	23.2
Melanesia	22.1
South-central Asia	21.8
East Africa	19.5
China	18.7
Central Africa	16.5

Rate per 100,000

Figure 9

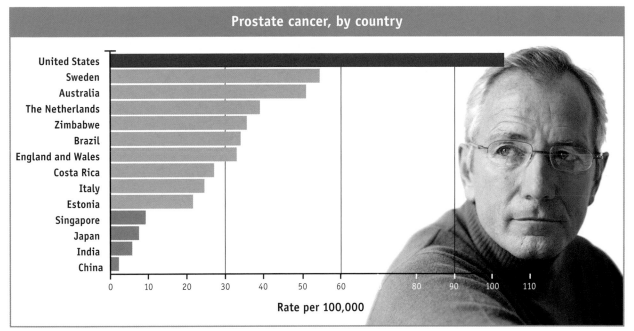

Prostate cancer, by country

United States
Sweden
Australia
The Netherlands
Zimbabwe
Brazil
England and Wales
Costa Rica
Italy
Estonia
Singapore
Japan
India
China

0   10   20   30   40   50   60   80   90   100   110

Rate per 100,000

Figure 10

obesity associated with excess calories create an inflammatory environment in our bodies. When combined with a fruit and vegetable deficiency, this fosters a climate favourable to cancer development (Figure 13).

Inflammation is very dangerous since it subjects cells to intense oxidative stress – a bombardment of free radicals that relentlessly attack the cell constituents that are absolutely essential to normal cell function.

Such an inflammatory climate is particularly devastating when it causes genetic mutations in cancer stem cells, a class of cancer cells that are fundamental in causing the onset of many types

(continued p. 148)

2007 Report of the Fonds Mondial de Recherche contre le Cancer (FMRC)

The largest study ever conducted on the link between lifestyle choices and cancer: *Foods, Nutrition, Physical Exercise and the Prevention of Cancer: A Global Perspective*

· **500,000** studies evaluated

· **5 years** of work

· Evaluation of risk factors for

17 types of cancer

10 recommendations made by **21 renowned specialists**, together with **234 oncologists and scientists**

Figure 11   Source: www.dietandcancerreport.org

Heredity is not the culprit

Heredity's minor contribution to the development of cancer is well illustrated by a study on 45,000 pairs of identical and non-identical twins. If cancer risk were due to inherited genes, identical twins with the same genes would be much more likely to contract cancer than non-identical twins. This is not what was observed: When one of the twins developed cancer during the study, less than 15% of identical twins developed the same cancer. Also, the simultaneous development of leukemia in identical twins is a relatively rare phenomenon: Despite the presence of the same genetic anomalies in two children, only 5% of twins contracted the same disease. In other words, although a certain proportion of cancers are inherited, it is primarily the non-hereditary factors that significantly influence their onset.

It was also observed that adopted children whose adoptive parents died prematurely of cancer were five times more likely to die from cancer themselves. However, those whose biological parents died prematurely from cancer did not have an increased cancer risk! In other words, habits acquired from living with adoptive parents (diet, exercise, smoking, etc.) have a much greater influence on cancer risk than genes inherited from biological parents.

Even in cases of certain inherited defective genes, it appears that the risk of cancer can be greatly influenced by lifestyle. For example, women carrying rare defective versions of BRCA1 and BRCA2 genes have a breast cancer risk eight to 10 times higher than the general population and an ovarian cancer risk 40 times higher. However, the risk of developing early breast cancer (before age 50) among women carrying these defective genes has tripled in those born before 1940, and in those born after 1940, it has increased from 24% to 67%. The major lifestyle changes that have occurred since World War II (decrease in physical activity, mass-production of food, increase in obesity) likely play a role in this increased risk. Overall, these observations show that lifestyle plays a predominant role in the risk of cancer, and is much more significant than hereditary factors. Adopting good habits, particularly in terms of diet and regular physical exercise, can largely mitigate cancer risk.

FMRC's recommendations

1 Stay as slim as possible, with a BMI between 21 and 23.

2 Be physically active for at least 30 minutes a day.

3 Avoid soft drinks and reduce to a minimum the consumption of calorie-rich foods.

4 Eat generous amounts of a variety of fruits, vegetables, legumes, and whole grain foods.

5 Reduce consumption of red meat (beef, lamb, pork) to about 500 g a week.

6 Limit daily consumption of alcohol to two glasses for men and one glass for women.

7 Limit consumption of salty pickled products.

8 Don't use cancer-preventing supplements.

9 Mothers should breast-feed their children for six months.

10 Cancer survivors should follow the recommendations given above.

Figure 12

of cancer and a major factor in its recurrence (see box, p. 150).

Obesity – Overweight and obesity are major risk factors for cancer, and maintaining a normal body weight must be a key priority of any preventive approach. In today's world, with the continuing decline in smoking and increase in the numbers of obese or overweight people, the cancer risk for obesity is fast approaching that of smoking and will probably soon exceed it.

Excess body fat is linked to a significantly increased risk of contracting at least seven types of cancer: esophageal, pancreatic, colon, breast (in menopausal women), endometrial (lining of the uterus), kidney, and gallbladder. While this increased cancer risk is especially pronounced in obese people (BMI over 30), it is also observed in those who are overweight (BMI between 25 and 30). It is therefore important to remain as slender as possible, with a body mass index of around 23, and to avoid gaining weight as we grow older. A recent analysis of various studies involving a total of 282,137 patients revealed that an increase in BMI from 23 to 28 – equivalent to a weight gain of about 15 kg for men and 13 kg for women – translates into a significantly increased risk for several types of cancer (Figure 14). These findings are consistent with the dramatic rise in cases of certain cancers, along with a parallel increase in the proportion of obese people in the population. For example, the incidence of

Harmful effects of industrial foods

DIET

Fruit and vegetable deficiency

Excess calories

Carcinogenic environment

Obesity

CANCER

Figure 13

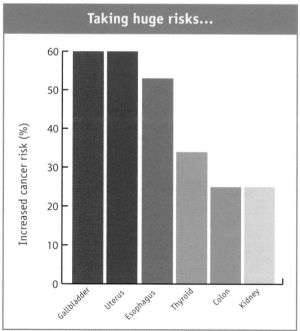

Taking huge risks...

Figure 14 chart: Increased cancer risk (%) — Gallbladder, Uterus, Esophagus, Thyroid, Colon, Kidney

Figure 14

Source: *Lancet* 2008; 371: 569-578

the most widespread form of esophageal cancer, esophageal adenocarcinoma, which is caused by gastric reflux that is often linked to obesity, has increased by more than 450% over the last 30 years. This makes it the fastest-growing form of cancer in America.

As for heart disease and Type-2 diabetes, the negative impact of obesity stems again from the huge metabolic imbalances caused by excess fat mass (Figure 15). Hypertrophy of adipose cells releases vast amounts of fat and inflammatory molecules into the bloodstream, causing the onset of insulin resistance (see Chapter 6) and increasing the production of free radicals. These

disturbances combine to create profound changes in the environment of pre-cancerous cells, producing conditions favourable to the onset of genetic mutations essential for the development of a mature cancer. Specifically, high insulin levels can stimulate cell growth by directly interacting with the proteins on the surface of these cells, or indirectly by increasing the levels of other proteins (like IGF) that boost cell growth. When combined with the high levels of free radicals produced by

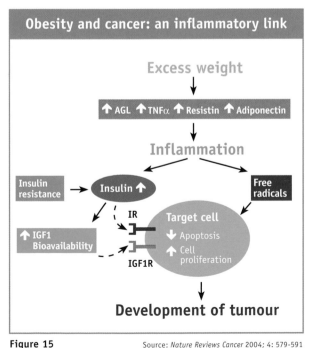

Figure 15   Source: *Nature Reviews Cancer* 2004; 4: 579-591

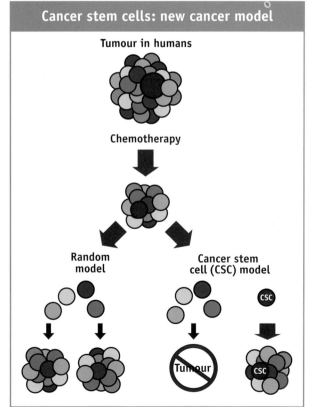

Figure 16

the inflammatory conditions near the cells, the excess insulin and IGF create volatile conditions that can only promote cancer development.

Fruit and vegetable deficiencies – In a number of prospective studies on the eating habits of thousands of people over a period of five to 10 years, researchers found that those who con-

sume large amounts of certain types of plants have a much smaller risk of contracting a range of cancers (Figure 17). In this chart, each line corresponds to a different study, with distinct populations. The consumption indicated reflects normal amounts, or eating each product an average of three to seven times a week. The results of the study are quite astounding: For example,

The root of the problem: cancer stem cells

"Your cancer is back." These are frightening words that patients hear too often after having fought cancer. It is generally bad news, not only because it means they will have to face the disease again, but mostly because a cancer that returns after a few months or years following treatment is even more dangerous than the initial one. So dangerous, in fact, that recurrences are largely responsible for most cancer deaths.

Until recently, it was believed that these recurrences were due to the presence of cancer cells that had survived chemotherapy or radiotherapy; each of the cells had the ability to recreate a cancer mass (random model) (Figure 16). However, today we believe that cancer recurrence is largely due to the presence of cancer stem cells, a sub-population of cells representing only a small proportion of the tumour mass, but that are very

resistant to drugs and can regenerate the tumour mass by producing a range of very aggressive cancer cells. As a result, while anticancer drugs may succeed in eliminating nearly all the cancer cells present in the tumour mass, it takes only a single cancer stem cell to escape the effects of these drugs and cause a recurrence.

We can compare cancer stem cells to bad weeds continuously trying to invade our gardens and lawns. No matter how short we cut the grass to eliminate any trace of dandelions or other undesirable weeds, they will return a few days later! The only way to effectively remove weeds is to pull them out by their roots; that is, eliminate what is absolutely essential for growth. The most recent research developments suggest that an effective way to destroy cancer stem cells is to target the environment in which they live, principally by preventing the creation of a climate likely to provide these cells with good conditions for growth.

Prospective studies showing the link between consumption of specific foods and incidence of cancer in human populations

Foods	Number of participants	Type of cancer	Reduced risk (%)
Cruciferous vegetables	47,909	Bladder	50%
	4,309	Lung	30%
	29,361	Prostate	50%
Tomatoes	47,365	Prostate	25%
Citrus fruits	521,457	Stomach, esophagus	25%
Green vegetables (dietary folate)	81,922	Pancreas	75%
	11,699	Breast (post-menopause)	44%
Lignans	58,049	Breast (post-menopause ER+)	28%
Carrots	490,802	Head and neck	46%
Apples, pears, plums	490,802	Head and neck	38%
Green tea	69,710	Colorectal	57%
Vegetable oils and nuts (dietary tocopherol)	295,344	Prostate	32%
Vitamin D/Calcium	10,578	Breast (premenopause)	35%

Figure 17

Plant communication

The incredible ability of plants to defend themselves against their aggressors is beautifully illustrated by the strategy of the acacia tree. When the giraffe – which is particularly partial to this tree's leaves – attacks it by eating the leaves, the tree reacts quickly by producing ethylene gas. This spreads to its surroundings and reaches other acacias within a radius of 50 m. Upon contact with the gas, the trees alter their metabolism and produce tannins, a class of particularly astringent molecules that dry out the animal's mouth, thereby discouraging it from continuing its meal. This "chemical language" thus acts as a warning device, preventing the animal from devastating the tree's foliage and ensuring the survival of the species (Figure 19).

A similar tactic is used by certain plants in response to damage caused by herbivorous insects like the American grasshopper (*Schistocerca americana*). During their "meal," these insects secrete a class of molecules, caeliferin, which the plant quickly recognizes as a signal that an enemy is present. The plants release a very complex mixture of odorous molecules that attract the natural enemies of crickets, enabling them to rid themselves of their attackers.

Plants are stressed by their environment

- Drought
- Soil deficiency
- Intense heat
- Adverse climatic conditions
- Virus, bacteria, fungus attacks
- Insect attacks

And they defend themselves
- to ensure their survival
- by their genomic plasticity
- by synthesizing defence molecules: phytochemical compounds

Figure 18

simply eating cruciferous vegetables at least three times a week reduces the risk of developing bladder or prostate cancer by 50%. Since prospective studies are the best way to determine the impact of diet on cancer risk, these observations show that a fruit and vegetable deficiency can be crucial in the development of this disease.

The protective effect of plants is due to their exceptional content of phytochemical compounds, a class of molecules synthesized by plants to protect themselves against aggressors and other hostile conditions present in their environment (Figure 18). For this reason, such compounds are often found in large quantities in the parts most likely to be attacked, particularly the fruits and roots (see box, p. 153). There is nothing abstract or theoretical about this

(continued p. 154)

The skin holds the key to cancer prevention

Several plant species store their DNA in their fruit, which if pollinated makes it possible for them to reproduce. Their high sugar content makes the fruit very attractive to us and to various aggressors! Plants have had to develop very sophisticated defence mechanisms to resist attack by various insects, bacteria, and fungi present in their immediate environment. Plants produce powerful insecticide and fungicide molecules that attack these parasites, enabling them to survive such hostile conditions. But, even more fascinating, these molecules can also play a significant role in preventing serious diseases, particularly cancer.

Grape skin is undoubtedly the best example of the effect that a plant's defence mechanisms can have on our health. In response to an attack, generally by microscopic fungi, vines react by producing a molecule called resveratrol, which accumulates in the grape skins and acts as a powerful fungicide to mitigate the damage caused by these fungi. The amount of natural fungicides in grape skin is therefore directly linked to the "stress" endured by the vine. For example, vines cultivated in the rainiest regions (such as the Niagara Valley) and whose grape has a thinner skin (the pinot grape) are more often attacked by fungi and as a result possess much higher levels of resveratrol.

The resveratrol content of grapes is essential not only to the vine; it also plays a major role in the health benefits of red wine. The long fermentation period of grape skin necessary to produce red wine makes it possible to extract large amounts of resveratrol – as much as 10 mg per litre. This concentration is enough to block the growth of a large number of cancer cells when studied in laboratories and to prevent the development of various types of cancers in animals.

However, the benefits of fruit skins are not only associated with grapes. A number of research studies have shown that the skins of certain other fruits consumed today such as apples, pears, peaches, plums, etc., contain most of the anticancer molecules present in the fruits as a whole. The same also applies to some vegetables: The anticancer compounds of potatoes, for example, are found only in the skin.

elevated content of phytochemical compounds in plants: More than half of the chemotherapy drugs being used today to save human lives come directly from plants (Figure 20)!

The presence of such phytochemical compounds is a basic characteristic of these plants, an adaptation that has been instrumental in the evolution of many plant species. Even a fruit with an appearance as plain as the avocado, often perceived as a good source of monounsaturated fats, contains an incredible variety of phytochemical molecules (Figure 21). As we can see, plants are undoubtedly the most complex foods in our diet, a seemingly limitless reservoir of molecules with multiple health benefits.

By depriving our body of a precious source of molecules that have numerous anticancer properties, we promote conditions favourable to cancer development.

The beneficial effects of plants largely compensate for the low-risk residual pesticides used to grow fruits and vegetables; these residues usually are present in too small amounts to damage health. The "carcinogenic potential" of these

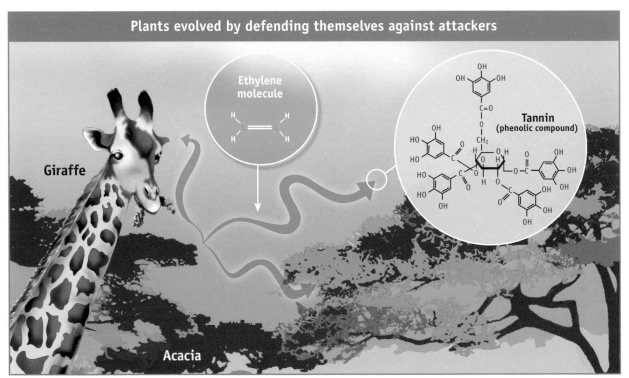

Figure 19

chemical products is often mentioned; this is evaluated on the basis of experimental models in which high doses of these products are tested. Well before the advent of industrial chemistry, our metabolism evolved in the presence of toxic molecules derived from consuming food of variable quality, and we have developed mechanisms to eliminate these products and maintain the integrity of our health. For example, P450 cytochromes in the liver metabolize these toxic products by breaking them down, thereby protecting us from their harmful action. Other enzyme systems, such as reflux enzymes (MDR, ABCB5, MRP) in the intestines, kidneys, or brain, prevent these toxic products from penetrating the body or a given tissue. This helps neutralize their potential danger by preventing them from attaining a level toxic to cells. These defence systems appeared very early in our evolution, more than 500 million years ago, and they are found in the most primitive

50% of anticancer drugs are plant-based

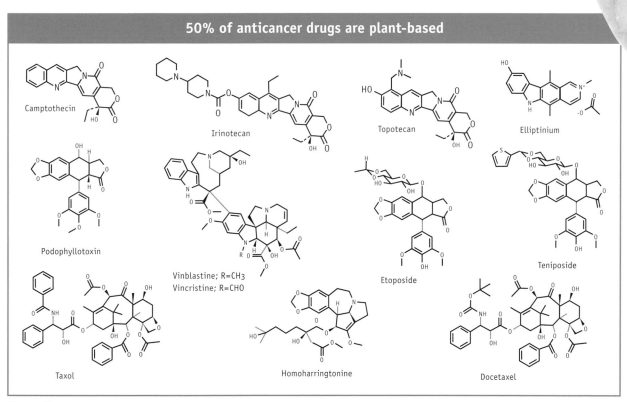

Camptothecin

Irinotecan

Topotecan

Elliptinium

Podophyllotoxin

Vinblastine; R=CH3
Vincristine; R=CHO

Etoposide

Teniposide

Taxol

Homoharringtonine

Docetaxel

Figure 20

bacteria where they protect cells from substances that could present a danger to their survival. The enzymes are so effective that tumour cells enlarge them to protect themselves against chemotherapy agents used in high doses of chemotherapy. This phenotype, or resistance signature, is even used as a diagnostic criterion in clinical resistance to chemotherapy. Such manifold resistance to drugs is one of the main factors responsible for the failure of chemotherapy treatments and patient deaths. If these enzymes can protect cancer cells against high doses of chemotherapy agents, they can obviously protect normal tissues against low doses of toxic chemical agents found in our

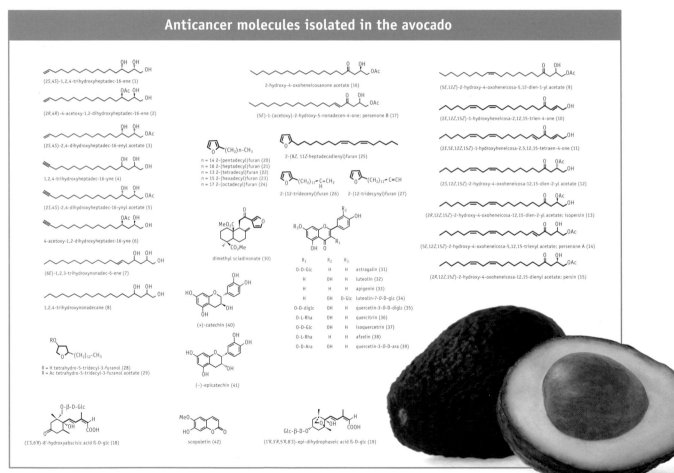

Anticancer molecules isolated in the avocado

Figure 21

Source: *Sem. Cancer Biol.* 2007; 17: 386-394

environment. Despite what many people think, the human body is far from vulnerable and weak; its biological evolution in a hostile environment has led it to develop powerful defence mechanisms against biochemical attackers.

Of all the pesticides consumed by humans, 99.99% are of natural origin: these are phytochemical compounds produced by plants to defend themselves against aggressors. An average person consumes about 1,500 mg of these phytochemical compounds daily, or 10,000 times more than trace amounts of synthetic pesticides associated with the consumption of plants (0.09 mg). A single cup of coffee contains more agents that can, at high doses, present greater carcinogenic potential than all the fruits and vegetables consumed by a person over an entire year (Figure 22). However, regular consumption of coffee is not associated with a rise in cancer, as many studies have shown. This indicates that these measurements of "carcinogenic potential" in a given molecule are of little use in evaluating the real impact of chemical products on tumour development due to the metabolic defence mechanisms developed during our evolution. The same applies to residual synthetic pesticides in agriculture: Their impact on the formation of tumours has not been convincingly demonstrated. We should distinguish between the situation of those whose job is to spread the pesticides – and must adequately protect themselves from high-level occupational exposure – and the considerably reduced exposure of consumers, at the opposite end of the food production chain. This does not mean we should abandon our fight against massive insecticide use to protect the health of the environment. On the contrary, it indicates that the potential risk to human health is still lower than the enormous benefits gained from regularly consuming fruits and vegetables.

Cancer prevention

Since mutant cells are present in our bodies throughout our lives, we risk developing cancer at any time. While this enforced co-habitation is dangerous, it is still possible to reduce the risks

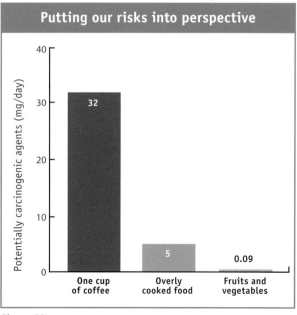

Figure 22

Source: *Mutat. Res.* 2000; 447: 3-13

posed by these pre-cancerous cells through lifestyle habits aimed at minimizing conditions favourable to the cells developing into a mature cancer, with all its destructive potential. Just as a lion tamer manages to stay close to the big cats by using a combination of cunning and force, it is possible to keep cancer at bay using every weapon at our disposal, especially food.

Eat an abundance of plant products

The large variety of phytochemical molecules present in plants is a crucial element of the beneficial properties of these foods, since these compounds can target several processes involved in cancer development (Figure 23). They may directly attack the cancer cells, or positively change the environment of cells to keep them in a latent and innocuous state, or increase the bioavailability of anticancer molecules. Whatever the case, their tens of thousands of phytochemical compounds make it possible to create an anticancer environment that will inhibit the development of this disease. While all plants are beneficial to health, some stand out for their unusual anticancer activity.

Cruciferous vegetables – Cruciferous vegetables (broccoli, cauliflower, cabbage, etc.) are among the most important foods for cancer prevention. The preventive effects associated with regular consumption of cruciferous vegetables are due to their high content of *glucosinolates*. As we chew these foods, these glucosinolates come into contact with myrosinase, an enzyme present in the plant that transforms glucosinolates into *isothiocyanates,* very reactive molecules that act on two key aspects of cancer development.

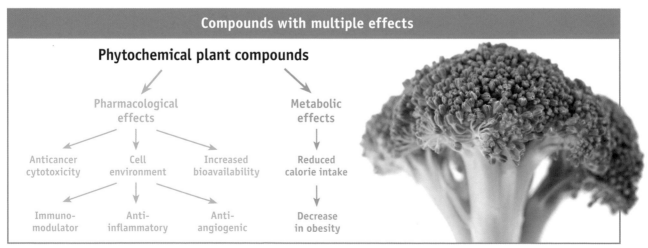

Figure 23

First, these molecules increase our defence system's action against carcinogenic substances, which speeds their elimination from the body, preventing them from damaging cell DNA. This effect is very important as several cancers are directly caused by insufficient action of these detoxification systems.

Some of these compounds, such as those found in broccoli or watercress, also have the property of preventing cancer cell growth by increasing the production of free radicals that kill these cells.

To maximize the production of anticancer molecules by cruciferous vegetables, we must pay special attention to how we cook them. Recent studies have shown that boiling broccoli, Brussels sprouts, cauliflower, or firm, round cabbage causes a significant loss (over 75%) of their glucosinolate content, as molecules escape from the vegetables into the boiling water. On the other hand, when these vegetables are steamed, microwaved, or stir-fried (in a wok, for example), their glucosinolate content remains identical to that of raw vegetables. Another important factor to bear in mind: It is important to reduce the cooking time of vegetables as much as possible to maximize the preservation of myrosinase activity. Cooking vegetables quickly, i.e, steaming or stir-frying them so they remain crunchy, will preserve most of their anticancer molecules. This is an easy habit to adopt, as cruciferous vegetables taste better when they are cooked for only a short time.

Allium – Several studies have shown that people who regularly consume vegetables from the garlic family (garlic, onion, chives, leeks) have a lower risk of developing several types of cancer, particularly those of the digestive system such as stomach and colon cancer. This protective effect is linked to the presence of *sulphur compounds* that hasten the elimination of carcinogenic toxic substances from our bodies. This reduces the risk that these substances will attack our DNA and cause mutations that can induce cancer. Garlic also has powerful anticancer compounds that fight microtumours lying dormant in us, by preventing cancer cell growth. Like cruciferous vegetables, garlic and its cousins must therefore be considered a first-line defence against cancer, true guardians of our health that strive to limit the damage caused by the various toxic aggressors we face daily.

Green tea – Green tea leaves are a very rich source of anticancer molecules called *catechins,* which can comprise almost one-third of the leaves' weight. This content is significant as the molecules have the property of preventing microtumours – which we develop spontaneously throughout our lives – from acquiring a new network of blood vessels essential for their growth. Without these new vessels, formed by the angiogenic process, cancer cells cannot get enough oxygen and nutrients to grow and are therefore condemned to remain in a latent and innocuous state. Our laboratory has shown that a single cup of green tea contains enough catechins to block the angiogenesis by interfering with the activity of certain proteins that are crucial in the formation of new vessels. When we drink green tea, our bodies are exposed to sufficient doses of anticancer molecules to block the angiogenesis, which can help prevent the development of microtumours and aggressive cancers. In addition, many scientific studies suggest that regular consumption of green tea is a major factor in reducing the risk of developing several cancers. For example, a recent study conducted with 69,710 Chinese subjects aged 40 to 70 showed a major reduction (57%) in the risk of colorectal cancer among avid green tea drinkers. Similarly, analysis of the habits of green tea drinkers among 49,920 Japanese aged 40 to 69 indicates that those drinking five cups a day had a 50% lower risk of developing advanced prostate cancer than those drinking less than a cup a day. Drinking green tea every day is a simple, effective and delicious way to use anticancer molecules of natural origin to prevent cancer.

Citrus fruits – Many studies have shown that the consumption of citrus fruits halves the risk of developing several types of cancer, specifically those of the digestive system (e.g., esophagus, mouth, and stomach). This anticancer effect is probably linked to the high level of *monoterpenes* and *flavanones* found in citrus fruits. These are two classes of anticancer compounds that interfere with several processes essential to the development of tumours. Monoterpenes block the activity of proteins involved in the growth of cancer cells, at the same time reducing their ability to invade the surrounding tissues. Flavanones can preserve the structure of blood vessels, which prevents inflammation and deprives tumours of a major source of growth stimuli.

Citrus fruits can also prevent cancer development indirectly by stimulating the anticancer activity of molecules present in other foods. For example, some grapefruit compounds do not intrinsically have anticancer activity, but nonetheless block the systems (cytochrome P450) involved in eliminating anticancer molecules from the body. They do so by increasing their life span in the bloodstream and thus their anticancer potential.

Super fruits – Some fruits contain high levels of *polyphenols* that give them special antioxidant potential. The best known are berries, which are extraordinary as much for their fine taste as for their health benefits. Strawberries, raspberries, blueberries, and blackberries are the main dietary sources of *ellagic acid* and *delphinidin,* two molecules that block angiogenesis. Ellagic acid is present in large amounts in strawberries, raspberries, and blackberries, while delphinidin is mostly found in blueberries and blackberries. The simultaneous presence of ellagic acid and delphinidin in blackberries is particularly beneficial, making these berries invaluable allies in the fight against cancer. Research conducted in our laboratory over the last few years has shown that these two molecules interfere with this process by blocking the activity of essential proteins. In this way they prevent the formation of new blood vessel networks near the tumours, depriving them of their oxygen supply and nutritional molecules. Since all cancers are absolutely dependent on this blood supply, ellagic acid and delphinidin can be considered very significant agents of prevention, capable of curbing the development of a wide range of cancers. Although these berries are seasonal, they can be frozen for future use as their anticancer molecules resist freezing well.

Some exotic fruits also contain large amounts of antioxidant polyphenols that can help cancer prevention. The best example is undoubtedly the pomegranate, a fruit that was grown in the Middle East (Iran and Iraq) some 6,000 years ago and was long considered by the people of this region an exceptional fruit both for its unique taste and many medicinal properties.

A pomegranate is made up of many hundreds of arils; these are grains formed from a red translucent pulp with a slightly bitter taste, which contain significant amounts of major anthocyanins and give the fruit its characteristically red colour. In addition there are complex hydrolysable tannins that are largely responsible for this fruit's strong antioxidant activity. The pomegranate's high content of punicalin, punicalagin, and ellagic acid derivatives spikes its antioxidant activity, which is three times higher than that of red wine or green tea. Feeding pomegranate juice to animals with prostate tumours substantially reduces tumour growth and dramatically decreases the animals' PSA levels, an indicator of how much the cancer has spread. This protective effect is also observed among humans: During a study conducted among patients with prostate cancer who had surgery or radiotherapy, daily consumption of 250 mL of pomegranate juice considerably delayed recurrence of the cancer.

This anticancer effect of pomegranate juice does not seem to be limited to prostate cancer: A recent study has shown that pomegranate juice was able to reduce by more than 60% the development of lung cancer induced by benzopyrene, a powerful carcinogenic substance.

To properly enjoy the taste of pomegranate, you must choose heavy fruits whose skin is smooth and shiny. The best way to peel a pomegranate is to score the skin in several places in a bowl of water and remove the pieces by pulling back the white membrane. You can also extract the juice by cutting the fruit in half and using a fruit juicer. Commercial pomegranate juice, including concentrate, is available in grocery stores.

Soy – Estrogens (female sex hormones) play a key role in activating breast cancer; when these hormone levels are too high, they stimulate excessive growth of the mammary glands and increase cancer risk (breast cancer is said to be hormone-dependent). Many studies suggest that the deleterious effects of estrogens could be reduced by regular consumption of foods rich in phytoestrogens. These phytoestrogens are plant-based molecules that resemble estrogens and prevent the hormones from interacting effectively with breast cells. They thereby reduce the negative effects of the estrogens and the cancer risk.

Isoflavones, molecules associated with soy, are the best-known phytoestrogens to date. Studies have shown that regular consumption of soy-based foods at a young age – that is before the marked increase in estrogen levels at puberty – considerably reduces the risk of contracting breast cancer. On the other hand, soy isoflavones do not have the same beneficial effects among women who have already contracted breast cancer, and could even have negative effects. These women must therefore consume soy in extreme moderation. It is also strongly recommended *not* to take isoflavones as supplements, since studies conducted to date show that these products can increase the risk of cancer instead of reducing it!

Tomatoes – Some observations have shown that the incidence of prostate cancer is lower in countries whose inhabitants consume a large amount of tomato-based dishes, such as Italy, Spain, and Mexico. This protection seems to be linked to the presence of *lycopene,* a pigment that can interfere with the growth of pre-cancerous prostate cells. To maximize the effect of lycopene, it is important to consume *cooked* tomatoes, ideally in a fatty substance like olive oil – in a sauce, for example. Cooking tomatoes in a fatty substance increases the amount of lycopene and helps our body cells absorb it.

Immunomodulators – Some foods also have the ability to favourably modulate the immune system, a property that can be beneficial in maintaining an environment resistant to cancer cell development.

Probiotics – Yogurt enriched with probiotics (*bifidobacteria* and *lactobacilli*) contains billions of beneficial bacteria. These can survive passage through the stomach to settle in the large intestine, where they can exert their beneficial effects, particularly on the immune system. For example, studies have shown that daily consumption of yogurt containing bifidobacteria and lactobacilli significantly increases the activity of certain immune cells involved in the defence against foreign invaders. Given that immune system activity is crucial in defending against microbes and also in protecting against certain cancers, these observations show the importance of intestinal bacteria in maintaining good health.

Mushrooms – Mushrooms are foods with multiple qualities: Not only are they nutritious, low in calories and very tasty, but they also contain molecules that stimulate the immune system and interfere with certain types of cancer growth. In grocery stores today, we can find cultivated mushrooms and their variants, the portobello and brown mushroom (cremini), as well as other tastier types like oyster mushrooms, and Asian mushrooms like shiitake and enokitake. These mushrooms are particularly healthful as they contain significant levels of complex molecules called *polysaccharides,* which can stimulate the immune system. Numerous studies have shown that the lentinan in shiitake mushrooms significantly increases the amount and activity of leukocytes, key cells in the immune system. This in turn increases the chances of controlling emerging tumours and preventing them from reaching a mature state.

The anticancer and immunostimulating activity of edible mushrooms does not seem to be limited to Asian species. Oyster mushrooms, for example, also contain compounds that appear to be effective in curbing the development of some cancers, particularly of the colon, by directly attacking the cancer cells and causing them to die through apoptosis. Similarly, cultivated mushrooms also contain molecules that can prevent some cancer cell growth, particularly breast cancer. This property is due to the ability of mushrooms to block the action of aromatase, an enzyme that plays a key role in the production of estrogens, the female sex hormones. Since most breast cancers are hormone-dependent – that is, their growth depends on these estrogens – blocking aromatase decreases estrogen levels and can prevent the growth of such cancers. It is also interesting to note that administering extracts of cultivated mushrooms to laboratory animals that have developed breast tumours causes a marked regression in the tumours. These observations are even more fascinating since the quantity of mushrooms required to reduce tumour growth corresponds to reasonable human consumption, or about 100 g per day. Including mushrooms in our diet makes it possible not only to add a new gastronomic dimension to our life, but also to enlist valuable allies in the prevention of certain cancers, specifically breast cancer.

Seaweed – Seaweed's anticancer properties are largely linked to their high content of *fucoxanthin* and *fucoidan,* two compounds that interfere with several processes essential to cancer cell growth.

Fucoidan is a complex sugar polymer present in large quantities in some seaweed, particularly kombu and wakame. This molecule prevents the growth of a large variety of cancer cells cultivated in the laboratory, and even kills them through apoptosis. In addition to this cytotoxic activity, fucoidan also seems to have a positive impact on the immune function by reducing inflammation and increasing "beneficial" immune system activity, thereby creating a more hostile, growth-limiting environment for cancer cells.

Fucoxanthin is a yellow pigment of the carotenoid family (beta-carotene, lycopene, etc.). Of all the dietary carotenoids tested to date, fucoxanthin has the most significant anticancer activity in both laboratory animals and isolated human tumour cells. It seems particularly active against prostate cancer cells. Its inhibiting effect is even more significant than that of lycopene, a carotenoid found mainly in tomatoes, long touted as playing a preventive role in the development of prostate cancer. Since seaweed is the only food source of fucoxanthin, there is no doubt that these plants should be part of any cancer prevention strategy involving diet, especially for prostate cancer.

Natural anti-inflammatories

The significance of inflammation in the development of pre-cancerous cells into a mature cancer suggests that everything should be done to minimize the presence of inflammatory conditions. Fortunately, some foods are especially likely to reduce inflammation.

Plants – Some plant foods contain molecules that prevent cancer cells from producing inflammatory molecules. The best examples of these anti-inflammatory molecules are resveratrol in red wine, curcuma in the Indian spice turmeric, and gingerol in ginger. Studies show that these three molecules can block COX-2 and that this anti-inflammatory activity plays a major role in the anticancer action of these foods. The anti-inflammatory activity of turmeric is particularly fascinating since this molecule certainly has the most distinct anticancer activities of the plant kingdom. More than 15 clinical trials are currently underway in the world's best hospitals to measure turmeric's effectiveness in treating various cancers (colon, pancreas, myeloma) and other inflammatory diseases.

This anti-inflammatory effect is not only limited to these foods; on the contrary, it is a characteristic of most plants. In our laboratory we have observed that several fruits and vegetables, especially blackberries and cranberries, also exhibit high anti-inflammatory activity.

Omega-3 – Another way to reduce chronic inflammation with food is to maximally increase our consumption of omega-3 fatty acids and reduce that of omega-6 acids. These two types of essential fatty acids are used by our cells to produce two types of molecules. Omega-3s produce two very powerful natural anti-inflammatory molecules, DHA and EPA. However, omega-6 fatty acids (present in meat and processed food) produce molecules that *promote* inflammation. Unfortunately, omega-3s are present in large amounts only in specific foods such as fatty fish (tuna, salmon, sardines) and some plants (flaxseed, chia, and walnuts), so the modern diet may contain 25 times more omega-6 acids than omega-3s. This creates an imbalance in our body, making it more susceptible to inflammation. There is no doubt that increasing the intake of omega-3 fatty acids and reducing that of omega-6s can re-establish this balance and prevent the creation of a climate of chronic inflammation in our tissues.

While long-chain omega-3 acids from fatty fish have received special attention over the last few years, we should not underestimate the significance of plant-derived omega-3s, from flaxseed, chia, or nuts. A recent study has shown that among overweight or obese men, a diet rich in linoleic acid causes a rapid and significant decrease (50%) in the blood levels of two powerful inflammatory molecules, TNF-a and interleukin-6. These observations indicate that adding foods rich in linoleic acid to the daily diet, such as flaxseed or chia, can cause a measurable anti-inflammatory effect, making its use a potentially very valuable strategy for combating inflammation and subsequent diseases.

Combining several plants possessing anticancer properties can only have positive repercussions in preventing the development of cancer. For example, it has recently been observed that in mice carrying a very aggressive tumour, adding a cocktail of plants with anticancer properties to their diet significantly reduced the tumour (Figure 24). There is no doubt that adopting a diet that includes many of these protector plants, combined with an increased intake of omega-3 fatty acids and a reduction of red meat and processed products, is essential for cancer prevention.

Vitamin D: Cancer prevention champion

Vitamin D was discovered in 1919, just after vitamins A, B, and C, its name coming from this alphabetical sequence. It plays an absolutely essential role in calcium absorption and bone growth, as well as in maintaining overall body functions. However, unlike other vitamins obtained through food, most of the vitamin D in our body (80-95%) is produced by the sun's action on the skin. UVB light rays transform a molecule called 7-dehydro-cholesterol into vitamin D3, which is converted in the liver and kidneys into 1,25-dihydroxyvitamin D, the active form of the vitamin.

The sun's major role in vitamin D production obviously poses a problem for populations in northern countries who have much less sun exposure in the winter. For example, studies have shown that inhabitants of Canada have vitamin D concentrations in the blood below the recommended levels, a deficiency that is particularly pronounced in winter.

This deficiency seems to increase the risk of certain cancers. For example, the incidence of breast cancer is generally higher in regions that are far from the equator (and receive less sun in the winter), such as the Scandinavian countries, Canada, and New Zealand, compared to regions that are sunny for most of the year (Africa in particular). Similarly, a study conducted among 48,000 men revealed that a vitamin D deficiency may be associated with an increase in the number of cancers and an increase in subsequent death rates, especially in cancers of the digestive system. In addition, studies have shown that people treated for colon cancer in the summer had a higher survival rate than those treated in the winter; this benefit is probably linked to an increase in vitamin D following exposure to the sun. A recent study shows that vitamin D levels in the blood could also improve the probability of surviving breast cancer: Women with insufficient levels of vitamin D during a diagnosis (below 50 nmol per litre) had twice the risk of a cancer recurrence.

The protective effects of vitamin D have been observed for several types of cancer. For example, an American study conducted among 15,000 men showed that subjects whose blood levels of vitamin D were below average saw their risk of prostate cancer more than double compared to those with significant levels of the vitamin. Spectacular results were also observed in another study conducted among 122,000 people: Those whose vitamin D intake was over 600 IU per day had half the risk of contracting pancreatic cancer than those whose daily intake was below 150 IU. A positive impact of vitamin D was also observed for breast cancer (50% reduction) and colon cancer (66% reduction). In addition, a recent study has shown that a daily intake of 1,000 IU of vitamin D by menopausal women reduced by more than 50% the general risk of cancer compared to those who did not receive the vitamin. As we can see, vitamin D is truly in a class by itself for cancer prevention!

In light of these results, we must increase our intake of vitamin D to prevent cancer effectively. The Canadian Cancer Society and several international experts have recommended increasing vitamin D intake from 200 IU to 1,000 IU per day to reduce the incidence of several cancers. From May to September, increasing the level of vitamin D is easy: Simply exposing your face and arms to the sun for ten minutes allows your body to produce some 10,000 IU! On the other hand, long exposure to the sun is strongly not recommended as it significantly increases the risks of skin cancer. The sun is therefore a double-edged sword that we must use intelligently to draw maximum benefit while avoiding its harmful effects.

From October to April, however, the lack of sunlight complicates the issue and we must turn to other sources of vitamin D. Fish like tuna and salmon contain significant levels and are therefore a good choice as they are also rich in omega-3s, the fatty acids that help in cancer prevention. Supplements containing 1,000 IU of vitamin D are also a simple, economical and effective way of increasing the intake of this vitamin.

Exercise: A little-known weapon in cancer prevention

In addition to the benefits of physical activity in the prevention of heart disease, studies have

Inhibiting tumour formation with a diet rich in anticancer fruits and vegetables

Untreated | **Treated with a mixture of anticancer vegetables**

Figure 24

shown that exercise is associated with a significant decline in the risk of contracting certain types of cancer. Detailed analysis of these studies, recently published by France's Fonds Mondial de Recherche contre le Cancer, shows that physical activity reduces the risk of colon cancer (50%), breast cancer (among menopausal women by 30 to 40%) and endometrial cancer. It may also have a protective effect against cancers of the lung, pancreas, and breast (in non-menopausal women), but this requires further study.

The benefits of regular exercise in cancer prevention are due to its many positive repercussions on the functioning of muscles and on the body in general (Figure 25). Exercise improves sugar intake by muscle cells, reducing the development of the insulin resistance phenomenon as well as the chronic pro-cancerous inflammation climate inevitably associated with this condition. At the same time, by reducing adipose mass, exercise also decreases the amount of sex hormones in the blood, thereby reducing the risk of hormone-dependent cancers, particularly of the breast and prostate. Weight loss also produces many positive effects by reducing the secretion of inflammatory molecules by the adipose cells; this helps

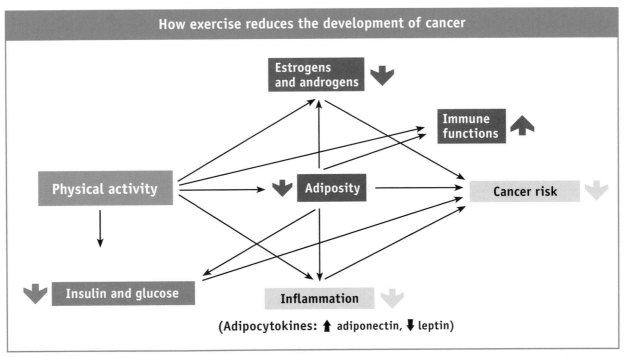

How exercise reduces the development of cancer

(Adipocytokines: ↑ adiponectin, ↓ leptin)

Figure 25

Source: *Nature Rev. Cancer* 2008; 8: 205-211

improve insulin sensitivity as well as making the immune system more efficient.

The powerful anti-inflammatory effect of regular physical exercise seems to play a predominant role in protecting against cancer development. In fact, muscles are not the only organs involved in body movement. Glands are also metabolically very active, and when stimulated by regular exercise, they activate several genes involved in maintaining anti-inflammatory conditions in the body. Conversely, the muscles

of sedentary people do not activate any of these protective mechanisms, which can only foster a climate of chronic inflammation (Figure 26). We can therefore consider physical inactivity a lifestyle factor, like obesity, that promotes chronic inflammation and the onset of chronic diseases, such as cancer, whose development depends largely on this inflammation.

Some people are discouraged by the idea of increasing their level of physical activity, wrongly believing it means they must practice an extreme

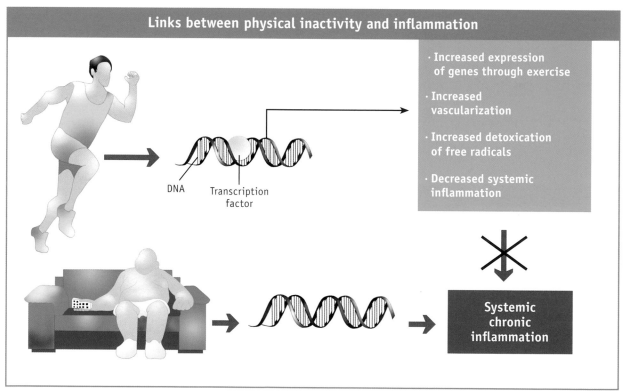

Links between physical inactivity and inflammation

DNA
Transcription factor

· Increased expression of genes through exercise

· Increased vascularization

· Increased detoxication of free radicals

· Decreased systemic inflammation

Systemic chronic inflammation

Figure 26

Source: *Nature* 2008; 454: 463-469

sport. But it is not necessary to become an Olympic champion to benefit from exercise! Walking, for example, is a simple and inexpensive form of exercise that can have very positive health repercussions, even in the short term. Studies have shown that women in breast cancer remission who are active – that is, they walk from three to five hours a week at a moderate pace – have 30% less risk of dying from the consequences of their cancer than those who are sedentary. How do you increase your level of physical exercise? All that is needed is to change your routine to create walking opportunities: for instance, by avoiding elevators and using stairs, getting off the bus one stop earlier, or parking farther from the office.

In addition, some daily activities like housework, mowing the lawn, or playing outside with children can lead to a significant expenditure of energy and also contribute to good health.

It goes without saying that more vigorous activities such as jogging, tennis, or cross-country skiing can only increase the benefits from exercise. However, it must be borne in mind that the most important initiative to take is exercising as often as possible, regardless of the intensity.

Summary

- Cancer is a complex disease that can only be prevented effectively by using all the weapons at our disposal. Among these, quitting smoking remains the most important measure for reducing the incidence of many types of cancer.
- Maintaining a healthy body weight, eating plant-rich foods, and exercising regularly make an unbeatable "cancer prevention trio" (Figure 27).

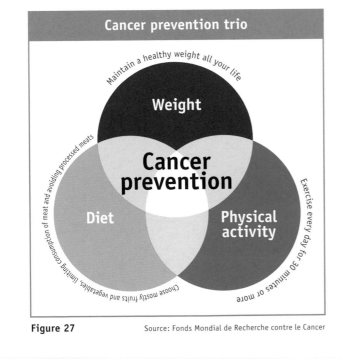

Cancer prevention trio

Maintain a healthy weight all your life

Weight

Cancer prevention

limiting consumption of meat and avoiding processed meats

Exercise every day for 30 minutes or more

Diet

Physical activity

Choose mostly fruits and vegetables,

Figure 27   Source: Fonds Mondial de Recherche contre le Cancer

The Brain is wider than the Sky
For put them side by side
The one the other will contain
With ease and You beside

Emily Dickinson (1830–1886)

Chapter 8

A Sound Mind in a Healthy Body: Preventing Alzheimer's through Diet

A marvel of evolution, the brain is certainly the body's most fascinating organ. An activity as commonplace as reading a book, planning a vacation, or simply talking with a friend is the result of extraordinarily complex processes involving the brain's nerve cells (neurons) of which there are about 100 billion. These neurons are divided into areas dedicated to specific functions, and each can make about 100,000 connections with its neighbours, adding up to a very sophisticated network. This network not only integrates information from the outside (senses, movements) but also develops complex phenomena like thought, emotions, language, and memory (Figure 1). Throughout the course of our evolution, the human brain has acquired a power unequalled in the living world, rendering humans the most extraordinary animals living on Earth.

In light of this, it should not be surprising that dysfunctions afflicting the brain have always been considered direct attacks on our private selves and our dignity – intrusions into the essence of what it means to be human. Caught off guard by the loss of mental stability, humans have long attributed such conditions to supernatural causes. Dementia (from the Latin *dementis,* meaning "loss of mind") was considered a visible manifestation of Evil, and in extreme cases, a sign of being possessed by the Devil. Only with the advent of the Renaissance did dementia stop being associated with the "spirit of Evil" to become gradually "diseases of the mind." These afflictions were finally recognized as "diseases of the brain's organs that prevent man from necessarily thinking and acting like the others" (Voltaire, *Philosophical Dictionary,* 1764). Too often used as a synonym for madness, dementia is still the medical term employed today to describe brain lesions that alter behaviour, personality, and all cognitive functions (reason, analysis, language). According to this definition, dementia is the consequence of cognitive and behavioural disorders, leading to a loss of autonomy in the person affected.

Alzheimer's disease

On November 25, 1901, in a Frankfurt hospital, Dr. Alois Alzheimer received a new patient, Frau Auguste Deter, a 51-year-old woman who was admitted due to memory problems and numerous behavioural disorders (jealousy, auditory hallucinations, agitation). She was unable to remember her husband's name or what she had eaten a few hours earlier, and her condition deteriorated to the point that she lost all contact with the outside world. Upon the patient's death in 1906, Dr. Alzheimer performed an autopsy of her brain, which revealed atrophied brain tissue and the presence of strange structures both inside and outside the neuron cells – plaque, which became the main characteristic of this

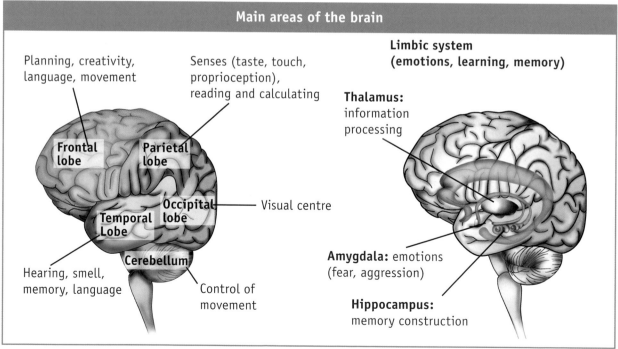

Main areas of the brain

Planning, creativity, language, movement

Senses (taste, touch, proprioception), reading and calculating

Limbic system (emotions, learning, memory)

Thalamus: information processing

Frontal lobe

Parietal lobe

Occipital lobe — Visual centre

Temporal Lobe

Cerebellum

Hearing, smell, memory, language

Control of movement

Amygdala: emotions (fear, aggression)

Hippocampus: memory construction

Figure 1

Source: www.ahaf.org

"new" form of dementia, to be called Alzheimer's disease.

In Canada, as in the rest of the world, Alzheimer's disease is the leading cause of dementia (Figure 2), far ahead of vascular dementia (a common consequence of stroke, which prevents blood from circulating to the brain and destroys neurons) or other types of serious, but more rare dementia. An estimated 24 million people in the world are currently afflicted by this disease. However, with nearly 4.6 million new cases a year associated with an ageing population (or one case every seven seconds), this number could reach an estimated 81 million by 2040. In the United States alone, the disease afflicts more than 5 million people, resulting in annual health costs of $60 billion.

The risk of contracting Alzheimer's disease increases considerably with age, and, given our growing life expectancy, the consequences of this disease will intensify. For example, while only about 1% of people age 60 have the disease, the rate doubles every five years, so that it afflicts almost 15% of people at age 80 and more than 30% after age 85 (Figure 3).

Alzheimer's disease is still very difficult to diagnose, and autopsies must be performed to confirm the presence of lesions symptomatic of the condition. The first stages are generally characterized by

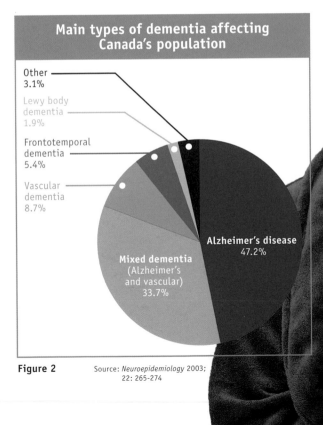

Main types of dementia affecting Canada's population

Other 3.1%

Lewy body dementia 1.9%

Frontotemporal dementia 5.4%

Vascular dementia 8.7%

Alzheimer's disease 47.2%

Mixed dementia (Alzheimer's and vascular) 33.7%

Figure 2   Source: *Neuroepidemiology* 2003; 22: 265-274

short-term memory loss, difficulty in performing certain simple tasks, and behaviours that could be interpreted as normal distractions (Figure 4). However, impaired cognitive function becomes increasingly obvious with the progression of the disease, leading to the onset of disorders – language, visual recognition, and the processing of external information. The ensuing confusion, often combined with major behavioural changes (hallucinations, agitation, withdrawal), indicates that the process of degeneration has reached an advanced stage. It now affects the brain's frontal lobes, an area that in some ways is the "seat of humanity" through the role it plays in memory, complex cognitive operations, language, and control of emotions. In the final stages of the disease, patients lose their ability to communicate or to recognize faces, and to control basic physiological functions (bladder, bowels). They will now need constant care until they die. On average, people with Alzheimer's disease live from four to 10 years once the diagnosis has been made, but can

A disease of ageing

Figure 3

Source: *Lancet* 2005; 366: 2112-2117

sometimes survive for 25 years. Death is generally due to a state of extreme weakness (inanition), malnutrition, or pneumonia.

The brain: A producer of free radicals

The brain is an organ that consumes a great deal of energy. Although the brain makes up only 2% of a person's weight, it consumes almost 20% of the oxygen used by the human body! While this extreme metabolic activity reflects the brain's ceaseless activity, the downside is that it also generates large amounts of "waste" called "free radicals." These free radicals are harmful to cells because they attack the structure of many of their constituents, particularly the genetic material (DNA), causing considerable damage and accelerating tissue ageing. Since an estimated 5% of the oxygen consumed by the brain leads to the creation of free radicals, the organ is particularly vulnerable to damage caused by these reactive molecules, a sensitivity exacerbated by the low antioxidant activity occurring in the brain.

Studies also show that, from age 40, oxidative stress can reduce the levels of proteins involved in proper neuron function. This may cause a slight loss in brain flexibility characterized by forgetfulness or increased difficulty in performing certain complex mental tasks. But in addition to these normal changes, the intense oxidative stress to which nerve cells are subjected can also influence the progression of Alzheimer's disease by

provoking metabolic defects in certain proteins located in and on the surface of neurons, causing them to aggregate and form neurotoxic deposits. These are largely responsible for the cerebral lesions characteristic of Alzheimer's disease (see box, p. 180).

The causes

The risk of contracting Alzheimer's disease ranges from 10% to 15%; in other words, up to 15 people in 100 are likely to develop it before reaching 85 years of age. Contrary to popular belief, hereditary factors are responsible for only a minority of Alzheimer cases (25%); the vast majority (75%) of cases are rather more random in nature, caused by a complex interaction between our genetic makeup and a panoply of factors linked to lifestyle (Figure 7).

We don't get to choose our family . . .

The influence of hereditary factors on the onset of Alzheimer's disease is well illustrated by data showing that first-degree relatives of a person with Alzheimer's disease have about a twofold greater risk of contracting it than other people (30% vs. 15%). This factor is particularly significant in early-onset Alzheimer's disease; that is, cases occurring before age 65. This is fortunately quite rare, at less than 5%, although cases of

(continued p. 182)

Ten warning signs

	Examples of abnormal behaviours	**Examples of normal behaviours**
1 Loss of memory that undermines familiar activities	• Often forgetting names of people close to you (friends, grandchildren, neighbours) • Forgetting recent personal events (birthdays, holidays, friends' visits)	• Difficulty remembering names of people you don't know well (actors, someone you met at a party, etc.) • Forgetting an appointment, a telephone number, etc.
2 Difficulty performing familiar tasks	• Inability to perform familiar activities like preparing meals, setting the table, etc.	• Distractions like forgetting to put water in the kettle, overcooking vegetables, etc.
3 Problems with language	• Forgetting easy and commonly used words (fork, toothbrush, etc.)	• Trying to find the right word to accurately describe a situation
4 Disorientation in time and space	• Getting lost in your neighbourhood and being unable to go home	• Getting lost during new trips, difficulty finding your car in a parking lot at a large shopping centre
5 Decreased judgment	• Not recognizing that a health problem requires medical treatment • Wearing light clothing in winter or heavy clothing in the sweltering heat	• Delaying going to a doctor, hoping that problems will soon take care of themselves

Figure 4

	Examples of abnormal behaviours	**Examples of normal behaviours**
6 Difficulty with abstract thinking	• Difficulty writing a cheque, not understanding what numbers mean	• Difficulty balancing the family budget!
7 Misplacing things	• Putting things in inappropriate places (iron in the freezer, wristwatch in the sugar bowl)	• Misplacing familiar things (keys, eyeglasses, wallet)
8 Changes in mood and behaviour	• Going from joy to anger quickly without an obvious reason	• Feeling impassive, sad, or angry when faced with a situation
9 Personality changes	• Exhibiting unusual behaviour, extreme suspicion, unjustified fear	• Changing one's habits and interests when ageing
10 Loss of interest	• Inability to perform familiar activities (gardening, sewing, playing cards, odd jobs, etc.), resulting in abandoning them and apathy	• Easily tiring of an activity

Source: www.alzheimer.ca

What is Alzheimer's disease?

Alzheimer's disease is characterized by two main nerve cell anomalies: *neurofibrillary tangles*, present in the neurons, and *amyloid plaque*s (or senile plaque), located outside these cells (Figure 5). The anomalies have become a subject of great interest, both in terms of understanding the causes of the disease and helping to discover drugs that interfere with these processes, in order to curb or slow down neurodegeneration.

Neurofibrillary tangles are caused by a change in the structure of a protein called *tau*, which causes it to aggregate and form fibrous structures inside the nerve cells. These structures are very toxic, preventing the transmission of substances within the neurons, blocking all communication with other neurons and subsequently killing these cells.

Amyloid plaques result from an extraordinarily complex process involving a protein present on the surface of neurons: the *amyloid precursor protein* (APP). During the process leading up to Alzheimer's disease, fragments of this protein (beta-amyloid peptide or Aß) are released to the periphery of the neurons, causing them to collect together and

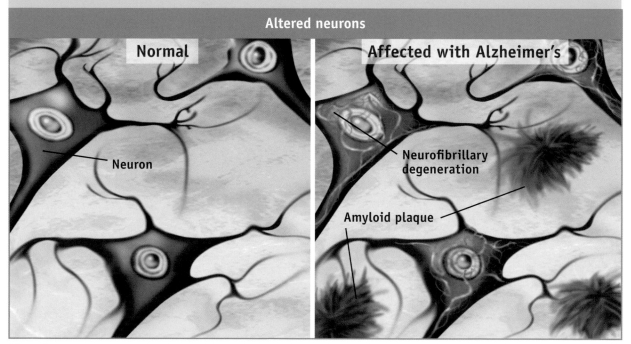

Altered neurons

Normal

Neuron

Affected with Alzheimer's

Neurofibrillary degeneration

Amyloid plaque

Figure 5

Source: www.ahaf.org

form insoluble deposits that gradually accumulate around the cells in the form of plaque. The presence of this plaque has catastrophic repercussions on the nerve cells, considerably increasing their vulnerability to oxidative and inflammatory stress and directly promoting their destruction. Brain cells of patients with Alzheimer's disease also contain very large amounts of oxidation products, which are especially prevalent near the amyloid plaques and in the neurofibrillary tangles. This process is significant and well illustrated since nearly all cases of Alzheimer's disease in the early stages are due to defective genes involved in peptide Aß formation. Similarly, people with Down syndrome (Trisomy 21) have an additional copy of the gene coding for APP (located in chromosome 21); after age 40 the vast majority of them will develop problems consistent with Alzheimer's disease.

Characteristic deposits of Alzheimer's disease are present mostly in those areas of the brain involved in memory and emotions, such as the hippocampus and the amygdala (Figure 1); for this reason amnesia is one of the first symptoms. Lesions then spread into neighbouring areas,

Impact of Alzheimer's disease on the brain

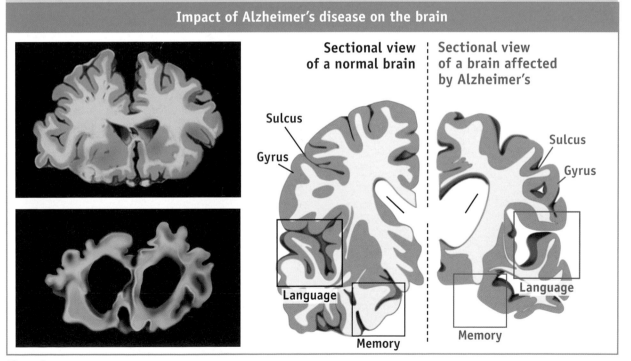

Sectional view of a normal brain

Sectional view of a brain affected by Alzheimer's

Sulcus
Gyrus
Language
Memory
Sulcus
Gyrus
Language
Memory

Figure 6

Source: www.ahaf.org

gradually destroying all knowledge (reason, visual recognition, etc.). After these deposits are formed, neuron cell death significantly reduces cerebral tissue mass over time (Figure 6). When compared to a healthy brain, the brain of a person with Alzheimer's is smaller in volume due to significant loss of peripheral cerebral tissue. This is accompanied by enlarged sulci and a significantly reduced volume of convolutions in the temporal lobe, the seat of memory and language.

Alzheimer's disease is therefore not simply "madness," a loss of contact with reality caused by an imbalance in cerebral function. Rather, it is a truly degenerative disease during which the brain shrinks in mass. For all these reasons, Alzheimer's disease is terrifying: By destroying the organ responsible for our personality and the essence of our human existence, it causes psychological, social, and physical death.

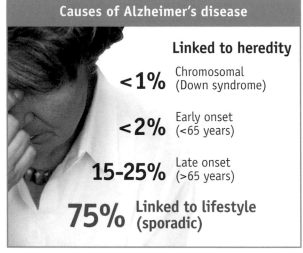

Causes of Alzheimer's disease

Linked to heredity

<1% Chromosomal (Down syndrome)

<2% Early onset (<65 years)

15-25% Late onset (>65 years)

75% Linked to lifestyle (sporadic)

Figure 7   Source: *Am. J. Alzheimers Dis. Other Demen.* 2007; 22: 37-41

people age 24 have been reported. The premature degeneration is caused by certain defective genes that participate directly in metabolizing peptide Aß (presenilin 1 and 2 and the amyloid precursor protein APP), with the tragic result of considerably accelerating the formation of the senile plaque that destroys neurons (Figure 8).

The hereditary factor most involved in the genesis of Alzheimer's disease is the gene coding for apoprotein E (ApoE), which helps carry lipoproteins and cholesterol in the bloodstream and is essential for regulating the amounts of peptide Aß present in the brain. The gene responsible for producing this protein is polymorphic, which means it exists in various forms in our genetic makeup, enabling the production of three distinct types of protein: ApoEε2, ApoEε3 and ApoEε4. The ApoEε3 variant functions normally, but many studies show that ApoEε4 is much less effective, significantly increasing the risk of contracting Alzheimer's.

Since our DNA contains two copies of each gene (one from each parent), six different ApoE combinations are possible (Figure 9). Most people have at least one copy of the normal protein (ε3), but a significant number of people (25%) have at least one copy of ε4, and 1% even have two copies. People with one copy of ε4 have a threefold higher risk of developing Alzheimer's, while the risk for those with two copies is 15 times higher (Figure 9). Specifically, the presence of ApoEε4 means that the first symptoms of Alzheimer's can occur five to 10 years earlier than in the general population among people with one ε4 copy of the gene, and 10 to 20 years earlier among those with two copies. More importantly, the presence of the ApoEε4 variant is neither sufficient nor necessary to develop Alzheimer's: Many people with a copy of this gene will never develop signs of the disease and even among people who have two copies of this gene, 50% will never contract Alzheimer's. ApoEε4 is a striking example of a gene that predisposes to a disease but whose destructive potential depends on the contribution of other factors, both genetic and external. Among these, the single most significant one is lifestyle.

. . . but we *can* choose our lifestyle

Alzheimer's disease does not appear overnight: Autopsies performed on the brains of people who died accidentally have shown that, by the age of 47, 50% already presented with the neurofibrillary tangles characteristic of this disease, particularly in the hippocampus. It seems that cerebral lesions are formed relatively early in life, and as a result we constantly run the risk of developing Alzheimer's. However, the percentage of people

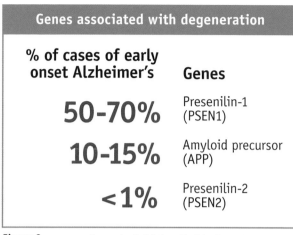

Genes associated with degeneration

% of cases of early onset Alzheimer's	Genes
50-70%	Presenilin-1 (PSEN1)
10-15%	Amyloid precursor (APP)
<1%	Presenilin-2 (PSEN2)

Figure 8   Source: *Am. J. Alzheimers Dis. Other Demen.* 2007; 22: 37-41

ApoE protein and Alzheimer's

Variants of the ApoE gene	% of the population	Increased risk of Alzheimer's disease
Ε2/Ε2	<2%	—
Ε2/Ε3	15%	—
Ε2/Ε4	<2%	—
Ε3/Ε3	55%	—
Ε3/Ε4	25%	**3 times**
Ε4/Ε4	<2%	**15 times**

Figure 9

who contract the disease at an advanced age (80 years) is much smaller (15%) than the 50% early lesions rate would suggest. This indicates that other factors, most probably lifestyle, can delay the development of this type of neuro-degeneration. As for the other chronic diseases mentioned earlier, identifying these causative factors can be one of the best weapons at our disposal to prevent, or at least delay for as long as possible, the onset of Alzheimer's.

An obvious example of the influence of life-style on the development of Alzheimer's is the wide variation in the incidence of this disease in different world populations. For example, while the inhabitants of Western countries, particularly in North America and Europe, are severely affected, elderly people living in other parts of the world, notably India and Africa, are much less affected by this disease (Figure 10). Certain regions of India, notably Ballabgarh in the north, have one of the lowest rates of Alzheimer's reported to date: a rate six times lower than that of Westerners. These international differences do not, however, appear to be due to genetic factors (the ApoEε4 gene, for example): A comparison of populations with similar genetic makeup

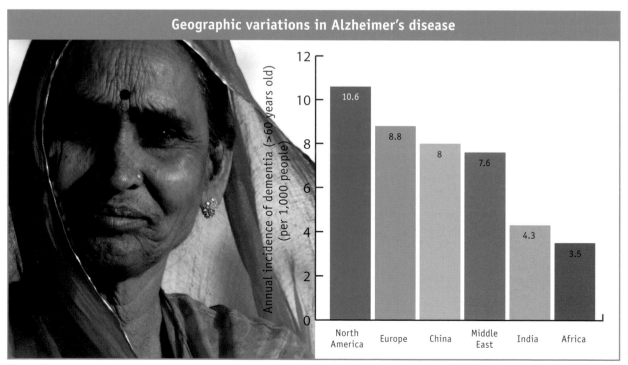

Figure 10

Source: *Lancet* 2005; 366: 2112-2117

shows major differences in the risk of developing dementia at an advanced age. Also, despite their common ancestry, the Yoruba of Nigeria and African Americans show very significant differences in their risk of developing a disease like Alzheimer's. The incidence of these diseases is more than 200% higher among African Americans (Figure 11). This increased risk of dementia associated with changes to lifestyle can even occur over a short period of time. For example, a study of migrant populations showed that Japanese people who emigrated to Hawaii had a significantly higher rate of Alzheimer's compared to their compatriots who stayed in Japan.

Serious memory loss

Of all the lifestyle factors, a poor diet, physical and intellectual inactivity, and smoking are now recognized as the leading factors promoting the development of Alzheimer's disease (Figure 12). The impact of diet is particularly interesting since it suggests that the risk of contracting this disease could be reduced by using preventive strategies similar to those described earlier for heart disease, diabetes, and cancer.

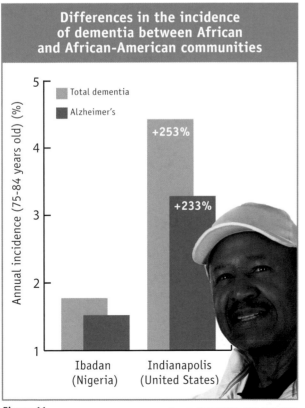

Differences in the incidence of dementia between African and African-American communities

Total dementia
Alzheimer's

+253%
+233%

Annual incidence (75-84 years old) (%)

Ibadan (Nigeria)
Indianapolis (United States)

Figure 11   Source: *Lancet* 2005; 366: 2112-2117

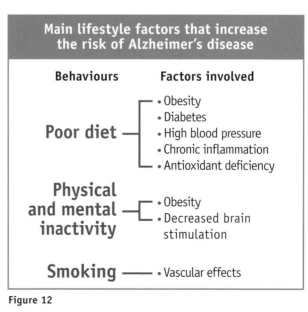

Main lifestyle factors that increase the risk of Alzheimer's disease

Behaviours	Factors involved
Poor diet	• Obesity • Diabetes • High blood pressure • Chronic inflammation • Antioxidant deficiency
Physical and mental inactivity	• Obesity • Decreased brain stimulation
Smoking	• Vascular effects

Figure 12

It is worth noting that most eating habits recognized as increasing the likelihood of contracting any of these chronic diseases are also associated with an increased risk of Alzheimer's.

Obesity – The excess weight associated with a poor diet not only fosters heart disease, diabetes, and cancer, but also contributes actively to cognitive decline and increased risk of Alzheimer's. Recent studies suggest that the brains of people in their fifties who suffer from obesity often exhibit anomalies characteristic of accelerated neuron ageing. This suggests they may run the risk of being affected by neurodegeneration throughout their lives. Obese people are twice as likely to develop dementia at an advanced age than slender people, and the risk is four times greater for people who carry excess fat in the abdomen. This increased risk is also observed with other factors associated with a poor diet such as hypertension or hypercholesterolemia. For example, people aged 50 who are affected by one or another of these three conditions are twice as likely to contract Alzheimer's disease 20 years later (Figure 13). If obesity is accompanied by hypertension and above-normal cholesterol, as is unfortunately often the case, the risk of Alzheimer's disease soars, becoming six times higher than for those showing none of these anomalies. This connection is not only observed among the obese: Overweight people (BMI of 25-30, or about half of the Western population) also have a greater risk of contracting dementia at an advanced age than slim people.

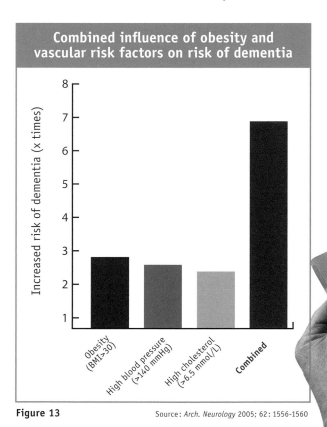

Combined influence of obesity and vascular risk factors on risk of dementia

Increased risk of dementia (x times)

- Obesity (BMI>30)
- High blood pressure (>140 mmHg)
- High cholesterol (>6.5 mmol/L)
- **Combined**

Figure 13   Source: *Arch. Neurology* 2005; 62: 1556-1560

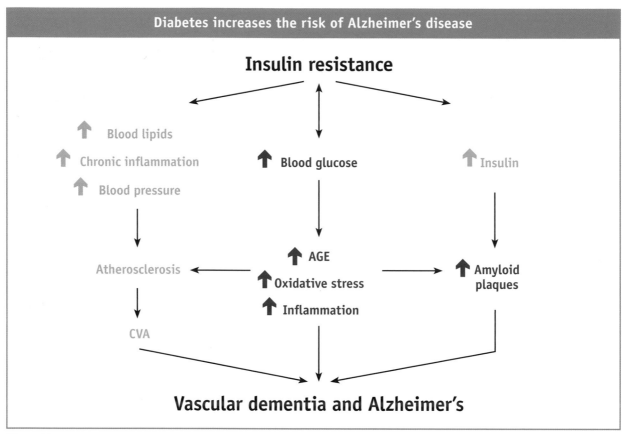

Figure 14

While the mechanisms linking overweight to Alzheimer's are not yet understood, these observations illustrate once again the degree to which obesity is a serious medical condition that can lead to a multitude of serious health problems.

Insulin resistance – Over 80% of patients with Alzheimer's disease exhibit symptoms of insulin resistance or have Type-2 diabetes, which suggests that these two diseases are closely related. Numerous observations have clearly established that imbalances in glucose metabolism are often associated with cognitive decline (particularly of the memory), including dementia. For example, a number of studies have shown that diabetics have twice the risk of contracting Alzheimer's disease; some studies have even reported that middle-aged diabetics (40 to 50 years old) have an increased risk of contracting Alzheimer's in old age by up to 400%! The negative impact of diabetes is probably due to the premature ageing of cerebral cells: Magnetic resonance studies have revealed that the brains of 60-year-olds who have been diabetics for less than 10 years already showed signs of atrophying. This was particularly prevalent in the region crucial for memory (the hippocampus): The studies showed that this reduction was actually associated with short-term memory loss.

As seen in Chapter 6, insulin resistance and Type-2 diabetes lead to multiple metabolic disorders, which seem to contribute to cognitive decline (Figure 14). On the one hand, an imbalance in blood lipids (triglycerides, cholesterol) promotes the formation of atheromatous plaque (atherosclerosis) and the development of hypertension. These two factors increase the risk of stroke, and consequently, cerebral damage that can degenerate into vascular dementia and Alzheimer's. On the other hand, too much blood glucose is very dangerous for the brain as it not only increases the risk of stroke – a consequence of oxidative stress and inflammation imposed on the blood vessels – but also promotes the formation of amyloid plaques, which hastens the progression of Alzheimer's. Finally, the surplus of insulin secreted by the pancreas to compensate for the resistance to this hormone contributes directly to the formation of amyloid plaques.

Premature ageing of the brain is therefore a direct consequence of the disorders associated with an imbalance in glucose metabolism, at the same time increasing the risk of cognitive decline and forms of dementia like Alzheimer's disease. Given the dramatic increase observed over the last few years in the number of people exhibiting such anomalies, it is disturbing to think that this rise in diabetes cases may soon be accompanied by a parallel increase in Alzheimer's disease and other serious neurological disorders. Recent studies indicate that over half of the people with Parkinson's disease, another affliction of the neurological system, show glucose metabolic anomalies and that Type-2 diabetes almost doubles the risk of contracting this disease.

Solutions: Preventing Alzheimer's disease

Alzheimer's disease is not an inevitable consequence of ageing, but rather a chronic disease whose development is closely linked to lifestyle habits. Like all the diseases mentioned in this book, it is possible to prevent or at least significantly delay the onset of Alzheimer's by paying particular attention to certain lifestyle factors. This preventive approach can lead to very positive outcomes: Since the incidence of Alzheimer's increases exponentially with age, rising dramatically after age 85, simply delaying its onset by five years may lead to a 50% reduction in cases by 2050.

Plants that help memory!

Many epidemiological studies indicate that the consumption of plant-based foods correlates with a reduced incidence of Alzheimer's. For example, daily consumption of fruits and vegetables is associated with a 30% decline in the risk of dementia – certainly another excellent reason to include these foods in your diet as much as possible!

Given the central role played by oxidative stress and inflammation in the etiology of Alzheimer's, it is evident that the many antioxidant and anti-inflammatory activities generally associated with plant products can actively contribute to their preventive effect. Adding antioxidants such as blueberries or pomegranate to the diet of mice that were genetically predisposed to developing Alzheimer's reduced their amyloid plaques and notably improved their cognitive functions! In addition to these properties, certain

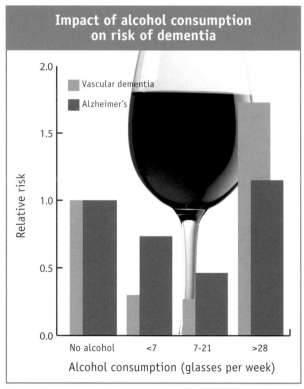

Impact of alcohol consumption on risk of dementia

Vascular dementia

Alzheimer's

Relative risk — Alcohol consumption (glasses per week): No alcohol, <7, 7-21, >28

Figure 15

Source: *Lancet* 2002; 359: 281-286

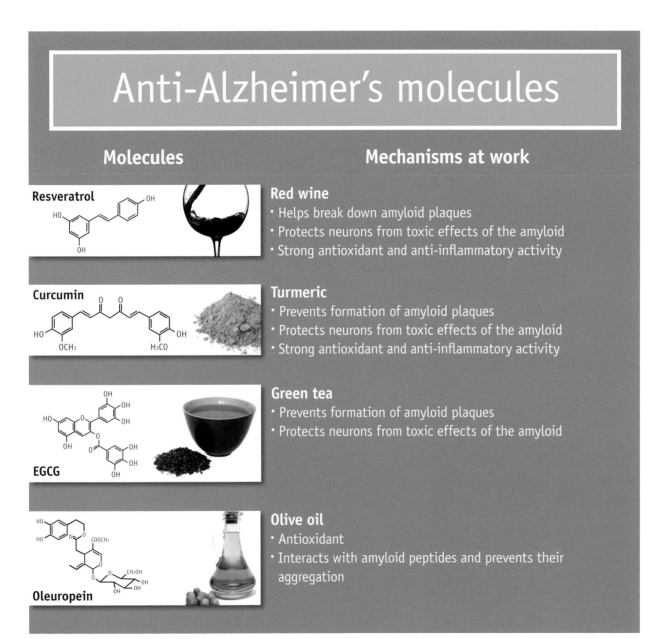

Anti-Alzheimer's molecules

Molecules

Mechanisms at work

Resveratrol

Red wine
- Helps break down amyloid plaques
- Protects neurons from toxic effects of the amyloid
- Strong antioxidant and anti-inflammatory activity

Curcumin

Turmeric
- Prevents formation of amyloid plaques
- Protects neurons from toxic effects of the amyloid
- Strong antioxidant and anti-inflammatory activity

EGCG

Green tea
- Prevents formation of amyloid plaques
- Protects neurons from toxic effects of the amyloid

Oleuropein

Olive oil
- Antioxidant
- Interacts with amyloid peptides and prevents their aggregation

Figure 16

plant-based foods act directly on the formation of amyloid plaques and as a result are provoking great interest among researchers (Figure 16).

Red wine – Studies have shown that moderate drinkers of red wine (one or two glasses a day) have a considerably reduced risk of contracting Alzheimer's, a protective effect seemingly associated with the presence of resveratrol in the wine. As well as its antioxidant and anti-inflammatory properties, resveratrol stands out for its ability to accelerate the breakdown of the beta-amyloid peptide, thus reducing the formation of plaque essential for the progression of this disease. However, the alcohol itself also contributes to the protective effect, since moderate consumption of wine, beer or spirits leads to a reduced risk of dementia, both vascular and Alzheimer's (Figure 15). This is undoubtedly linked to the positive effect of alcohol on the cardiovascular system. But, as with heart disease, abusive consumption of alcohol in all its forms (more than four glasses a day) significantly increases two types of dementia, illustrating once again the degree to which alcohol is a double-edged sword that must be used intelligently.

Turmeric – Clearly the most anti-inflammatory molecule in the plant kingdom is turmeric, from turmeric spice, or *Curcuma longa*. It can prevent peptide Aß aggregation, simultaneously reducing the formation of amyloid plaques,

thereby protecting the neurons against its toxic effects. These mechanisms likely play a role in the low incidence of Alzheimer's disease in India, a country where large amounts of turmeric are consumed. A recent study has shown that people who frequently eat curry dishes, and therefore turmeric, are less subject to age-related cognitive decline.

Other spices and seasonings contain properties that may help to prevent Alzheimer's. The best-known examples are sage (*Salvia officinalis*) and its close relative rosemary (*Rosmarinus officinalis*). These two herbs are recognized for their antioxidant and anti-inflammatory potential. Shakespeare was praising its virtues around 1600: "There's rosemary, that's for remembrance. Pray, love, remember." (*Hamlet,* Act IV, Scene 5). The rosemary acid contained in these herbs has recently been identified as a molecule that can protect neurons against the toxic effects of peptide Aß. This may explain the improved cognitive function produced by these herbal extracts, as observed in certain studies.

Green tea – Many laboratory studies have shown that the polyphenols in green tea, notably epigallocatechin gallate (EGCG), have many neuro-protective properties that may help to prevent neurodegenerative diseases such as Alzheimer's and Parkinson's. Studies show that daily consumption of two or more cups of green tea significantly reduces the risk of contracting

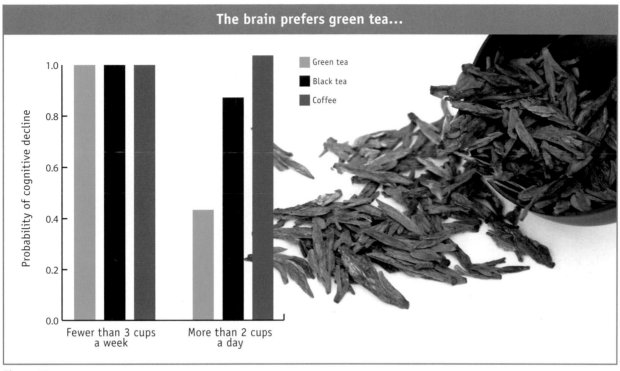

The brain prefers green tea...

Green tea
Black tea
Coffee

Probability of cognitive decline

Fewer than 3 cups a week

More than 2 cups a day

Figure 17

Source: *Am. J. Clin. Nutr.* 2006; 83: 355-361

Parkinson's disease. The potential impact of regular consumption of green tea on the risk of Alzheimer's is fascinating: Recent studies conducted among the elderly have shown that people who drink more than two cups of green tea daily are likely to lose significantly less cognitive function (almost 60%) compared to those who drink it only rarely (under three cups a week). Conversely, people who regularly drink black tea or coffee do not show any reduction in the risk (Figure 17).

Olive oil – Epidemiological studies indicate that adopting a Mediterranean-style diet is linked to a significant decline in the risk of contracting Alzheimer's disease. The cornerstone of this diet, olive oil, seems to play a key role in the protective effect. On the one hand, the high monounsaturated fat content of olive oil increases HDL cholesterol levels (the good type!) and has a beneficial effect on the brain since low amounts of HDL are associated with cognitive decline and dementia, according to several studies. On the other hand, olive oil stands out from the other vegetable oils for its polyphenol content, including oleocanthal, hydroxytyrosol, and oleuropein. These molecules possess anti-inflammatory activities, and in the case of oleuropein, directly interact with peptide Aß, which may prevent it from aggregating and subsequently forming amyloid plaques.

Omega-3s: "Intelligent" fats

Abundant consumption of foods rich in saturated or trans fats significantly increases the risk of Alzheimer's disease, an effect linked to increased atherosclerosis caused by these fats (see Chapter 5) and their direct impact on the formation of amyloid plaques. Autopsies performed on subjects aged 40 and over have established a link between blood cholesterol levels and the increased presence of amyloid plaques. Among people aged 40 to 55, simply increasing the blood cholesterol from 4.7 to 5.2 mmol (which means moving to a higher risk level for heart disease) tripled amyloid plaque formation! These observations coincide with many studies showing that regular users of statins – drugs that reduce LDL-cholesterol levels – had a lower risk of Alzheimer's.

Conversely, other types of fats, notably the polyunsaturated omega-3 fats, have often been posited as substances that may actively help prevent Alzheimer's. This protective effect is logical since we have known for a long time that omega-3 fatty acids are absolutely essential for brain and retina cell development, and are vital to the transmission of nerve impulses. A fetus in particular craves these fats in its final trimester, accumulating about 70 mg of omega-3s a day. Many studies have shown that pregnant women who consume omega-3s during this period improve the visual acuity and motor function of their children.

The positive effect of omega-3s on neuron function also seems to play a decisive role in preventing Alzheimer's. Numerous studies have shown that people who consume very high levels of docosahexaenoic acid (DHA, present in fatty fish), the main long-chain omega-3 fatty acid, had a significantly lower risk of contracting this disease. It has been observed that, among people who do not have the ApoE variant associated with the disease (75% of the population), consuming at least one portion of fatty fish per week reduced the risk of developing Alzheimer's by 35% compared to those who almost never consume it. These results concur with the observation that the brains of Alzheimer's patients have a lower DHA content than those of healthy people, particularly in the hippocampus and the frontal lobe. While the precise mechanisms responsible for this protective effect need to be specifically identified, it seems that DHA protects the neurons against the neurotoxic effects induced by

amyloid plaques, thereby preserving their function. However, since a reduced risk of Alzheimer's disease has also been observed for short-chain omega-3 fats present in vegetable oil (flax, canola, chia), it is tempting to assume that the anti-inflammatory effect of these fats may also help prevent the disease. Such an effect is even more likely, since studies have shown that regular users of synthetic anti-inflammatories are also less likely to contract Alzheimer's disease.

Put your neurons to work . . . and your body in general!

Regularly practicing cognitive tasks is another crucial factor in delaying the age at which the first symptoms of Alzheimer's may appear. For example, we have long known that the risk of this disease is lower among people who were stimulated in their childhood, a phenomenon believed to be linked to the creation of a high amount of neuron connections. This is, in effect, a "cognitive reserve" that counterbalances the degeneration that occurs in old age. Such a beneficial effect is not limited strictly to childhood: adults engaging in mentally challenging activities at work or play also have a reduced risk of Alzheimer's. It is therefore likely that constant intellectual stimulation reinforces the neuron connections, particularly in the memory zones (the hippocampus), thereby fiercely resisting the destruction of neurons through ageing.

Regular physical activity is a major preventive factor, and exercise alone may reduce the risk of Alzheimer's disease by 30%. It is never too late to start: The elderly who are physically inactive can considerably reduce their risk of contracting Alzheimer's by increasing their daily level of physical activity. As John Adams, the second president of the United States, said: "Old minds are like old horses. You must exercise them if you wish to keep them in working order!"

Summary

- Like all chronic diseases, the development of Alzheimer's is strongly influenced by lifestyle habits, particularly vascular risk factors (e.g., hypertension, atherosclerosis, diabetes, obesity, smoking), diet, and physical exercise.
- Eating a diet rich in fruits, vegetables, and fish (omega-3s) and foods possessing strong anti-inflammatory activity (plants, turmeric), and being physically and intellectually active, is a simple and effective way of significantly reducing the risk of contracting this disease.

I married an archaeologist
because the older I grow
the more he appreciates me.

Agatha Christie (1890–1976)

Chapter 9

Ageing Gracefully and in Good Health

The gradual loss of biological functions accompanying ageing is an unavoidable consequence of the incredible amount of energy our body cells must expend throughout our lifetime. The frenetic consumption of oxygen necessary to maintain cell function is associated with the production of large quantities of free radicals. These are highly reactive molecules that cause great damage to the main constituents of our cells. As seen in previous chapters, adopting healthy lifestyle habits largely counterbalances the damage these molecules cause, allowing the ageing process to continue normally; that is, with a steady loss of cell function not necessarily leading to the onset of chronic diseases. Conversely, an unhealthy lifestyle exacerbates the negative effects of this metabolic stress, too often leading to the rapid development of serious diseases that threaten longevity (Figure 1).

Striving to grow old in good health should not be confused with a quest for immortality.

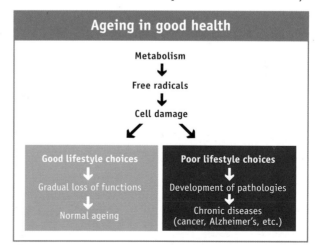

Figure 1

While old age may well be "the only disease you don't wish to be cured of" (Orson Welles), the goal is to prevent the normal ageing process from being prematurely interrupted by serious disease and thereby enjoying life to the maximum.

Adopting good lifestyle habits essential to healthy ageing should be an absolute priority for anyone determined to make the most out of life. Yet paradoxically we seem more preoccupied with the visible effects of ageing – our physical appearance and especially our skin – than with their repercussions on how our bodies function. While only a minority of people may be adopting the key lifestyle habits likely to stave off chronic diseases, the pursuit of ways to halt or minimize the signs of physical ageing has never been so popular. The cosmetics industry generates annual revenues of about $200 billion, and an increasing percentage of these earnings comes from anti-ageing products and numerous non-surgical techniques aimed at lessening the physical signs of ageing (Figure 2). We live in a society in which appearance takes precedence over inner well-being. "Looking younger than your age," regardless of the cost, is a greater concern than preventing diseases as serious as cancer or Alzheimer's.

However, preventing disease can still be compatible with maintaining an attractive appearance. We have long known that our complexion or general physical appearance very often provides infallible clues about our state of health. Historically, the skin has been a mirror of nutritional deficiencies in either vitamins or essential fatty acids, and certain studies have shown that "looking older than your age" can be linked to an increased risk of premature death. This relationship is not surprising since we now know that numerous lifestyle factors contributing to the prevention of chronic diseases can also have a decisive impact on the skin's appearance. In short, health can be synonymous with beauty!

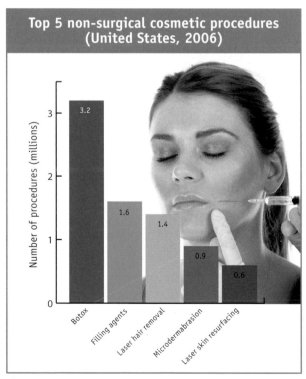

Figure 2

Skin: The largest organ of the human body

The skin is not simply a protective layer; it is the human body's most impressive organ, covering an area ranging from 1.5 to 2 m² and representing about 15% of body weight. With its three main layers – the epidermis, dermis, and hypodermis (Figure 3) – the skin's thickness can vary considerably depending on its location on the body. It may measure less than 0.5 mm in the eyelids, yet more than 6 mm on the sole of the foot. Each of these layers plays a key role in the many functions of the skin: It may serve as a chemical, physical, or biological barrier protecting other organs from the environment by excreting waste, by controlling body temperature, or through tactile perception (Figure 4).

Skin ageing: The causes

Like all body organs, the skin undergoes multiple changes throughout its existence, a process easily recognizable from major changes in its appearance, colour and texture. During ageing, cutaneous cell renewal diminishes significantly, creating an imbalance between normal cell growth and the elimination of dead cells on the skin's surface. Within the dermis, the collagen and elastin fibres begin to fragment at around age 30. This diminishes the skin's resistance, elasticity, and supportiveness, leading to a general slackening,

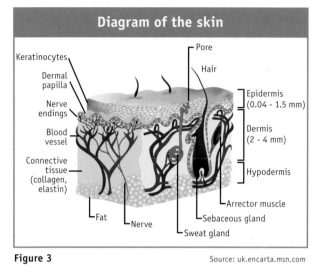

Diagram of the skin

Keratinocytes
Dermal papilla
Nerve endings
Blood vessel
Connective tissue (collagen, elastin)
Fat
Nerve
Pore
Hair
Epidermis (0.04 - 1.5 mm)
Dermis (2 - 4 mm)
Hypodermis
Arrector muscle
Sebaceous gland
Sweat gland

Figure 3   Source: uk.encarta.msn.com

which we see as fine lines and wrinkles, particularly facial expression lines (Figure 5). While this process may be normal, it can be accelerated considerably by other ageing factors that make us look older than our actual age (Figure 6).

UV rays – Excessive sun exposure is undoubtedly the main factor in premature skin ageing, a phenomenon known as photoageing. Almost all Caucasians, by the age of 15, exhibit signs of premature cutaneous ageing in areas exposed to the sun, while in the unexposed areas these signs normally appear at around age 30.

The sun's negative impact is due to the damaging effects of ultraviolet A and B rays (UVA and UVB), two types of radiation that induce multiple changes in the skin's constituents (Figure 7). UVB rays, comprising only about 5% of ultraviolet

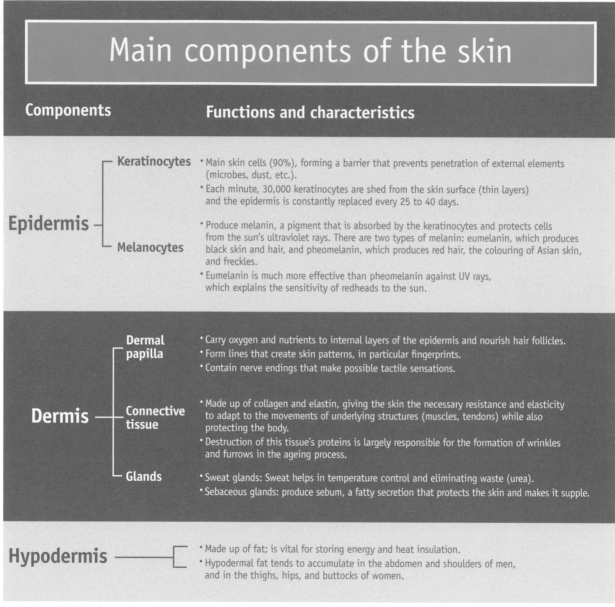

Main components of the skin

Components	Functions and characteristics
Epidermis — Keratinocytes	• Main skin cells (90%), forming a barrier that prevents penetration of external elements (microbes, dust, etc.). • Each minute, 30,000 keratinocytes are shed from the skin surface (thin layers) and the epidermis is constantly replaced every 25 to 40 days.
Melanocytes	• Produce melanin, a pigment that is absorbed by the keratinocytes and protects cells from the sun's ultraviolet rays. There are two types of melanin: eumelanin, which produces black skin and hair, and pheomelanin, which produces red hair, the colouring of Asian skin, and freckles. • Eumelanin is much more effective than pheomelanin against UV rays, which explains the sensitivity of redheads to the sun.
Dermis — Dermal papilla	• Carry oxygen and nutrients to internal layers of the epidermis and nourish hair follicles. • Form lines that create skin patterns, in particular fingerprints. • Contain nerve endings that make possible tactile sensations.
Connective tissue	• Made up of collagen and elastin, giving the skin the necessary resistance and elasticity to adapt to the movements of underlying structures (muscles, tendons) while also protecting the body. • Destruction of this tissue's proteins is largely responsible for the formation of wrinkles and furrows in the ageing process.
Glands	• Sweat glands: Sweat helps in temperature control and eliminating waste (urea). • Sebaceous glands: produce sebum, a fatty secretion that protects the skin and makes it supple.
Hypodermis	• Made up of fat; is vital for storing energy and heat insulation. • Hypodermal fat tends to accumulate in the abdomen and shoulders of men, and in the thighs, hips, and buttocks of women.

Figure 4

rays, are undoubtedly best known for their ability to cause the irritations (rashes), characteristic of sunburn, and for their role in the development of skin cancer, notably melanomas. By acting on the epidermis, these rays directly affect the DNA of skin cells, wreaking havoc and promoting the onset of mutant cells, the first stage of carcinogenesis. Overexposure to these rays also creates free radicals and inflammation, two processes that provide these precancerous cells with an environment favourable to their development. UVB rays are therefore the ultimate carcinogenic agent. They can simultaneously cause the

mutations necessary for the onset of cancer cells and modulate the cell environment to promote cancer cell progression.

Much more abundant than UVB rays, UVA rays (95% of solar rays) have long been considered harmless to the skin, given their very weak energy levels. However, we now know that these rays penetrate the skin more deeply, causing significant damage by triggering a series of events that profoundly disrupt the connective tissue. UVA rays create free radicals in the dermis, inducing an inflammatory response that culminates in the production of enzymes (metalloproteinases).

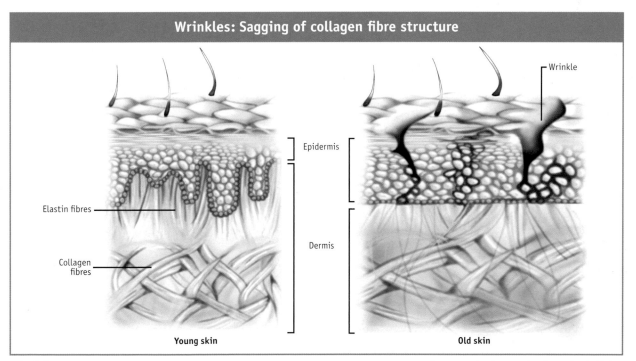

Wrinkles: Sagging of collagen fibre structure

Young skin

Old skin

Epidermis
Dermis
Elastin fibres
Collagen fibres
Wrinkle

Figure 5

Source: www.jouviance.com/eng/images/aged_skin.jpg

Main factors involved in skin ageing

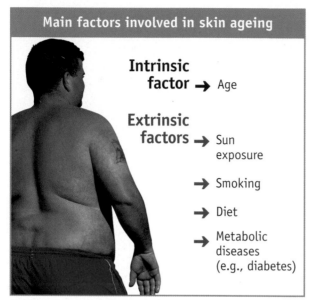

Intrinsic factor → Age

Extrinsic factors → Sun exposure

→ Smoking

→ Diet

→ Metabolic diseases (e.g., diabetes)

Figure 6

These break down the collagenous matrix and trigger an accumulation of non-functional fragments. The effect is well illustrated by an electronic microscopic examination of collagen fibres from skin that has been exposed to the sun for several years, revealing significant fibre damage (Figure 8). The breakdown of the dermis matrix also expands the blood vessels, which can become visible on the skin surface, a phenomenon known as telangiectasia (rosacea).

The synergistic action of UVA and UVB rays on the skin makes the sun a formidable aggressor in prematurely ageing the skin and triggering cancer. These phenomena are closely linked: Skin cancer very often develops on skin that has been subjected to photoageing.

UV rays: Toxic aggressors

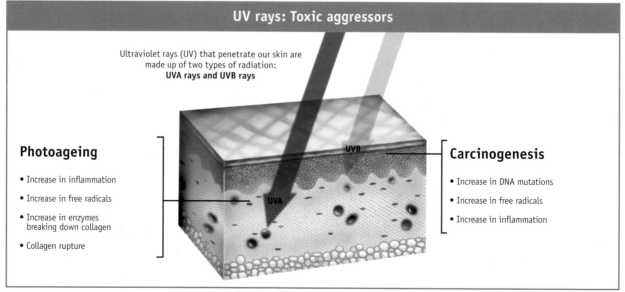

Ultraviolet rays (UV) that penetrate our skin are made up of two types of radiation: **UVA rays and UVB rays**

Photoageing

• Increase in inflammation

• Increase in free radicals

• Increase in enzymes breaking down collagen

• Collagen rupture

UVB

UVA

Carcinogenesis

• Increase in DNA mutations

• Increase in free radicals

• Increase in inflammation

Figure 7

Source: adapted from www.fda.gov

Smoking – While most people are aware that smoking is a main factor in the development of most chronic diseases, few know it is also a leading cause of premature ageing of the skin. For example, smokers risk developing excessive wrinkles that are about 300% more prominent than those of non-smokers, an effect already visible just 10 years after taking up regular smoking. The impact of smoking is particularly devastating when combined with abusive sun exposure: A person age 65 who has been smoking since age 15, with regular sun exposure, is 12 times more likely to develop excess wrinkles than a non-smoker (Figure 9). This accelerated ageing is due primarily to the vascular effects of tobacco. By reducing the blood flow to the skin capillaries, tobacco lowers the oxygen and nutrient intake, thereby interfering with skin cell renewal, which contributes to wrinkle formation. The effect becomes more pronounced when cigarette smoke also damages collagen fibres and the elastin of the dermis, reducing tissue elasticity, a key factor in premature skin ageing.

The phenomenon of accelerated skin ageing associated with UV rays and smoking should not only be looked at from the esthetic point of view. Cutaneous ageing is also linked to a decline in skin functions such as defence, scarring, sensory

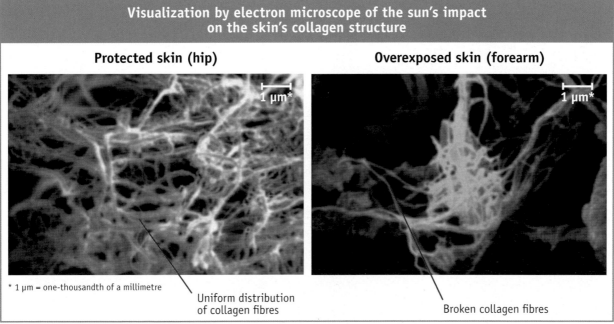

Visualization by electron microscope of the sun's impact on the skin's collagen structure

Protected skin (hip)   **Overexposed skin (forearm)**

1 µm*

1 µm*

* 1 µm = one-thousandth of a millimetre

Uniform distribution of collagen fibres

Broken collagen fibres

Figure 8

Source: *J. Invest. Derm.* 2003; 120: 842-884

perception, and thermoregulation, as well as to a marked increase in cancer risk. Preventing photo-ageing with sunscreens that block both UVB and UVA rays, and giving up smoking, have consequences not only on physical appearance but on skin health in general.

Solutions: Preventing premature ageing of the skin

Since the process of skin ageing depends on the same mechanisms as those at work in other organs, it is not surprising that the beneficial foods that can delay this process are the same as those involved in chronic disease prevention. A study conducted among people who had undergone repeated sun exposure as part of their daily activities showed that consumption of products rich in saturated fats (butter, whole milk products) and sugar correlated with a higher incidence of wrinkles. Conversely, people who consumed large amounts of vegetables, olive oil, legumes, and fish tended to have fewer wrinkles (Figure 10). The role of diet in the appearance and health of the skin vividly illustrates the extraordinary influence of food on bodily health in general.

While the relationship between diet and skin appearance has been only cursorily studied, certain foods seem to play a particularly important role in preventing cutaneous ageing.

Green tea – Green tea is undoubtedly the plant-based food whose beneficial effects on the skin have been best determined. Many studies have shown that adding green tea to the diet of laboratory animals prevented photoageing and skin cancer.

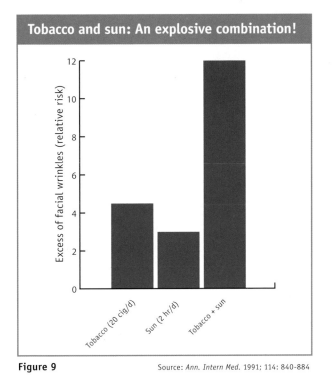

Tobacco and sun: An explosive combination!

Excess of facial wrinkles (relative risk)

Tobacco (20 cig/d) · Sun (2 hr/d) · Tobacco + sun

Figure 9   Source: *Ann. Intern Med.* 1991; 114: 840-884

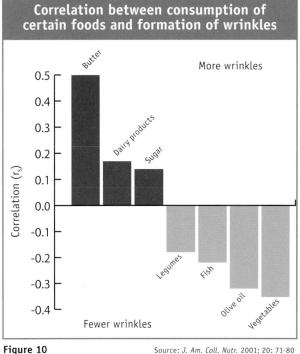

Correlation between consumption of certain foods and formation of wrinkles

Correlation (r_s)

Butter — Dairy products — Sugar — More wrinkles

Legumes — Fish — Olive oil — Vegetables — Fewer wrinkles

Figure 10   Source: *J. Am. Coll. Nutr.* 2001; 20: 71-80

Its protective effect is largely due to the inhibiting action of epigallocatechin gallate (EGCG), the main polyphenol in green tea, on many events involved in these phenomena. The EGCG's antioxidant and anti-inflammatory action is instrumental in preventing carcinogenesis induced by UV rays. In addition, it blocks the production of damaging collagen enzymes (metalloproteinases) caused by repeated exposure to UVA rays, thus preventing the collagen loss linked to ageing. While the effect of green tea on the skin has not yet been well documented, it does seem to have a beneficial action on photoageing and the carcinogenesis processes induced by UV rays.

Super fruits – The remarkable antioxidant content of certain fruits may also help to slow skin ageing. An example is extract of pomegranate

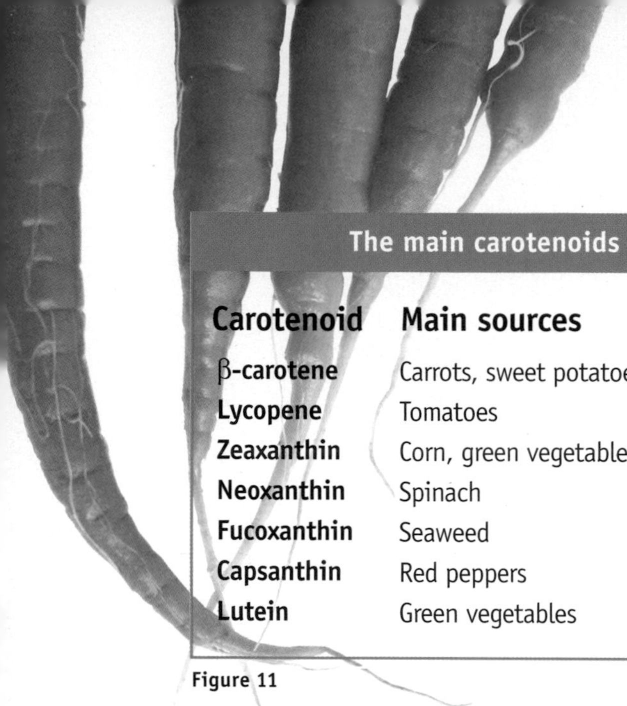

The main carotenoids	
Carotenoid	**Main sources**
β-carotene	Carrots, sweet potatoes, watercress
Lycopene	Tomatoes
Zeaxanthin	Corn, green vegetables
Neoxanthin	Spinach
Fucoxanthin	Seaweed
Capsanthin	Red peppers
Lutein	Green vegetables

Figure 11

(*Punica granatum*), a fruit long used in the Middle East, India, and Iran for treating cutaneous inflammations. This extract blocks the inflammations caused by the effects of UVA and UVB rays on skin cells, preventing the development of cutaneous lesions. Similarly, adding grape extract to the diets of laboratory animals inhibits the skin damage caused by UV rays, an effect due at least partly to the presence of resveratrol in the grapes. This molecule's strong antioxidant and anti-inflammatory activity interferes with the harmful action of free radicals in the skin, preventing activation of the processes involved in photoageing. The resveratrol has even more positive effects, as the molecule possesses extraordinary anticancer properties, blocking the growth of a large range of cancer cells including those found in the skin.

Olive oil – In addition to the essential role it plays in the diets of people living in the Mediterranean basin, olive oil has always been considered beneficial to the skin. In ancient times, Greeks even bathed in olive oil to preserve their beauty! This effect does not appear limited to the topical use of the oil, but may also apply to dietary use. Olive oil's high content of antioxidant and anti-inflammatory polyphenols protects against oxidative stress and may also reduce the impact of free radicals on the fibrous structure of the skin.

Vegetables – Certain classes of molecules found in large amounts in vegetables possess a property that slows skin ageing by interfering with the production of free radicals. The best documented example is undoubtedly carotenoids. These are the pigments responsible for the orange, yellow, or red colouring of many plants (Figure 11). Studies have shown that increased dietary intake of foods rich in carotenoids is associated with improved UV-ray protection. Carotenoids, which are the main source of antioxidant molecules, are found in large amounts in the skin. Of all the carotenoids, lycopene (a molecule present in large amounts in tomatoes) is by far the most effective in neutralizing the free radicals produced by the action of UV rays. This may slow skin ageing. One study demonstrated that daily consumption of tomato paste led to about 30% increased protection from the sun, as well as significantly boosting collagen levels – two crucial factors in maintaining the integrity of the skin.

The identification is only just beginning of other plant substances that may also curb photo-ageing, but the results are promising. Silibinin, a molecule present in artichokes and known for a long time as an effective agent for preventing liver cancer, is certainly a good example. Studies have shown the molecule to be very active in preventing skin carcinogenesis induced by UVB rays. This illustrates once again the degree to which the preventive effects of plant-based foods on the development of internal organ pathologies can also help prevent external skin damage.

Wabi-sabi

Our preoccupation with appearance – which harks back to the ideals of beauty and perfection of Greek civilization – often makes us forget the significance of inner beauty. In striving to prevent the premature ageing of the skin by adopting a healthy lifestyle, we are reminded of the inseparable nature of these two aspects: External appearance very often reflects an inner harmony, and good health normally stems from a high-quality diet combined with a non-toxic environment free of aggressors such as UV rays or cigarette smoke. Therefore we must regard the prevention of skin ageing not as an objective in itself, but rather as a beneficial "side effect," intimately linked to a lifestyle aimed at preventing chronic diseases.

Recognizing the close connection between our physical appearance and the ageing of our bodies in general helps us to accept the physical changes inherent in growing older. We can thus more gracefully appreciate the imperfections and inevitable signs of our slow but gradual journey from birth to death. We can perhaps draw inspiration from *wabi-sabi*, which is the essence of the Japanese esthetic. According to this philosophy, the beauty of objects and individuals lies in their imperfections, their ephemeral and incomplete nature. Ageing, associated with the patina of time, is regarded with admiration and respect, as a sign of maturity, wisdom, and experience. Such a view of life makes it possible to accept the natural arc of growth, degeneration, and death. It allows us to regard the physical signs of ageing not as imperfections, but as indicators of the wealth of human experience.

Summary

- The skin, like all body organs, undergoes many changes while ageing, but this process is accelerated markedly by tobacco use and prolonged sun exposure.
- The adoption of a healthy lifestyle based on a diet rich in fruits and vegetables, combined with the absence of smoking and moderate sun exposure, is the best remedy for premature ageing of the skin.

Eat a good meal prepared lovingly
Beware of poorly cooked foods
Never eat between meals
Make sure food is correctly cut
And that it is served with the proper sauces.

Confucius

Chapter 10

Living to Eat:
Cuisine as Cultural Expression

The main chronic diseases affecting us – cardio-vascular, Type-2 diabetes, cancer, and Alzheimer's – are very often perceived as the inevitable consequences of ageing, a price to pay for the amazing life expectancy we have enjoyed throughout the past century. Based on such a fatalistic approach, ageing is necessarily associated with a decline in our state of health and a loss in our quality of life. This is a phenomenon about which we can do nothing except hope that the miracles of medicine will alleviate the pain of these diseases and add a few more years to our lives.

As we have seen throughout this book, such a pessimistic view is incorrect: While ageing undeniably leads to a gradual decline in bodily functioning, we can largely prevent the development of chronic diseases by paying special attention to certain lifestyle factors, particularly our eating habits. Combined with the extraordinary means available to us through curative medicine, this preventive approach is the best weapon for blending longevity and quality of life, thereby helping us enjoy the richness of life to the fullest.

A life like Methusaleh's

Living for more than 100 years has been regarded as a remarkable achievement throughout the history of humanity, a very rare feat viewed with curiosity, fascination, and respect. In certain cases, such remarkable longevity has even acquired a legendary status, as exemplified by central figures in the Judeo-Christian tradition, notably Adam (930 years), Seth (912 years), and Methusaleh (969 years).

Longevity fascinates us even today as evidenced by the number of publications describing the extraordinarily long lives of inhabitants of the Okinawa Archipelago in Japan, the Greek island of Crete, Sardinia, Costa Rica's Nicoya Peninsula, and the small Adventist municipality of Loma Linda in California. While we try to attribute the remarkable life expectancy of these populations to some "secret" – a special food or miracle diet that protects them against disease – we now know that their longevity is due to a combination of lifestyle factors. All peoples who achieve exceptionally long lives share the same characteristic of living an optimal lifestyle, based on the five main principles stated in the introduction of this book:

- Don't smoke;
- Maintain a normal body weight;
- Eat an abundance of plant products such as fruits and vegetables and whole grains;
- Exercise regularly; and
- Eat a minimal amount of food laden with saturated fats (red meats, whole milk products) and simple sugars (sweets, desserts), as well as calorie-rich, mass-produced foods, or what is generally known as junk food.

Of all these principles, diet is undoubtedly what exerts the greatest influence on disease risk,

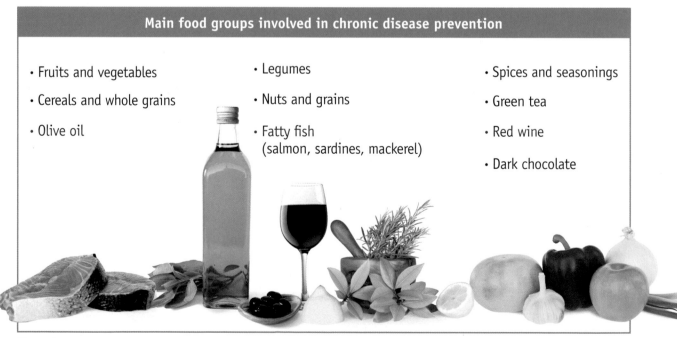

Main food groups involved in chronic disease prevention

- Fruits and vegetables
- Cereals and whole grains
- Olive oil

- Legumes
- Nuts and grains
- Fatty fish (salmon, sardines, mackerel)

- Spices and seasonings
- Green tea
- Red wine
- Dark chocolate

Figure 1

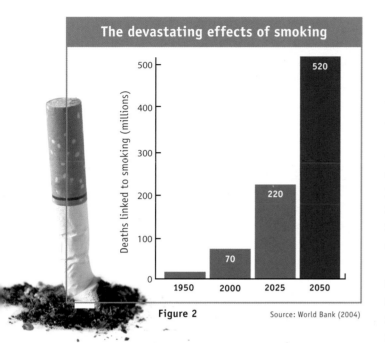

The devastating effects of smoking

Deaths linked to smoking (millions)

520

220

70

1950 2000 2025 2050

Figure 2   Source: World Bank (2004)

practice, the presence of plants in all these diets makes possible an infinite number of combinations. For example, in the traditional Okinawa diet, over 90% of calories come from the carbohydrates in plant foods. This percentage is completely different in the typical diet of the Mediterranean basin (Crete, Sardinia), where olive oil accounts for almost half of the daily calories. We should, therefore, not dwell excessively on the percentage of carbohydrates, lipids, or proteins in the diet, but rather make sure that we get these nutrients mainly from plant-based rather than animal-based foods (Figure 1).

On the other hand, foods laden with saturated fats and/or simple sugars, as well as high-calorie industrial products, cause multiple imbalances in the equilibrium of physiological functions. Since this promotes the development of chronic diseases, these foods should occupy only a minor place in the diet.

Such a diet is diametrically opposed to the one currently in vogue in Western countries, and this difference plays a key role in the high incidence of chronic diseases afflicting our societies. There is nothing theoretical or abstract about their devastating impact. For example, the inhabitants of Okinawa, with their traditional way of life, have one of the longest life expectancies in the world (81 years) and lead the world in centenarians (35 for every 100,000 inhabitants, or more than four times that of the United States). Yet, unprecedented changes in Okinawans' eating habits are in the process of reversing this trend. The island's

and indirectly on the likelihood of living for a long time in good health. Of the foods recognized as being beneficial to health, we cannot overemphasize the importance of plant-based products. Whether they consist of fruits and vegetables, whole-grain cereal products, spices and seasonings, olive oil, dark chocolate, or certain beverages like green tea or red wine, their remarkable content of protective phytochemical molecules is vital in maintaining good physical and mental health. People today tend to believe – wrongly – that there is no good way to eat in order to effectively prevent the development of major chronic diseases. On the contrary, not just one, but many, diets are beneficial to health! In young inhabitants have over the years developed a particular fondness for eating at fast-food restaurants located near U.S. military bases. As a result, they are now exhibiting obesity and heart disease levels comparable to those of Western countries. An unfortunate consequence is that the life expectancy of Okinawa's male inhabitants has plummeted from first to twenty-sixth place in Japan's national rankings. The same phenomenon can be observed in Crete, where abandoning the traditional diet at the expense of a Western diet has lead to a phenomenal increase in obesity and its concomitant diseases. In other words, while there are many ways to eat well to prevent the development of diseases, today's Western diet is not one of them. On the contrary, it is a major risk factor invariably leading to health problems.

Given the phenomenal contribution of the Western lifestyle to the development of all chronic diseases discussed in this book, it goes without saying that modifying certain lifestyle factors is absolutely essential in significantly reducing the incidence of these diseases. Fortunately, people who really want to take charge and improve their life expectancy can benefit from a plethora of studies conducted in the last few years, and adopt new habits that can have remarkable repercussions on their health.

Tobacco: The benefits of butting out

It is estimated that more than 500 million people will die over the next few years from smoking-related diseases, the leading cause of death worldwide (Figure 2). These statistics are even more disturbing given that, in half of the cases, death strikes people in the prime of their life, reducing life expectancies by 20 to 25 years. Tobacco's devastating effects are due to the soaring increase in the risk of contracting many serious diseases, particularly of the heart and lungs. For example, among heavy smokers (35 cigarettes or more a day), the risk of heart disease has quadrupled and the lung cancer risk has increased forty-fold, while the risk of other lung diseases (chronic obstructive lung disease, emphysema) has skyrocketed by a factor of 115! The increased cancer risk associated with smoking is particularly alarming: In addition to lung cancer, cigarettes increase the risk of contracting 14 other types of cancer! Overall, it is estimated that cigarettes directly cause 65% of all deaths of smokers.

While the many destructive effects of smoking are well documented, less well known is how quickly the damage caused by cigarettes can be reversed when we stop smoking. For example,

Smoking in the twenty-first century

An analogy can be drawn between the current obesity crisis and the smoking situation that prevailed 40 years ago. We already knew then that smoking radically increased the risk of lung cancer, and many scientists had started sounding the alarm, trying to make the population aware of the dangers of this bad habit. They were contending with a very powerful industry, and only after a great deal of effort was expended was it possible to finally have cigarette advertising banned. A social consensus seems to have been reached about the need to limit the use of these products through tighter legislation. The huge decline in the percentage of smokers in the population shows these efforts have not been in vain, and there is no doubt that the benefits of reduced smoking will be felt over the next few decades.

Scientific data about the catastrophic effects of obesity on health are currently as solid as those that existed earlier about the damaging effects of smoking. However, while it may be hard to imagine seeing advertising for cigarette brands on prime-time television today, we still watch very aggressive ads for high-sugar and high-fat food products without flinching – even though their consumption promotes excess weight and ultimately leads to obesity and its concomitant chronic diseases. The situation is particularly paradoxical given that this advertising largely targets children, the future of our society. That is despite the fact that we know the alarming increase in child obesity will compromise children's health in the long term, thereby depriving us of some of their vitality and knowledge.

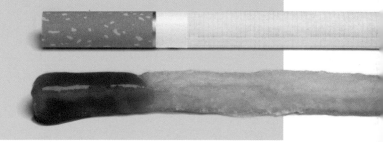

recent studies show that the increased mortality from cardiovascular diseases observed among women smokers declines significantly (by 60%) within just five years of quitting. For lung diseases and lung cancer, the impact of quitting is also very marked, with a 20% risk reduction within five years of stubbing out the final cigarette. Even more noteworthy, in the long term – 20 years after quitting – the risk of former smokers developing these diseases is almost identical to that of people who have never smoked. These observations illustrate the human body's incredible capacity to right itself and reverse in a few years the significant damage caused by the highly toxic substances in cigarette smoke. Quitting smoking not only means ending a bad and expensive habit, but it is also the action that has the most positive impact on life expectancy.

Controlling body weight: Taming the obese person within

It is always amusing to look at photos from the 1980s or earlier to see just how clothing, hairstyles, or even the design of cars has changed over the years. But what is less fun is seeing just how much slimmer people were back then! The phenomena of overweight and obesity, at one time quite rare, have increased considerably over the last 25 years, such that today two-thirds of Western populations are overweight.

Excess weight and obesity associated with excessive consumption of calories best illustrate the dangers of today's mass-produced diet. We still dwell too often on the *external* aspects of fat gain and fail to take into account the number of works or articles discussing the physical or psychological aspects related to excess weight. However, scientific data gathered over the last few years about the consequences of excess fat on how the body functions show it is high time we became concerned about the *internal* effects and their repercussions on health (see box, p. 215). Overweight is a major factor in the onset of all chronic diseases affecting the population: Type-2 diabetes, cardiovascular diseases, many types of cancer, and Alzheimer's. Like quitting smoking, the maintenance of a normal body weight (a BMI

of about 23) should be a key objective in chronic disease prevention.

Adipose mass is not something inert or static, just serving to accumulate surplus energy from food; it is, on the contrary, a very dynamic organ, a gland secreting significant amounts of hormones and inflammatory molecules that influence how all body organs function. Just as we would be concerned (with good reason) about the appearance of a growth on any part of our body, the excessive growth of adipose mass must be seen as a visible manifestation of profound changes in the equilibrium of our vital functions. It is a sign of major metabolic upheaval with many ramifications for the development of different diseases.

The evolutionary pressure of survival, which makes us very effective at storing the energy contained in food in the form of fat, also predisposes us to obesity, due to the culture of excess in which we live. Our society's overconsumption of high-calorie foods produces a surplus of energy that is almost impossible to counterbalance with physical exercise, especially as people are becoming increasingly sedentary. For example, to burn off the calories from a simple snack of a bag of potato chips, candy bar, and soft drink we would need to walk for more than two and a half hours or cycle for an hour and a half! That is indeed a high price to pay for a 10-minute snack.

The way to fight the influence of our "obesogenic" environment is not to deprive ourselves by following one of the many weight-loss diets

currently in fashion. Generally, these very low-calorie diets cause an intense feeling of hunger that may be alleviated in the short term, but in the long term only generates despondency and frustration. Such diets are generally ineffective in losing weight due to our remarkable genetic ability to extract the tiniest amount of energy from food. More important, they end up destroying our special relationship with food by making us feel guilty and undermining the pleasure of eating.

The only realistic approach to maintaining an ideal weight is to avoid the influence of these excessively caloric industrial foods and adopt a diet to which our metabolism has adapted over the course of evolution; that is, we should aim for a diet consisting mainly of plant products such as fruits and vegetables and whole grains. The cornerstone of all world cuisines, this combination of plant foods enables the internal mechanisms involved in appetite control to function optimally and thus avoid the energy overload inevitably associated with processed foods.

Plants: When nature means well

Fruits and vegetables: Good partners together

We have to marvel at the diversity, abundance, and profusion of colours of the fruits and vegetables sold in our markets, particularly during the harvest seasons. The stalls spill over with luxuriant green broccoli and cabbage, contrasting with the vibrant red tomatoes. Squash of all types and shapes compete for space with cucumbers and eggplants, alongside multicoloured peppers and handsome leeks just pulled from the earth. All of these fabulous plants are tangible manifestations of the earth's incredible fertility, reminding us just how vital these foods have been and continue to be to the human diet.

Plant-based foods are truly in a class by themselves for disease prevention because of their remarkable content of vitamins, minerals, fibres, antioxidants, and other phytochemical compounds. All chronic diseases affecting the population today are linked more or less to some kind of plant deficiency, an effect that is more pronounced when accompanied by the overconsumption of industrial foods, thus fostering obesity. Such a combination is truly the worst-case scenario for health. Metabolic imbalances caused by calorie overload create an inflammatory climate favourable to the development of chronic diseases, and this is not being offset, due to the lack of a valuable source of antioxidant and anti-inflammatory molecules when plants are absent from our diet.

While all plants are beneficial to health, certain ones stand out for their significant health benefits. Cruciferous vegetables, for example, are truly outstanding in preventing many types of cancer and as a result are essential for the maintenance of good health. Fruits rich in antioxidants also deserve special attention in any disease-prevention strategy through diet: They possess an enormous ability to neutralize the negative effects of free radicals, a major aggressor for the body to face throughout its life.

Yet, despite all their fine qualities, plant foods are still avoided by a large segment of the population today: Just 35% of people consume the minimum requirement of five portions of fruits and vegetables a day. This situation is explained, paradoxically, by the high content in these foods of molecules beneficial to health. Unlike other substances essential to the functioning of the human body – such as sugar, fat, and salt – whose tastes are favourably recognized by our brain, the beneficial molecules in plants produce a bitter taste. This is negatively interpreted by our primeval instincts inherited from a distant evolutionary past (the reptilian brain). The dislike of bitterness stems from the fact that most plant poisons are bitter and humans had to develop, very early in our evolution, defence mechanisms to avoid them. However, we can outwit the primitive within by combining the bitter taste of these foods with other flavours, as is the case in all great world cuisines.

We absolutely must make the most of our farmers' hard work and embrace these remarkable foods in order to enjoy their health benefits and extraordinary gastronomic qualities.

Whole grains: Returning to the source

Our taste buds have become so used to products made from refined flour that we forget just how little these foods have in common with the cereals from which they came. When cereal grains are whole, they are filled with many nutrients beneficial to health, and it is precisely for their ability to ensure survival that these plants were chosen by the first farmers 10,000 years ago. Agriculture as we know it today would have never emerged if the harvests had been used to make white bread: The lack of essential nutrients would have quickly caused serious deficiencies and threatened human survival. While our diversified diet today allows us to consume refined flour without suffering deficiencies, we must nonetheless bear in mind that these foods are basically a source of starch (and therefore sugar), deprived of the basic elements that make whole grains so attractive.

Besides their higher fibre and higher nutrient content, the main benefit of these whole grain products is that they slow the absorption of sugar from the starch of cereals, thereby making it possible to stabilize glycemia. This property is important as the wide glycemic fluctuations caused by these refined flour-based products induce multiple metabolic disorders that can lead to excess weight and the development of many chronic diseases, notably Type-2 diabetes.

Maximally integrating whole-grain-based products into the daily diet is one of the lifestyle changes that can have the most positive impact on our health and well-being.

Legumes: Extraordinary plants

Legumes, along with whole grain cereals, are the first plants to have been domesticated by humans. From a nutritional perspective, this combination is crucial as it provides to the body all the essential amino acids: Legumes give us lysine while cereals deliver methionine. It is interesting to note that the benefits of a cereal-legume combination have been discovered empirically by all the different populations that depended on these foods for their survival. Examples of this are chick peas and semolina (couscous) in the Mediterranean, rice and lentils in India, rice and soy in Asia, and corn and beans in Central America.

The remarkable content of protein, fibre, vitamins, and phytochemical compounds in legumes makes these amazing plants very beneficial to our health.

Olive oil: Mediterranean gold

Appreciated for its gustatory qualities for more than 5,000 years by the inhabitants of countries bordering the Mediterranean Sea, olive oil is now considered not only an essential culinary ingredient, but also a fat with one of the most positive effects on health maintenance in general. Olive oil is truly a unique oil, both for its remarkable monosaturated-fat content and for the presence of certain phenological compounds capable of a high antioxidant activity. Researchers have recently identified the presence of oleocanthal in olive oil; oleocanthal is an anti-inflammatory molecule similar to ibuprofen – the active pain-killing ingredient in Motrin and Advil!

Olive oil plays a key role in heart disease prevention and is one of the main factors responsible for the longevity of the inhabitants of Mediterranean countries. Given olive oil's health benefits, we should rejoice in the wide selection of oils currently available in our grocery stores. Although the choice of olive oil is first and foremost a question of personal taste (and budget), it is nonetheless important to opt for virgin or extra-virgin olive oil, both for its superior taste and its numerous health benefits. These oils are extracted by mechanical means, which preserves the flavour, aroma, vitamins, and antioxidants present in the original olives. Conversely, when only the words "olive oil" appear on the bottle, the oil is generally of poor quality, produced by industrial refining; it was probably extracted with

organic solvents that destroy some of the anti-oxidant molecules found naturally in olives.

Red meat: The benefits of moderation

Once regarded as a luxury commodity reserved for holidays and special occasions, red meat dominates today's Western diet. For example, the average American consumes 123 kg of meat a year while Indians consume only five kg. Excess red meat can be harmful to health not only because it leads to the absorption of saturated fat and an excess of calories, which inevitably increases the risk of overweight, but also because it promotes the development of certain serious diseases, particularly colon cancer. In its latest report, the Fonds Mondial de Recherche contre le Cancer has recommended limiting red meat consumption to 500 g a week.

In all culinary traditions around the world, the flavourful taste of meat has been used for millennia to complement the flavour of vegetable dishes such as couscous, pot-au-feu, or various stir-fried Asian dishes. As well, the rich flavours of meat (*umami*, among others) wonderfully enhance the taste of broths and sauces.

This is an excellent way to boost our plant intake, thereby diversifying our diet.

From an environmental perspective, reducing meat consumption is a little-known way to do something positive for the health of our planet. Cattle alone are responsible for 18% of all greenhouse gases emitted into the atmosphere, which is a more significant amount than that caused by transportation (12%)! In addition to its impact on global warming, intense cattle raising takes up one-quarter of the world's land surface, requiring almost 10% of available water. Since it takes seven kg of plants to produce one kilo of meat, one-third of the planet's arable land is used only to feed cattle.

Omega-3: The king of fats

Regularly including fatty fish such as salmon, sardines, and mackerel in our diet is an excellent way to diversify it while benefiting from their remarkable content of EPA, DHA and long-chain omega-3 fatty acids – all vital to proper body functioning.

Few food-based molecules are so beneficial to so many processes essential to

good physical and mental health. These processes include brain cell development and functioning, and regulating the heart rate, not to mention the anti-inflammatory effect, which prevents the development of numerous pathologies. Since insufficient intake of omega-3 fatty acids is undoubtedly one of the main dietary deficiencies currently affecting industrialized countries, consuming fatty fish two or three times a week can have a considerable impact on health.

The benefits of omega-3 fatty acids are not restricted to the long-chain form: Many studies have shown that short-chain omega-3 fatty acids, found in significant amounts in oilseed grains such as flaxseed and chia, also have dramatic anti-inflammatory effects. They can reduce by half the production of very potent inflammatory molecules such as TNF or interleukin-6. Adding freshly ground flaxseed to your breakfast cereal is a simple way to significantly increase omega-3 intake and benefit from the positive

impact of these fats on preventing cardiovascular diseases.

Chia grains do not have to be ground to be absorbed by the digestive tract and can be added directly to breakfast cereals, yogurt, and salads. *Chia fresca,* for example, is a very popular drink in Mexico and in Central America: Mix two teaspoons of grains in a cup of water to form a slightly gelatinous liquid, add some lime and sugar, and enjoy. Its distinctive flavour makes for an excellent summer drink!

Spices and seasonings: a matter of taste

Nothing better illustrates the importance of pleasure in the human diet than the essential role of spices and seasonings in all traditional world cuisines. The use of pepper, ginger, turmeric, and thousands of other spices identified over the centuries testifies to the innate human desire to discover new tastes and new ways of preparing dishes, to extend the eating experience beyond simply taking in calories. When European explorers first discovered the world of spices, they enabled a growing number of people to savour the remarkable taste of these plant products, which were long the prerogative of inhabitants of the Asian continent. This opened the door to what undoubtedly was the first form of "market globalization." The infatuation with spices, often regarded as veritable treasures, has never faded throughout history: In the year 408 when Alaric, king of the Visigoths, laid siege to Rome, the city's starving inhabitants agreed to pay for their freedom with 5,000 pounds of gold, 30,000 pounds of silver, 4,000 silk garments, 3,000 pounds of pelts, and 3,000 pounds of pepper!

We often forget that spices were first and foremost plant products made by the plant to protect itself against aggressors in its environment. Like fruits and vegetables, these molecules have multiple biological, antioxidant, and anti-inflammatory properties that can affect the development of diseases.

In North America, we often use fat, sugar, or salt automatically to flavour our foods. But we can change these habits by capitalizing on the beneficial properties of spices and seasonings to give a delectable aroma to our daily meals. At the same time, we can take advantage of their health benefits. So disease prevention can also be a matter of good taste!

Green tea: A reflection of human culture

Considered for 2,000 years a healthful drink and a symbol of humanity, tea is rivalled only by wine in humanity's celebration of nature's wealth.

This excerpt from a poem by Lu Tung (790–835), a Chinese poet known as a "tea lover," celebrates the pleasure evoked by drinking endless cups of tea brewed in a Yixing teapot:

The first cup caresses my lips and my throat
The second banishes all my loneliness
The third clears my head

The fourth makes me perspire lightly, dispersing past ills through my pores
The fifth cleanses every element of my being, my skin and my bones
The sixth transports me to the land of the Immortals

As with wine, the best way to learn about tea is to try many different kinds. Wines vary greatly in taste, depending on the grape variety and soil; some people enjoy Cabernet, others Merlot, Tempranillo, or Shiraz. The same diversity is found in tea: Some are herbal, others floral, earthy, tannic, or spicy. It is not advisable to drink tea made only from tea bags, which are often the residue of tea production, but rather to broaden the range of flavours by trying as many types of loose tea as possible, available from import stores. At a price of $5 to $25 per 50 g, at two g per cup, the best teas in the world cost between $0.20 and $1 per cup, or a fraction of what a soft drink or cup of coffee costs. Do not hesitate to explore this world of pleasure, available at such little cost! Tea names alone can fire up the imagination: Snow Bud, Precious Dewdrop, Dragon Well. Let yourself be carried away by the scents of an Anji Bai Cha, a Gyokuro, a Tie Guan Yin, or a Da Hong Pao.

There are many ways to savour tea, depending on the cultures and regions of the world. However, the most elegant and refined methods have been developed in China and Japan. The first method uses a cup called Chung, used to brew and drink the tea. The tea is placed in the cup, water is added, and the cover adjusted to allow the infusion to steep. After four or five minutes, the cover is moved slightly and the tea is drunk straight from the cup, using the cover to keep the leaves inside. Chung cups are works of art with delicate porcelain and splendid glazes. The tea leaves can expand freely and release their scent to the fullest, and they can be infused several times.

The second method, used in China and Japan, employs a small clay or porcelain teapot, with a capacity of about 150 mL. The best ones, made from stoneware clay, come from the Jiangsu region of China where the soil has the best properties for making teapots. These teapots, called Yixing, are works of art, with wonderful shapes, elegant and fluid lines, and a variety of colours ranging from blue to yellow, but mostly red-brown. The Japanese prefer to use enamel teapots, which are also elegant, but the esthetic emphasis is on the beauty of the glaze. Choose a teapot, place two grams of tea at the bottom, then add water brought

Here are a few tips to take advantage of tea's benefits:

· Visit a tea merchant, in person or on the Internet; ask for their advice to introduce you to this expansive world.

· Try a variety of teas with different aromas and tastes to establish your preferences; start with a dozen to decide on your tastes. You will prefer certain ones, your friends will love others; keep those you prefer and give the others to friends.

· Treat yourself and buy a lovely clay Yixing or ceramic Japanese teapot, a few small cups and a serving tray.

· Brew one full teaspoon of tea per 250 mL of hot water for about seven minutes; adjust to your taste. It is normal for tea to taste slightly bitter because of the polyphenols.

· Schedule tea breaks at home or at work.

· Choose a relaxing and soothing environment for enjoying this fine beverage.

· Savour this moment of introspection if you are drinking tea by yourself.

· Relish this moment of friendship if you are sharing it with a friend.

· Treasure this moment of culture and humanity, with 20 centuries of history behind it.

to a boil and let it steep for five to eight minutes. Pour the tea completely into a small cup that has the same volume as the teapot. Enjoy the colour of the infusion, the richness of the aroma, and the complexity of the flavour. Sip the tea slowly, and while savouring it, enjoy the beauty of the cup, the teapot, and the tray on which you have prepared it. For serving, a tray made from plain wood is often used; it has a visible grain, without superfluous decorations. The tray allows you to carry the tea and enjoy it comfortably.

Learn how to create this moment of introspection if you drink tea alone or share the moment with a friend. In all tea-drinking cultures, tea is associated with the hospitality and warmth of the human community. Make it a daily habit.

Red wine: A touch of class

Along with dark chocolate, moderate consumption of red wine is undoubtedly one of the most popular health recommendations! Our passion for wine may be explained by its undeniable contribution to the pleasure of eating, by the way its taste blends with that of food, and the relaxed and intimate atmosphere associated with drinking a bottle of good wine. No one wants to spoil a good wine with a mediocre meal (or vice versa), so the desire to have a glass of wine while eating is generally associated with good-quality food, often cooked with fresh ingredients. Wine is the enemy of junk food!

Beyond its festive nature, an essential aspect of red wine that contributes to disease prevention is its exceptional polyphenol content – molecules that possess multiple antioxidant and anti-inflammatory properties that help prevent the development of chronic diseases. One of these molecules, resveratrol, also has the remarkable property of increasing the longevity of several animal species. This is probably the characteristic that contributes to the benefits attributed to drinking wine in moderation. The fact that a drink as delicious as red wine contains so many molecules with multiple health benefits is a true gift of nature!

Dark chocolate: Food of the gods

No plant-based food can elicit as much passion as chocolate, the fruit of cacao (*Theobroma cacao*). This "food of the gods" was cultivated by the Olmecs and Mayans more than 2,000 years ago. In doing so, they rendered us a great service, for cacao paste is one of the major sources of antioxidants reported to date.

To take advantage of the benefits of these molecules one must, however, eat chocolate containing a minimum of 70% cocoa paste, and avoid milk chocolate: Milk proteins interact directly with antioxidants, preventing their absorption in the intestines.

Although over the years chocolate has become synonymous with sugar, it is also6 good to learn about other blends of flavours more representative of the chocolate that was consumed by the Aztecs. Melt 70% cocoa chocolate in a double-boiler, add Esplette peppers, some cinnamon, or pepper, and let harden by placing the mixture in small moulds. Or you can melt the cocoa and instead add freshly grated ginger, orange peel, or even basil!

Physical exercise: More than just a matter of muscles!

We have known for a long time that sedentary people are generally in poorer health than those who exercise regularly. The importance of physical activity to good health is not a new concept: It was mentioned in Chinese and Indian medical treatises dating back 3,000 years!

The sedentary nature of the inhabitants of modern societies is astonishing: An estimated 70% of the population gets less than 30 minutes of moderate physical exercise a day. This situation is most unfortunate as a sedentary lifestyle increases the risk of contracting at least 35 serious health disorders, notably cardiovascular diseases, certain types of cancer such as colon and breast, Type-2 diabetes, and other degenerative diseases like Alzheimer's.

The close relationship between lack of exercise and the development of chronic diseases is caused by mechanisms similar to those responsible for the damaging effects of obesity. Inactivity and obesity create a climate of chronic inflammation in the body, characterized by overproduction of inflammatory molecules that disturb the normal function of many organs. For example,

inflammation of the adipocytes is linked to the development of insulin resistance and the onset of Type-2 diabetes. Inflammatory molecules released near the blood vessel linings encourage the development of atherosclerosis lesions, while in the brain these inflammatory conditions can alter neuron function and accelerate the onset of neurodegenerative diseases. The major contribution of inflammation to cancer development is in creating a generalized climate of chronic inflammation, considerably increasing the risks of abnormal cells growing uncontrollably, leading to cancer. Getting regular exercise not only keeps you in shape and maintains muscle mass integrity, it is also a form of anti-inflammatory shock therapy with very positive consequences for the entire body.

We should not underestimate the major impact of physical exercise on our mental and psychological equilibrium. Being physically active is undoubtedly the best way to learn about recognizing your limits, and also of savouring victory while accepting setbacks and confronting fears with courage, perseverance, and resilience.

Junk food: The less the better!

Concern about the repercussions of food on health does not mean we should totally demonize foods that do not meet the highest criteria, including the products of the junk food industry. Eating healthily does not mean we are joining a

kind of "orthorexic sect" in which the pleasures associated with potato chips, fries, hot dogs, or other "treats" are banished forever! We must be realistic: We live in an environment awash with enticing sweet, fatty, or salty foods (sometimes all three at the same time) and it is only human to indulge occasionally. But chronic bad habits generate chronic health problems. We do not become obese or sick by *occasionally* eating fast food: The modern mass-produced diet is bad for health not because people consume a hot dog and fries three times a year, but because they may do so three times a week. We can take a defensive approach to the abundance of processed products all around us and see these foods for what they are: occasional pleasures.

Supplements are not the solution

For certain people, health problems related to a poor diet are easy to resolve: Just take supplements to make up the missing essential elements rather than examining what you eat. This is definitely a lucrative trend: Almost 50% of North Americans regularly take supplements, generating annual sales of nearly $15 billion. This fad is especially remarkable as there is no scientific study showing that supplements are able to compensate for a chronic deficiency in fruits and vegetables. In fact, the numerous studies conducted over the past twenty years do not convincingly show a real benefit from taking multivitamin supplements in lowering cancer rates. On the contrary, we have observed an increased risk for developing certain types of cancer from taking high doses of vitamins A and E. For this reason the Fonds Mondial de Recherche contre le Cancer recommended in its last report that we not look to supplements for cancer prevention.

This medicalization of the diet, in which foods as complex as fruits and vegetables are simply reduced to sources of vitamins, minerals, or phytochemical compounds that can be easily replaced by pills, is ludicrous. A diversified diet, rich in plants, can supply the body with up to 20,000 different molecules. All of these interact to maintain our physiological and homeostatic equilibrium and reduce the risk of developing chronic diseases. The absorption and distribution of the molecules in our body are also strongly influenced by the food matrix – that is, all the other pharmacologically non-active components that modulate the absorption, distribution, and elimination of biochemically active molecules in a plant product. The nature of the fats, proteins, and sugars, as well as of the salt, fibre, pH, and other content, will also modulate the effectiveness of absorption. For most plants, evolution has made it possible to optimize this matrix. The fact that humans can consume a plant as food is due not only to the presence of molecules beneficial to heath, but also to the existence of the matrix that enables the absorption of these active molecules.

The pharmaceutical industry determines the excipients (products added for the coating, preservation, taste, and colour of the pills) that will best enable the absorption of a drug. And this "coating" of active molecules present in plants is not an insignificant matter: Pharmacokinetic and pharmacodynamic studies represent investments in the tens of millions of dollars in drug development. Obviously, such complexity is absolutely impossible to reproduce in supplements, which adds to their ineffectiveness.

Supplements are not a solution to the high incidence of chronic diseases associated with a bad diet. Despite the essential roles of phytochemical compounds, omega-3 fatty acids, and vitamins in maintaining good health, the modern diet is not a medical problem that can be resolved by simply absorbing a few food-based chemical molecules. To approach food from such a reductionist perspective is

to believe in magic, to deny the complexity of the human body and the delicate balance that enables our vital functions to work harmoniously together. Even worse, it undermines the major role that food has played in human history, particularly our incredible ability to use food as a source of pleasure and as a cultural symbol essential for the cohesion of people. We may have evolved by eating to live, but we have only become truly human by living to eat.

Living to eat

In China, it is customary to greet someone not by saying "hello," but rather by saying "Chi fan le ma" (have you eaten?). This polite greeting illustrates the important place that food occupies in the daily life of Chinese people, a preoccupation wonderfully reflected by the festive nature of their meals, with the sharing of many plates at lively, noisy tables.

In the West, we have a tendency to perceive this type of behaviour as strange, an anomaly contrary to our perception of the place food should occupy in our daily lives. For Westerners, especially North Americans, eating is a necessary but not very important act, one human need among others that must be satisfied quickly. Convinced that the comfort, wealth and abundance typical of our lifestyle are all-important, we have developed a certain arrogance toward behaviours that differ from ours. However, it is in fact our present lifestyle that undermines the traditional relationship between humans and food!

In reviewing the major stages in the history of the human diet, we have to marvel at our remarkable adaptability and the wealth of ingenuity our distant ancestors exercised throughout evolution to obtain the food essential for survival. From the first great apes who tried to improve their lot by walking upright to the first hominids who added meat to their diet to the first hunters who used an increasingly productive brain to become formidable predators despite their small size – all these ways of acquiring food directly contributed to the emergence of the human race. Our great curiosity about food led to the invention of agriculture, making it possible to identify new foods and discover food combinations that produce the most pleasure and health benefits – a new cultural dimension. This phenomenal treasure trove of empirical knowledge, passed on from generation to generation, constitutes the most incredible experience realized on this earth, and an invaluable heritage. Much more than simply a matter of survival, the history of human food is the history of humanity itself.

Unfortunately, the junk food industry is in the process of squandering this heritage. By treating foods as products meant for little more than meeting energy needs, mass-production reduces food to a consumer product like any other, with little regard for its cultural and historical dimensions. Once sacred, the act of eating has become meaningless. Food is becoming less and less important in our everyday concerns as we aim to satisfy our needs in the fastest way possible from among the myriad processed products available. Meal preparation is often the first thing we eliminate due to the lack of time that characterizes our era. However, this is more a reflection of our lack of interest in food than a true lack of time. On average, Canadians devote less than one hour a day to meals and more than two hours to watching television. The same applies to price: It is much more expensive to eat industrial products than unprocessed foods. In 2007, a study conducted in Montreal showed that for a family of two adults and two children, a grocery basket containing, among other things, fruits, vegetables, legumes and dairy products cost an *exorbitant* $6.11 per day per person.

There should be no illusion: The goal of the junk food industry is completely contradictory to everything food has represented throughout

human history. Its aim, in assuming responsibility for feeding us, is not to promote the pleasure of eating well or to emphasize the importance of cooking with unprocessed ingredients such as fruits and vegetables. On the contrary, it is to persuade people that eating is a need that can be met quickly, several times a day, with calorie-rich products that satisfy our natural inclination for sugar, fat, and salt. This approach is particularly devastating for children: While childhood represents a vital stage of exploring a multitude of food smells, tastes, and textures, thereby developing an intimate and respectful relationship with food and ways to prepare it, the continual presence of excessively calorie-laden foods with a uniform taste interferes with the acquisition of basic gastronomic knowledge. For this reason, the junk food industry mainly targets young people and in doing so has established itself very successfully in all parts of the world, even those with rich culinary traditions like Europe and Asia. By redefining the notions of taste at a very young age, this type of diet completely eliminates the cultural dimension that for millennia has been associated with food. It has been replaced with the ephemeral pleasure of an act designed only to satisfy the most basic needs.

Taking advantage of abundance

It is human nature to consider something scarce as valuable and to show little interest in anything that is abundant. In the West, spices from Asia, particularly pepper, were for centuries regarded as valuable commodities, due to their distant origins and scarcity – the preserve of the rich and powerful. But nowadays, spices are readily available at any neighbourhood grocery store, and are relatively inexpensive!

A similar situation has occurred with food generally, at least in the richer parts of the planet. While for millennia the main problem humans had to face was survival in periods of food scarcity and hunger, we now live, for the first time in history, in an era of extraordinary food abundance. Yet, instead of taking advantage of this abundance to improve our condition, we increasingly lose interest in foods and their effect on health. The speed with which the modern diet seems to be causing the progression of many serious diseases shows the danger of this approach, and how completely unsuited it is for the way our metabolism has adapted throughout evolution. As paradoxical as it may seem, the present overabundance of food must surely be considered a threat to our health and well-being, just as food scarcity once was. While our metabolism has gradually adapted to food scarcity by developing effective mechanisms for using the energy contained in food, we are physiologically powerless faced with an overabundance of food. The only way to counteract the deleterious effects of overeating is to redefine the place of food in our lives, to adapt culturally to this overabundance, not by eating excessively, but by

exploring new culinary horizons and rediscovering the pleasures of eating.

Eating is the ultimate social act, a special moment that has always been associated with sharing and holidays. From Greco-Roman banquets and other gatherings to the celebrations that today mark the harvests of tomatoes (Spain), onions (Berne, Switzerland), and blueberries (Lac-St-Jean, Quebec) and other countless products of the earth, all these holidays show the importance of the connections between people and food. The monotony of today's diet, in which the pleasure of eating is mostly associated with the presence of sugar, fat, and salt, makes us forget just how much the quest for new tastes and sensations is an integral part of the human experience. The eating of bull's testicles in Spain, scorpions and other insects in China, reptiles like alligators or rattlesnakes in the United States . . . these acts show our curiosity and boldness in identifying new food sources and pushing the limits of taste (and bad taste). Sometimes this boldness may even constitute a risk to our lives, the best example being the delectable puffer fish. Considered a very refined dish in Japan, the puffer fish can become poisonous if not properly cooked. For this reason, only licensed chefs may prepare it, as the skin must avoid any contact with certain organs of the fish; these contain a potent poison, tetrodoxin, that blocks sodium channels, causing violent death within minutes.

Thus, eating represents a complex and stimulating experience, an exercise that embraces the

world. We can only marvel at the new directions taken by Hervé This in his molecular cuisine; or the wonderful dishes emerging from the culinary deconstructed approach of Ferran Adrià; or the molecular oenology developed by François Chartier; or the remarkable talents of Mibu Ishida. Learning about cuisine is always enriching, reflecting our species' perpetual quest to take advantage of nature's riches for our own pleasure.

The world in which we live abounds in remarkable food resources from all over the globe. We are fortunate in enjoying access to plants from Bangkok's markets, *tapas* from Spain, the *mezze* of Lebanon, and the beauty and elegance of Japanese *kaizeki*. In all the great culinary traditions of the world, dishes are not only healthy and delicious but also works of art! We must celebrate this beauty and wealth while learning something about the history and culture that have allowed us to achieve such a level of refinement.

To rediscover the pleasure of eating well is to take advantage of this remarkable variety in world cuisine and to explore the wonderful rich tastes and textures of these ancient cuisines. Drawing on the most wonderful experience ever realized by humans, eating well and staying healthy is the tangible expression of our ingenuity in constantly improving our daily lives. More than a basic need, eating is a unique, cultural act, demonstrating the special relationship between humans and nature. To eat well is to celebrate our humanity.

The references listed represent only a small fraction of the abundant literature on the links between lifestyle and chronic illnesses. They can, nevertheless, offer a good starting point for those readers wishing to explore this exciting subject in more detail.

Chapter 1

Global burden of disease and risk factors, Lopez A.D., Mathers C.D., Ezzati M., Jamison D.T., Murray C.J.L., Eds, Oxford University Press, New York, 2006.

Oeppen J., Vaupel J.W. Broken limits to life expectancy. Science 2002; 296: 1029-1031.

Yates L.B., Djoussé L., Kurth T., Buring J.E., Gaziano J.M. Exceptional longevity in men: modifiable factors associated with survival and function to age 90 years. Arch Int. Med. 2008; 168: 284-290.

Khaw K.-T. Healthy aging. BMJ 1997; 315: 1090-1096.

Popkin B.M. The world is fat. Sci Am. 2007; 297: 88-95.

Willett W.C. Eat, drink and be healthy: The Harvard medical school guide to healthy eating. Free Press, New York, 2001.

Chapter 2

Human diet: Its origin and evolution. Ungar P.S. et Teaford M.F. Eds, Bergin & Garvey, Westport, 2002.

The emergence of agriculture: a global view. Denham T. et White P. Eds. Routledge, New York, 2007.

Cordain L., Eaton S.B., Sebastian A. et al. Origins and evolution of the Western diet: health implications for the 21st century. Am. J. Clin. Nutr. 2005; 81: 341-354.

Leonard W.R. Food for thought: dietary change was a driving force in human evolution. Sci. Am. 2002; 287:106-115.

Wolf K. Visual ecology: coloured fruit is what the eye sees best. Curr. Biol. 2002; 12: R253-R255.

Becoming human: evolution and the rise of intelligence. Scientific American Special Edition, September 2006.

Larsen C.S. Animal source foods and human health during evolution. J. Nutr. 2003; 133: 3893S-3897S.

Tishkoff S.A., Reed F.A., Ranciaro A. et al. Convergent adaptation of human lactase persistence in Africa and Europe. Nature Genetics 2007; 39: 31-40.

Balter M. Plant science: Seeking agriculture's ancient roots. Science 2007; 316:1830-1835.

Chapter 3

Goff S.A., Klee H.J. Plant volatile compounds: sensory cues for health and nutritional value? Science 2006; 311: 815-819.

Scott K. Taste recognition: food for thought. Neuron 2005; 48: 455-464.

Chandrashekar J., Hoon M.A., Ryba N.J..P, Zuker C.S. The receptors and cells for mammalian taste. Nature 2006; 444: 288-294.

Flier J.S., Maratos-Flier E. What fuels fat. Sci Am. 2007; 297:72-81.

Cummings D.E., Overduin J. Gastrointestinal regulation of food intake. J. Clin. Invest. 2007; 117: 13-23.

Yamaguchi S., Ninomaya K. Umami and food palatability. J. Nutr. 2000; 130: 921S-926S.

Wooding S. Evolution: a study in bad taste? Curr. Biol. 2005; 15: R805-R807.

Bachmanov A.A., Beauchamp G.K. Taste receptor genes. Annu Rev. Nutr. 2007; 27: 389-414.

Coll A.P., Farooqi I.S., O'Rahilly S. The hormonal control of food intake. Cell 2007; 129: 251-262.

Chapter 4

Kopelman P.G. Obesity as a medical problem. Nature 2000; 404: 635-643,

Willett W.C., Dietz W.H., Colditz G.A. Guidelines for healthy weight. New Engl. J. Med. 1999; 341: 427-434.

Rosen E.D., Spiegelman B.M. Adipocytes as regulators of energy balance and glucose homeostasis. Nature 2006; 444: 847-853.

Chakravarthy M.V., Booth F.W. Eating, exercise, and "thrifty" genotypes: connecting the dots toward an evolutionary understanding of modern chronic diseases. J. Appl. Physiol. 2004; 96: 3-10.

Christakis N.A., Fowler, J.H. The spread of obesity in a large social network over 32 years. New Engl. J. Med. 2007; 357: 370-379.

Bouchard C. The biological predisposition to obesity: beyong the thrifty genotype scenario. Int. J. Obesity 2007; 31: 1337-1339.

Prentice A.M. Early influences on human energy regulation: thrifty genotypes and thrifty phenotypes. Physiol. Behav. 2005; 86: 640-645.

Willett W.C. Eat, drink and be healthy:The Harvard medical school guide to healthy eating. Free Press, New York, 2001.

Schlosser E. Fast food nation: The dark side of the all-American meal. Houghton Mifflin, New York, 2001.

Chapter 5

Ross R. Atherosclerosis: an inflammatory disease. New Engl. J. Med. 1999; 340: 115-126.

Di Castelnuovo A., Costanzo S., Bagnardi V., Donatti M.B., Iacoviello L., de Gateano G. Alcohol dosing and total mortality in men and women. Arch. Int. Med. 2006; 166: 2437-3445.

De Lorgeril M., Renaud S., Mamelle N. et al. Mediterranean alpha-linolenic acid-rich diet in secondary prevention of coronary heart disease. Lancet 1994; 343: 1454-1459.

Serafini M., Bugianesi R., Maiani G., Valtuena S., De Santis S., Crozier A. Plasma antioxidants from chocolate. Nature 2003; 424: 1013

Buijisse B., Feskens E.J.M., Kok F.J., Kromhout D. Cocoa intake, blood pressure and cardiovascular mortality: The Zutphen elderly study. Arch. Int. Med. 2006; 166: 411-417.

Lawes C.M.M., Hoorn S.V., Rodgers A. Global burden of blood-pressure-related disease, 2001. Lancet 2008; 371: 1513-1518.

Hansson G.K. Inflammation, atherosclerosis, and coronary heart disease. New Engl. J. Med. 2005; 352: 1685-1695.

Hu F.B., Willett, W.C. Optimal diets for prevention of coronary heart disease. JAMA 2002; 288: 2569-2578.

Després J.-P., Lemieux I., Bergeron J. et al. Abdominal obesity and the metabolic syndrome: contribution to global cardiometabolic risk. Arterioscler. Thromb. Vasc. Biol. 2008; 28: 1039-1049.

Visioli F., Borsani L., Galli C. Diet and prevention of coronary heart disease: the potential role of phytochemicals. Cardiovasc. Res. 2000; 47: 419-425.

Liu S., Manson J.E., Stampfer M.J. et al. Whole grain consumption and risk of ischemic stroke in women: A prospective study. JAMA 2000; 284: 1534-1540.

Willett, W.C. Eat, drink and be healthy:The Harvard medical school guide to healthy eating. Free Press, New York, 2001.

Chapter 6

Kahn S.E., Hull R.L., Utzschneider K.M. Mechanisms linking obesity to insulin resistance and type 2 diabetes. Nature 2006; 444: 840-846.

Hotamisligil G.S. Inflammation and metabolic disorders. Nature 2006; 444: 860-867.

Lieberman L.S. Dietary, evolutionary, and modernizing influences on the prevalence of type 2 diabetes. Annu. Rev. Nutr. 2003; 23: 345-377.

Qi L., Hu F.B. Dietary glycemic load, whole grains, and systemic inflammation in diabetes: the epidemiological evidence. Curr. Opin. Lipidol. 2007; 18: 3-8.

Fung T.T., Hu F.B., Pereira M.A. et al. Whole-grain intake and the risk of type 2 diabetes: a prospective study in men. Am. J. Clin. Nutr. 2002; 76: 535-540.

Barclay A.W., Petocz P., McMillan-Price J. et al. Glycemic index, glycemic load, and chronic disease risk: a meta-analysis of observational studies. Am. J. Clin. Nutr. 2008; 87: 627-637.

Buchanan T.A. How can we prevent type 2 diabetes? Diabetes 2007; 56: 1502-1507.

Zimmet P., Alberti K.G.M.M., Shaw J. Global and societal implications of the diabetes epidemic. Nature 2001; 414: 782-787.

Muoio D.M., Newgard C.B. Molecular and metabolic mechanisms of insulin resistance and b-cell failure in type 2 diabetes. Nature Rev. Mol. Cell Biol. 2008; 9: 193-205.

Ramasamy R., Vannucci S.J., Du Yan S.S., Herold K., Yan S.F., Schmidt A.M. Advanced glycation en products and RAGE: a common thread in aging diabetes, neurodegeneration, and inflammation. Glycobiology 2005; 15: 16R-28R.

Hu F.B., Manson J.E., Meir J. et al. Diet, lifestyle, and the risk of type 2 diabetes mellitus in women. New Engl. J. Med. 2001; 345: 790-797.

Willett, W.C. Eat, drink and be healthy:The Harvard medical school guide to healthy eating. Free Press, New York, 2001.

Chapter 7

Hanahan D., Weinberg R.A. The hallmarks of cancer. Cell 2000; 100: 57-70.

Food, Nutrition, Physical Activity and the Prevention of Cancer: a global perspective. WCRF/AICR Export report, 2007.

Anand, P., Kunnumakara, A.B., Sundaram, C., Harikumar, K.B., Tharakan, S.T., Lai, O.S., Sung, B., Aggarwal, B.B. Cancer is a preventable disease that requires major lifestyle changes. Pharm. Res. 2008; 2097-2116.

Calle E.E., Kaaks R. Overweight, obesity and cancer: epidemiological evidence and proposed mechanisms. Nature Rev. Cancer 2004; 4: 579-591.

McTiernan A. Mechanisms linking physical activity with cancer. Nature Rev. Cancer 2008; 8: 205-211.

Benetou V., Trichopoulou A., Orfanos P. et al. Conformity to traditional Mediterranean diet and cancer incidence: the Greek EPIC cohort. Br. J. Cancer 1998; 99: 191-195.

Ames B.N., Gold L.S. Paracelsus to parascience: the environmental cancer distraction. Mutat. Res. 2000; 447:3-13.

Renehan A.G., Tyson M., Egger M., Heller R.F., Zwahlen M. Body-mass index and incidence of cancer: a systematic review and meta-analysis of prospective observational studies. Lancet 2008; 371:569-578.

Holick M.F. Vitamin D: its role in cancer prevention and treatment. Prog. Biophys. Mol. Biol. 2006; 92: 49-59.

Kirsh V.A., Peters U., Mayne S.T. et al. Prospective study of fruit and vegetable intake and risk of prostate cancer. J Natl Cancer Inst. 2007; 99 :1200-1209.

Yang G., Shu X.O., et al. Prospective cohort study of green tea consumption and colorectal cancer risk in women. Cancer Epidemiol Biomarkers Prev. 2007; 16:1219-1223.

Michaud D.S., Spiegelman D., Clinton S.K., Rimm E.B., Willett W.C., Giovannucci E.L. Fruit and vegetable intake and incidence of bladder cancer in a male prospective cohort. J Natl Cancer Inst. 1999; 91: 605-613.

Chapter 8

Cummings J.L. Alzheimer disease. New Engl. J. Med. 2004; 351: 56-67.

McCarty M.F. Toward prevention of Alzheimer disease: potential nutraceutical strategies for suppressing the production of amyloid beta peptides. Med. Hypotheses 2006; 67: 682-697.

Pasquier F., Boulogne A., Leys D., Fontaine P. Diabetes mellitus and dementia. Diabetes Metab. 2006; 32: 403-414.

Kodl C.T., Seaquist E.R. Cognitive dysfunction and diabetes mellitus. Endocrine Rev. 2008; 29: 494-511.

Ferri C.P., Prince M., Brayne C., et al. Global prevalence of dementia: a Delphi consensus study. Lancet 2005; 366: 2112-2117.

Hendrie H.C., Ogunniyi A., Hall K.S. et al. Incidence of dementia and Alzheimer disease in 2 communities: Yoruba residing in Ibadan, Nigeria, and African Americans residing in Indianapolis, Indiana. JAMA 2001; 285: 739-747.

Chandra V., Ganguli M., Pandav R., Johnston J., Belle S. and DrKosky S.T. Prevalence of Alzheimer's disease and other dementia in rural India: The Indo-US study. Neurology 1998; 51: 1000-1008.

Yaffe K., Kanaya A., Lindquist K. et al. The metabolic syndrome, inflammation and risk of cognitive decline. JAMA 2004; 292: 2237-2242.

Morris M.C., Evans D.A., Bienias J.L. et al. Dietary fats and the risk of incident Alzheimer disease. Arch. Neurol. 2003; 60: 194-200.

Steele M., Stuchbury G., Münch G. The molecular basis of the prevention of Alzheimer's disease through healthy nutrition. Exp. Gerontol. 2007; 42: 28-36.

Verghese J., Lipton R.B., Katz M.J. et al. Leisure activities and the risk of dementia in the elderly. New Engl. J. Med. 2003; 348: 2508-2516.

Singh-Manoux A., Gimeno D., Kivimaki M., Brunner E., Marmot M.G. Low HDL cholesterol is a risk factor for deficit and decline in memory in midlife: The Whitehall II study. Arterioscler. Thromb. Vasc. Biol. 2008; 28: 1556-1562.

Rossi L., Mazzitelli S., Arciello M., Capo C.R., Rotilio G. Benefits from Dietary Polyphenols for Brain Aging and Alzheimer's Disease. Neurochem Res. 2008.

Kivipelto M., Ngandu T., Fratiglioni L. et al. Obesity and Vascular Risk Factors at Midlife and the Risk of Dementia and Alzheimer Disease. Arch Neurol. 2005;62:1556-1560.

Chapter 9

Ames B.N., Shigenaga M.K., Hagen T.M. Oxidants, antioxidants, and the degenerative diseases of aging. Proc. Natl. Acad. Sc. USA 1993; 90: 7915-7922.

Stahl W., Sies H. Bioactivity and protective effects of natural carotenoids. Biochim. Biophys. Acta 2005; 1740: 101-107.

Hsu S. Green tea and the skin. J. Am. Acad. Dermatol. 2005; 52: 1049-1059.

Morita A. Tobacco smoke causes premature skin aging. J. Dermatol. Sci. 2007; 48: 169-175.

Afaq F., Mukhtar H. Botanical antioxidants in the prevention of photocarcinogenesis and photoaging. Exp. Dermatol. 2006; 15: 678-684.

McCullough J.L., Kelly K.M. Prevention and treatment of skin aging. Ann. N.Y. Acad. Sci. 2006; 1067: 323-331.

Purba M., Kouris-Blazos A., Wattanapenpaiboon N. et al. Skin Wrinkling: Can Food Make a Difference? J. Am. Coll. Nutr. 2001; 20: 71–80.

Boelsma E., Hendriks H.F.J., Roza L. Nutritional skin care: health effects of micronutrients and fatty acids. Am. J. Clin. Nutr. 2001;73:853–864.

Rabe J.H., Mamelak A.J., McElgunn P.J.S., Morison W.L., Sauder D.N. Photoaging: Mechanisms and repair. J. Am. Acad. Dermatol. 2006;55:1-19.

Chapter 10

Kenfield S.A., Stampfer M.J., Rosner B.A., Colditz G.A. Smoking and smoking cessation in relation to mortality in women. JAMA 2008; 299: 2037-2047.

Heidemann C., Schulze M.B., Franco O.H., Van Dam R.M., Mantzoros C.S., Hu F.B. Dietary patterns and risk of mortality from cardiovascular disease, cancer, and all causes in a prospective cohort of women. Circulation 2008; 118: 230-237.

Handschin C., Spiegelman B.M. The role of exercise and PGC1α in inflammation and chronic disease. Nature 2008; 454: 463-469.

Pollan M. In defense of food: an eater's manifesto. The Penguin Press, New York, 2008.

Petrini C. Slow food nation: Why our food should be good, clean, and fair. Rizzoli Ex Libris, New York, 2007.

BSIP: Belmonte130; Manceau 51

Corbis: Kevin Carter/Megan Patricia Carter Trust/Sygma 79; P. Desgrieux/photocuisine 228

Flickr: Ed Uthman 98 (http://creativecommons.org/licenses/by-sa/2.0/deed.fr_CA)

Getty Images: 89, 152, 245; Absodels 18; Karl Ammann 26; Mark Andersen 21; B2M Productions 227; Sandra Baker 97; James Balog 45; Jean Louis Batt 65; Al Bello 94; Patrick Bernard 90; Luc Beziat 67; Burgess Blevins 16; Paul Bradbury 76; Bridgeman Art Library 73; Andrea Chu 65; CMSP 189; DAJ 250; Donna Day 86; Peter Dazeley 30, 31; Martin Diebel 57, 235; Digital Vision 17, 72, 76; Gerry Ellis 31; Issaque Fujita/A. collection 12; Tim Graham/Getty Images 165; GSO Images 203; Holly Harris 66; ML Harris 155; Andreas Heumann 93; Gary Houlder 214; IMAGEMORE Co. Ltd. 60; Amanda Koster Productions 146; Utagawa Kunisada 75; Clarissa Leahy 15; Cheryl Maeder 222; Liz McAulay 11; Stuart McClymont 71; Ryan McVay 157; George Marks 234; National Geographic/Getty Images 260; James Nelson 259; Jose Luis Pelaez Inc 135; Photodisc 057; Tim Platt 70, 74; Prehistoric 34; Christopher Robbins 10; Rubberball 11; Sabine Scheckel 3; Hugh Sitton 257; Tom Stoddart 77; Stockbyte 15, 48, 126, 193, 213, 249, 254; Tom Stoddart 80; Joy Tessman 35; Time & Life Pictures/Getty Images 81; Roy Toft 29; Paul Thomas 25; Luis Veiga 42; Wade 64, 136; Axel Weiss 145; Stephen Wilkes 68; Holly Wilmeth 46; Cary Wolinsky 048

Groupe Librex: 7, 8, 21, 40, 41, 48, 53, 54, 55, 56, 57, 76, 84, 85, 86, 87, 92, 104, 105, 117, 118, 121, 138, 139, 142, 152, 159, 168, 170, 172, 173, 178, 205, 207, 209, 224, 225, 231, 232, 238, 242, 246, 252

Jacques Migneault: 28

Jupiter Images: 14, 21, 22, 56, 57, 81, 102, 105, 109, 123, 129, 143, 174, 176, 185, 186, 190, 201, 207, 206, 216, 220, 231, 240, 256, 261; Burke/Triolo Productions 200; Brian Hagiwara 243; Natasha K. 237; Maximilian Stock Ltd. 114

Laboratoire de médecine moléculaire, Montréal: 180

Science Photo Library: David Gifford 27; Mehau Kulyk & Victor De Schwanberg 91; Oak Ridge National Laboratory/ US Departement of Energy 63

Shutterstock: 21, 53, 72, 113, 116, 141, 211; 7382489561 199; Aga 38; Kitch Bain 28; Franck Boston 241; bpatt81 96; David Burden 39; Daemys 50; Lisa Eastman 103; Vania Georgieva 59; Ciaran Griffin 103; Daniel Hebert 96; Julian 28; Junial Enterprises 197; Natalia Klenova 39; Alex Kosev 105; Stanislav Mikhalev 76; Mushakesa 163; Kirsty Pargeter 19; Photoroller 22; Styve Reineck 28; Aivars Rimsa 207; Izaokas Sapiro 21; Alexander Shalamov 175; Roman Sigaev 167; Yakovchuk Vasyl 105

Super Stock: Mauritius 24